IMAGES
of America

FORT OGLETHORPE

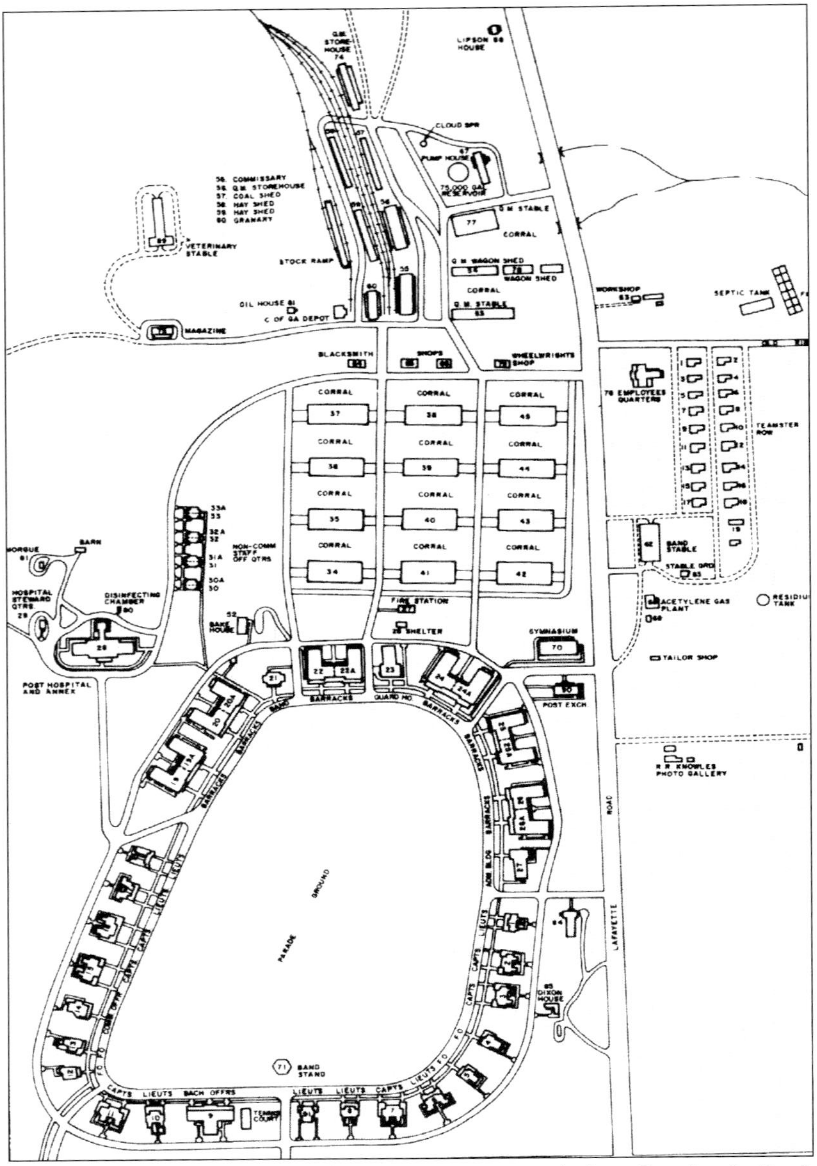

This map shows the original Fort Oglethorpe Army Post, including Barnhardt Circle, the post hospital, quartermaster building, stables, and rail lines. Another map on page 63 shows how the post was expanded, both east of the original post and south into the adjoining Chickamauga and Chattanooga National Military Park during 1943–1945, when the Women's Army Corps was stationed at Fort Oglethorpe. (National Archives and Records Administration.)

On the Cover: Formed in 1900, the 6th U.S. Cavalry Association originally held reunions in different cities. Fort Oglethorpe was designated as the official home of the 6th Cavalry in 1919, and all subsequent reunions have been held there. This photograph depicts the 1949 reunion, with members and their families gathered on the steps of the post chapel following the memorial service honoring those cavalrymen who had died in the past year. (Sixth Cavalry Museum.)

IMAGES
of America

FORT OGLETHORPE

Gerry Depken and Julie Powell

ARCADIA
PUBLISHING

ISBN 978-0-7385-6605-4

Published by Arcadia Publishing
Charleston, South Carolina

Printed in the United States of America

Library of Congress Control Number: 2009923877

For all general information contact Arcadia Publishing at:
Telephone 843-853-2070
Fax 843-853-0044
E-mail sales@arcadiapublishing.com
For customer service and orders:
Toll-Free 1-888-313-2665

Visit us on the Internet at www.arcadiapublishing.com

We thank our husbands, Craig and Jim, for their invaluable support for this project. Their uncomplaining assistance is appreciated more than words can say.

Contents

ACKNOWLEDGMENTS

The authors wish to extend their thanks to all who helped bring this book to publication. We especially thank our editor, Katie Shayda. You were a pleasure to work with, and we really appreciate your efforts to keep us on track and on time! So many people have shared photographs and stories with us. We want to express special appreciation to all the citizens of Fort Oglethorpe, who reached back into their memories for names and dates. Thank you, too, to the archivists, historians, and librarians who have shared their collections: Chattanooga-Hamilton County Bicentennial Library (CHCBL); Chickamauga and Chattanooga National Military Park (CCNMP); Doyle Phillips Collection, courtesy of Maggie Armstrong (DP); Hutcheson Auxiliary (HA); Hutcheson Regional Medical Center (HRMC); James "Smokey" Holder Collection, courtesy of Marie McDaniel (JH); National Archives and Records Administration (NARA); Sixth Cavalry Museum (SCM), Chris McKeever, executive director; City of Fort Oglethorpe (CFO); and Wayne and Rena Honeycutt (WRH). Special thanks go to Leigh Powell (LP) for her excellent photography. Our families have been wonderful support teams, and without their enthusiasm and encouragement, this book would not have been possible. There are so many more who shared their memories—they will have to await another book!

INTRODUCTION

First an army post and later a town, Fort Oglethorpe was founded in 1902 and continues to thrive today. The post was named for Gen. James Oglethorpe, who founded the Georgia colony in 1733. The origins of the army post can actually be traced back to 1898, when military troops were based on Chickamauga Battlefield, training for the Spanish-American War. The area where they trained was called Camp Thomas.

The army needed more space for its instruction and maneuvers, but there was concern over the integrity of the park. In 1902, eight hundred thirteen acres were acquired immediately north of the park, and Fort Oglethorpe Army Post was established. Pres. Theodore Roosevelt visited the post that year.

The Civil War and Reconstruction had taken a terrible toll on the area. By 1900, the region still had not recovered from the physical damage to the land, the political ramifications of sectional reprisal, and the destruction of roads, railroads, and other infrastructure. The post became an important economic factor in the recovery of the greater Chattanooga and northwest Georgia area.

The central part of the post development was Barnhardt Circle, named for Col. George C. Barnhardt. The parade grounds/polo field, named, at a later date, Johnston Field in honor of Col. Gordon Johnston, commanding officer at Fort Oglethorpe from 1931 to 1933, was surrounded by structures. Married officers and their families occupied single and double family housing on the southern end of the circle. The Band Barracks, six troop barracks, guardhouse, and administration building were located at the northern end. Homes on the circle have neoclassical and Queen Anne architectural characteristics, which became popular following the Columbian Exposition of 1892. The houses are built of wood and have large welcoming front porches. Captains and lieutenants lived in duplexes, and the field grade officers had single-family dwellings. The Bachelor Officers Quarters barrack was located on the south end, across from the bandstand.

During World War I, the military base expanded onto the battlefield, as was permitted by Congress. Three separate camps were created. Camp Greenleaf, commanded by Col. Henry Page, trained 24,000 doctors and medical personnel to man the ambulance, medical, and sanitary corps. Officer training was conducted under Col. Herbert Slocum at Camp Warden McLean, and infantry and engineer training was taught at Camp Nathan B. Forrest, first under Col. J. N. Pickering and later under Col. Spencer Cosby, commander of the 605th Engineers. The 6th Cavalry was also here for a short time.

Enemy aliens were confined to the post during World War I. Among them were well-known chefs who cooked for the Officers Club and Germans who were known for the delicious bread they baked. Dr. Karl Muck and Earnest Kunwald, famous symphony conductors, were both detained in the enemy alien compound.

Between the two world wars, the Civilian Military Training Corps (CMTC), Civilian Conservation Corps (CCC), and the Reserve Officers Training Corps (ROTC) trained at Fort Oglethorpe. Their financial contribution to the local economy was significant. During this period, local carpenters built barracks. Local tailors advertised custom-made uniforms, and tanneries and tack shops were numerous. The cavalry and these special corps members spent their army paychecks locally. All this helped the community prosper. The later relocation and widening of Lafayette Road and the construction of Battlefield Parkway were two additional catalysts for economic growth.

During World War II, the post again expanded into Chickamauga Battlefield. Several units trained at Fort Oglethorpe, including the 3rd Cavalry in 1942, under Col. Howell Estes. Col. Duncan Richart was commanding officer of the post at that time. The 16th Cavalry was also at Fort Oglethorpe briefly in 1942. At Fort Oglethorpe, portable medical units, the forerunner of Mobile Army Surgical Hospitals (MASH), were developed.

Prisoners of war were again detained at the post, including those captured abroad and transferred to the United States. Harold Silcox, city council member, remembers when the POWs were interred at Fort Oglethorpe. Occasionally, a POW would wander away on his return to camp after a workday and would come knocking at the family's back door. Silcox says, "My mother would invite the prisoner in, and would seat him at the table with the family. After we had all enjoyed a nice meal together, she would call the Military Police (MPs) to come get their missing prisoner."

The mild climate and agricultural life made the South a reasonable location for these prisoner internments. The camps had sanitary facilities, infirmaries, kitchens, and bakeries. There were outdoor facilities where the POWs could engage in various sports. The men did a lot of their own baking and cooking and had gardens where they grew their own fresh vegetables.

Some of the prisoners worked for the local farmers in the area. They were paid for their labor with coupons, which they could then redeem at the Post Exchange. The prisoners eventually saved enough coupons to build their own indoor sports complex. These camps were enclosed with two rows of barbed-wire fences.

In April 1942, the 6th Cavalry left for Europe as a fully mechanized unit, to be assigned to Gen. George Patton's Third Army. Patton referred to the "Fighting Sixth" as his eyes and ears, as they performed reconnaissance work for him.

The post changed drastically in 1943 when the women arrived. Fort Oglethorpe became the third and largest training center for the Women's Army Auxiliary Corps (WAAC) under director Oveta Culp Hobby. Hobby served three years, and then oversaw the transfer of the WAAC from an auxiliary to the Women's Army Corps (WAC). Pres. Franklin Delano Roosevelt reviewed the WAACs on April 7, 1943, on an unannounced visit to the post. On July 5, 1943, Hobby was appointed director of the Women's Army Corps.

Lana Turner, Loraine Day, and Susan Peters filmed part of the movie *Keep Your Powder Dry* on the grounds of the army post. Sgt. Alvin York came to visit his two sons, who enlisted there, and Bing Crosby, Walter Pidgeon, Al Jolson, and John Payne also visited Fort Oglethorpe. Mary Churchill, daughter of the British prime minister, was a guest military observer. While the WAC units were stationed at Fort Oglethorpe, department stores sold women's custom-made uniforms and WAC dolls and jewelry. Lake Winnepesaukah attracted soldiers, WACs and their families, and visitors to enjoy some time at the amusement park.

Lt. Col. Elizabeth Strayhorn was commissioned as commanding officer of Fort Oglethorpe Army Post on April 22, 1944. She was the first female post commander in the United States. Over 50,000 WACs were trained and processed through the base. Gen. George C. Marshal, U.S. Chief of Staff, inspected the WAC training center in April 1944.

When the war ended, the women's center was closed, and the post was used to muster out members of the military to civilian life. Fort Oglethorpe was then declared surplus. As Sgt. James H. Bryant played "Taps," the flag at Fort Oglethorpe was lowered for the last time on December 31, 1946. Buildings and land were sold to the public, veterans given first choice.

Local residents recognized that the core of a town, with water, electricity, streets, houses, and businesses, was already in place, and they petitioned the state legislature for a charter. The town of Fort Oglethorpe was incorporated in February 1949, the first town in Georgia to be incorporated after the war.

On April 20, 1979, the houses on Barnhardt Circle were placed on the National Register of Historic Places. The City of Fort Oglethorpe established the local historic district in 1991. In 1999, Fort Oglethorpe celebrated its 50th anniversary as a town. Students at Lakeview-Fort Oglethorpe High School helped grow golden marigolds, which the garden clubs planted in beds around the city to commemorate the town's golden anniversary.

Many of the original buildings in Fort Oglethorpe are in use today. Stately Barnhardt Circle homes, once residences of the officers and their families, are now occupied by a new generation. One of the captain's quarters is now a bed-and-breakfast, and the Band Barracks has become a vacation rental facility. Three of the stables remain and serve as commercial buildings. The movie theater and post chapel are now parts of the Baptist and Presbyterian churches standing at the entrance to Barnhardt Circle. The post gymnasium and Post Exchange (PX) are now being used by local businesses.

The post hospital became Hutcheson Memorial Tri-County Hospital, serving Walker, Catoosa, and Dade Counties. The original post hospital had 14 beds for soldiers and their families. As of 2009, Hutcheson Regional Medical Center boasts 179 beds and is a state-of-the-art medical facility.

The bandstand still stands proudly on the parade grounds. Honeycutt Baseball Field is now used by a new generation of young ball players, and additional playing fields have been built. The Sixth Cavalry Museum is also located on the parade grounds. Apartments occupy the original guardhouse, and the Bachelor Officers Quarters has been converted into an apartment building. On the site of two of the original barracks, apartment buildings built in a style similar to the old barracks are present.

Houses on Sergeants Row have remained true to their original design and are used primarily as businesses associated with Hutcheson Regional Medical Center. One of the lovely homes once served as the residence of the president of the hospital.

The city of Fort Oglethorpe continues to grow and flourish, with increased population, new businesses, and a bright future ahead.

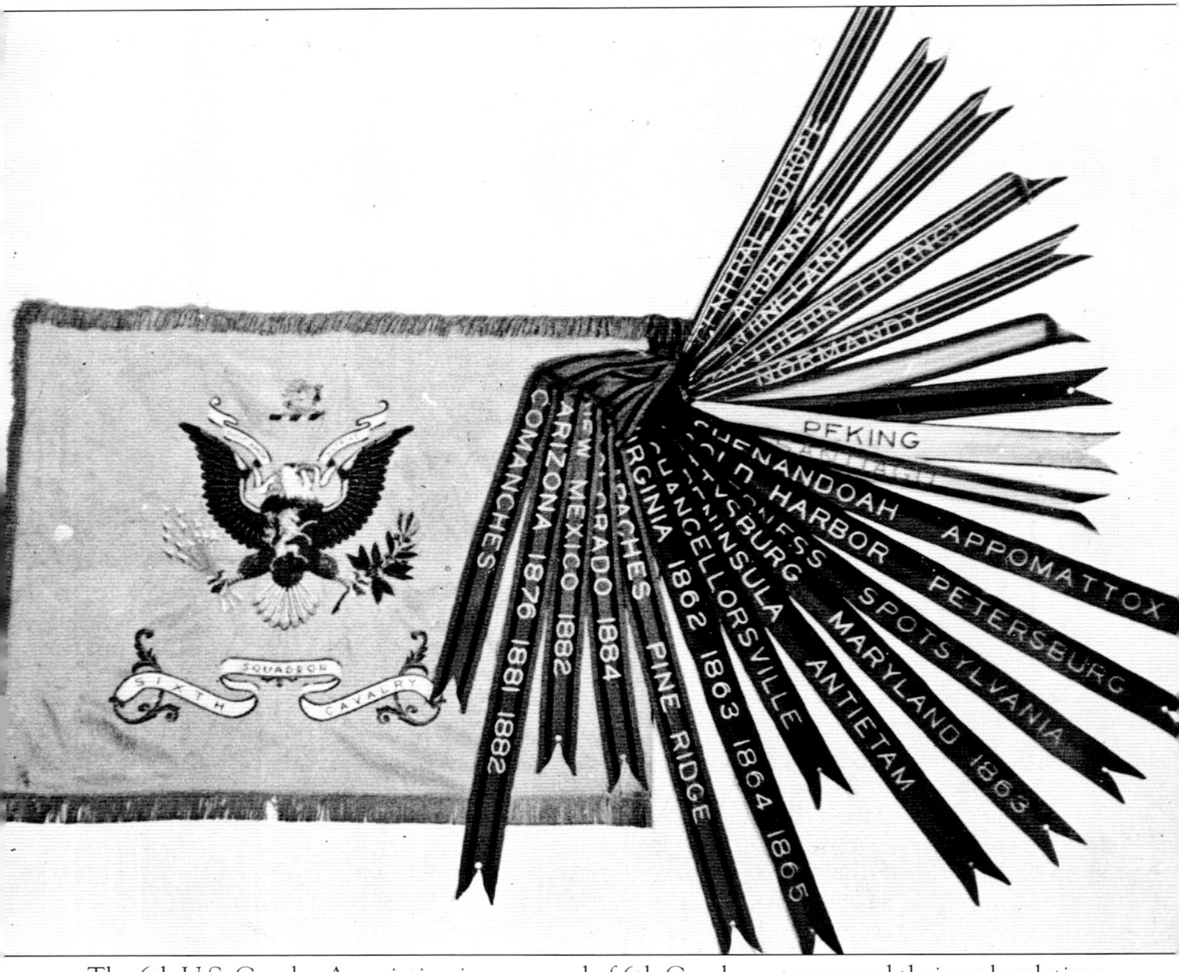

The 6th U.S. Cavalry Association is composed of 6th Cavalry veterans and their male relatives. The 6th Cavalry squadron flag is shown here with the unit crest on the chest of an eagle. Streamers from the Civil War, the Western Campaigns against the Native American, Santiago, and Cuba, and the Spanish-American War, Peking and the Boxer Rebellion, the Mexican Expedition against Poncho Villa, World War I American Expeditionary Force, Normandy, and the European Theater in World War II under Gen. George Patton attest to the long service of the "Fighting Sixth." (SCM.)

One

Establishing the Post

Next to Chickamauga and Chattanooga National Military Park was Fort Oglethorpe Army Post. Along with training exercises, the post provided ceremonial troops for park events. The park was so popular with visitors that Chattanooga built a streetcar line to bring visitors to the area. Earl Wright, a local citizen, built a livery stable, where he rented horses and buggies to the arriving visitors.

One group included Pres. Theodore Roosevelt and his entourage. Hacks and surreys were selected to take the guests on a tour through the park to view a special landmark. However, the president demanded a horse to ride. The Secret Service selected a gentle mare and had her saddled and tied to the hitching post near the parade buggies. Earl Wright, though, borrowed a handsome, spirited black steed from a prominent resident and outfitted the horse with his own silver-trimmed saddle and bridle that had been a gift to him from "Wild" Bill Cody. He tied that horse nearby.

The president saw the mare, then eyed the impatient steed. He asked whose mount it was, and Wright replied, "It's yours, Mr. President, if you so desire." President Roosevelt quickly mounted the horse and rode to the head of the parade.

"Follow me," he shouted, then turned and galloped off, leaving the parade behind in a cloud of dust. When President Roosevelt arrived at the site, the waiting crowd cheered loudly for their president and hero, the Rough Rider Teddy Roosevelt.

The post was established in 1902 on land acquired so the troops could be moved from the park. Residences for officers and their families surrounded the parade grounds on Barnhardt Circle. There were quarters for bachelor officers and band members. The guardhouse and enlisted men's barracks were on the north side of the circle.

North of Barnhardt Circle were stables, the quartermaster building, and blacksmith shop. The east gate was flanked by the post chapel and later the theater; the Post Exchange and gymnasium were on Lafayette Road.

In the 1930s, brick Georgian-style homes, called Sergeants Row, were built on Thomas Road, northwest of the hospital.

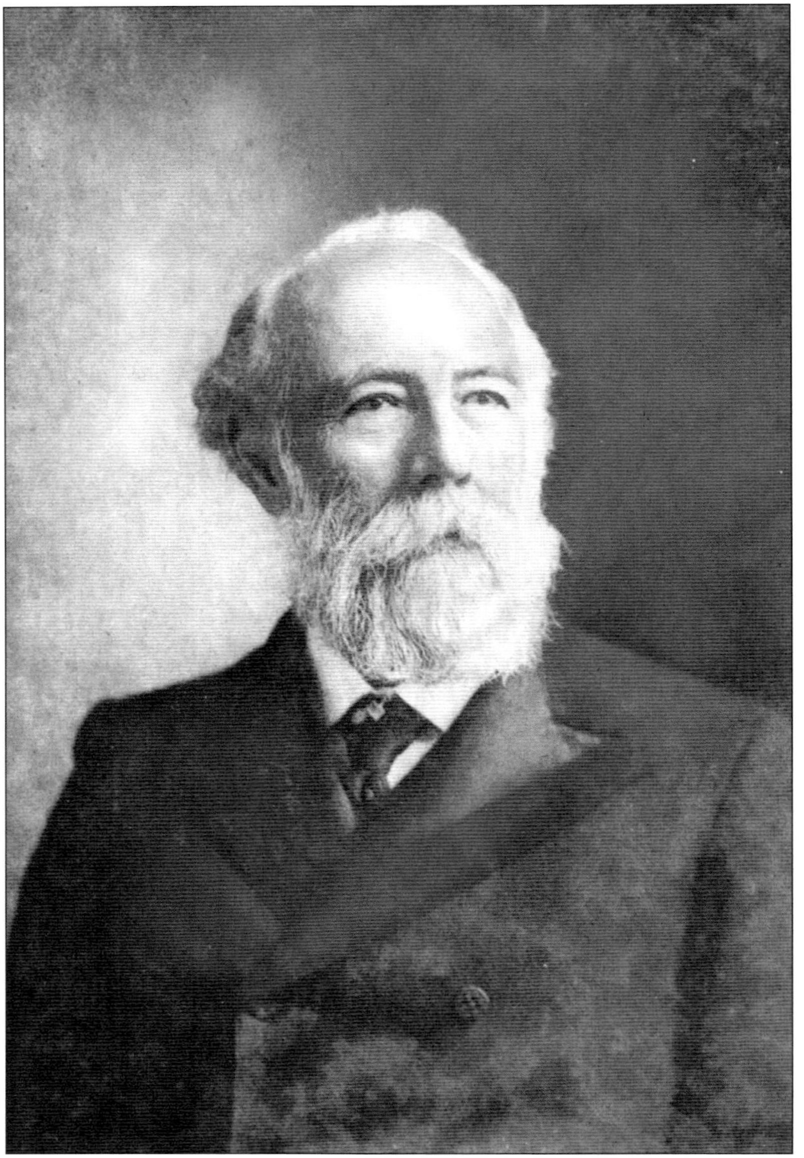

Gen. Henry Van Ness Boynton led Union troops at the Battle of Chickamauga. After the war, Boynton became a reporter for the Cincinnati *Commercial Gazette* and was stationed in Washington, D.C. He became a leading figure championing the establishment of Chickamauga National Military Park. He served as chairman of the committee that brought together military and civilian parties from both the North and the South. In addition to their efforts to preserve the battlefield on which they fought, they assisted the federal government with solving discrepancies in the war maps of Chickamauga in the Official Records of the War of the Rebellion. This committee oversaw the development of the military park. Federal legislation resulted in the creation of Chickamauga and Chattanooga National Military Park in 1890. Additional legislation provided for the use of the battlefield lands by National Guard and federal troops for training purposes. The proximity of the military park to the railroads in Chattanooga and the additional space north of the park suggested that a permanent post could be created nearby. (CHCBL.)

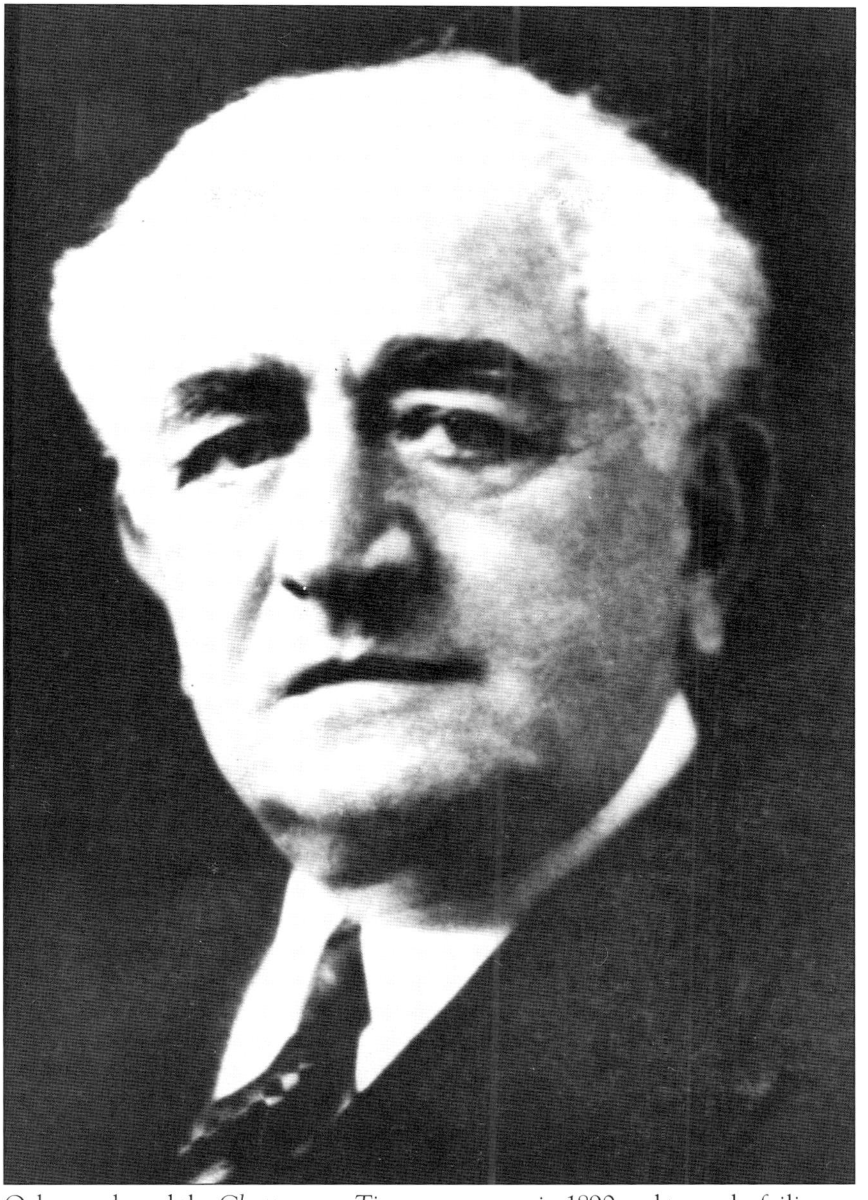

Adolph Ochs purchased the *Chattanooga Times* newspaper in 1890 and turned a failing paper into an independent and successful publication. He was one of several visionaries who believed in the future of the town, which survived the war and occupation by both Confederate and Union troops. In time, Ochs became the unofficial city host to visitors and businessmen interested in locating in Chattanooga. He was an active supporter of the creation of a military park at Chickamauga and worked for the success of that project. In 1896, he purchased the *New York Times* and moved north. Through his widening influence, he contributed time and resources to the park creation. His interest in the park movement also brought the voice of the *New York Times* to the protection of Central Park in New York City. His continued civic contributions in the Chattanooga area included securing 3,500 acres on Lookout Mountain for the national park to preserve the battle sites there. (CHCBL.)

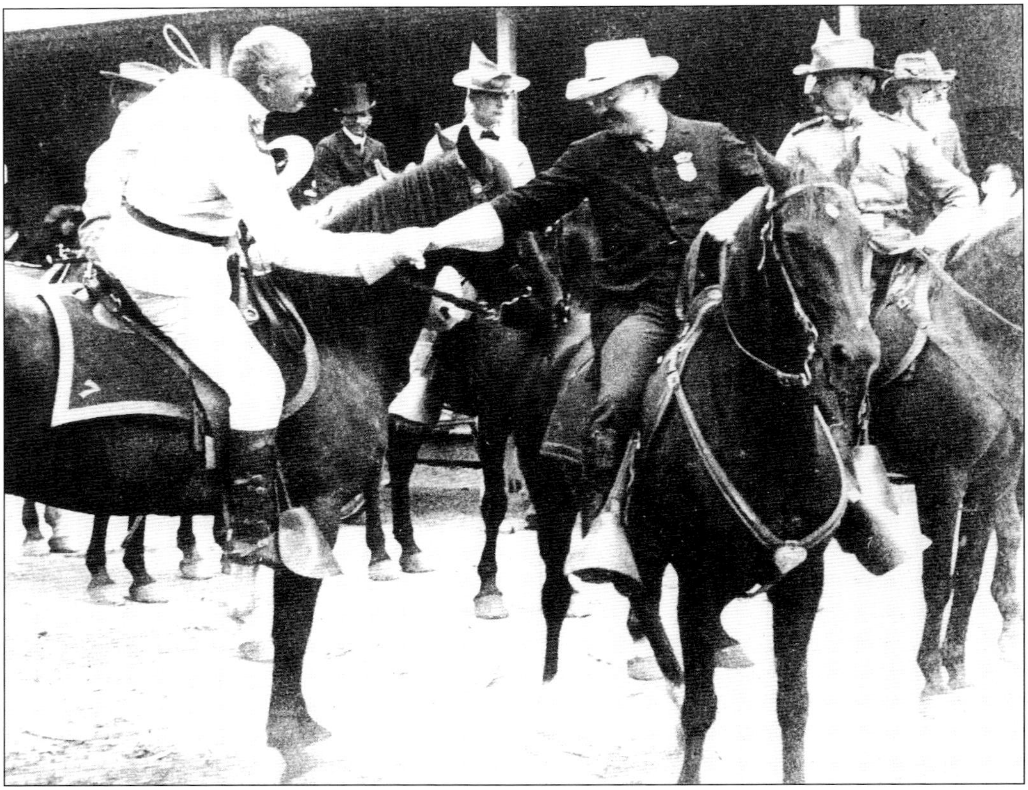

Pres. Theodore Roosevelt spoke to the Brotherhood of Locomotive Firemen in Chattanooga on September 8, 1902. He toured the Chickamauga Battlefield with Gen. Henry Boynton. Here Roosevelt (center) is shaking hands with Lt. Capt. Winfield Scott Edgerly. Col. Theodore Baldwin, right, was the commander of the 7th Cavalry, the first cavalry unit to be stationed at the new post. The 7th acted as Roosevelt's honor guard while in the park. (CHCBL.)

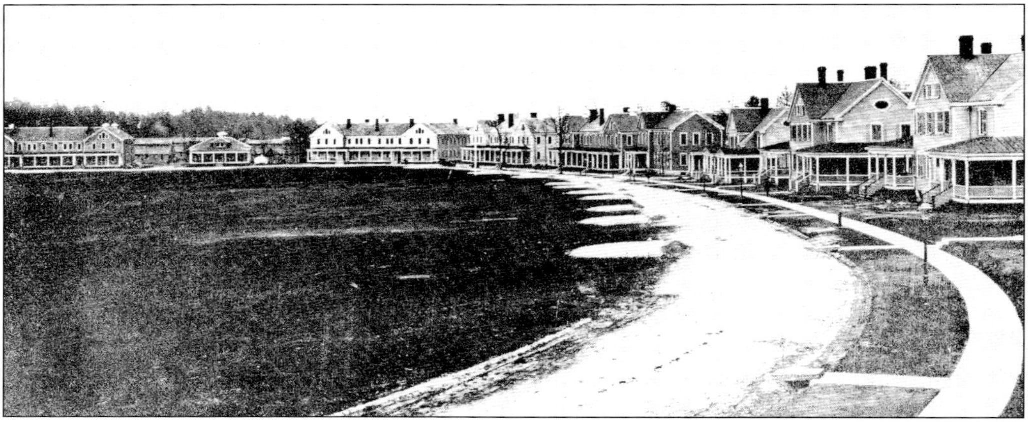

This 1905 postcard shows a sweeping panoramic view of the east and north sides of Barnhardt Circle, the area encompassing the parade grounds of Fort Oglethorpe. From the right, three officers' houses in the residential area of the post are shown. The fourth building, the Post Headquarters, begins the northern end, which contains troop barracks, the guardhouse, and, north of these buildings, the stables for the cavalry horses. (CHCBL.)

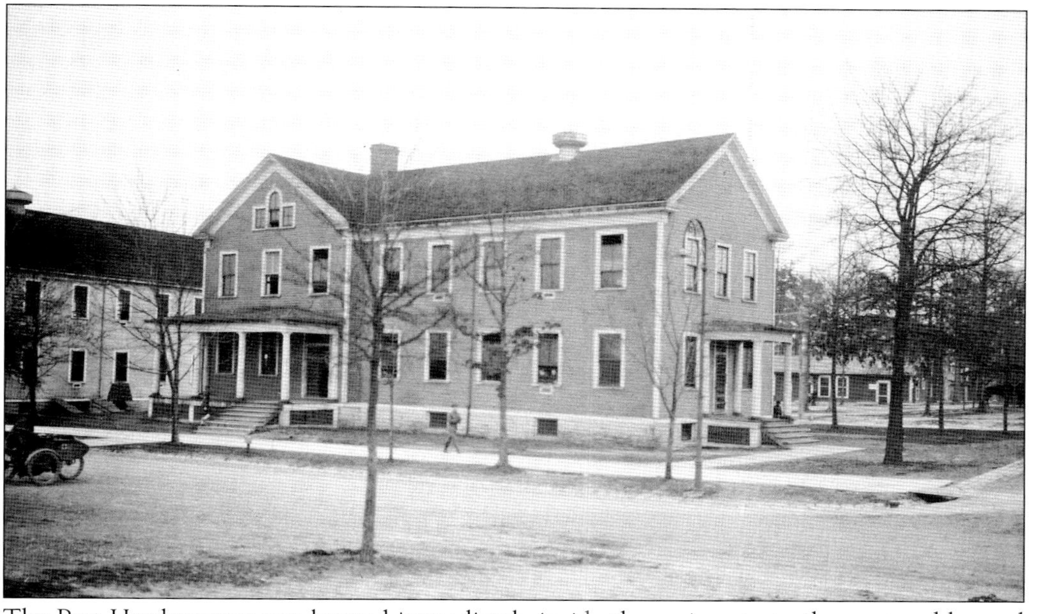

The Post Headquarters was located immediately inside the main gate to the post and housed the offices of the commandant and his staff. The headquarters troop was housed on the second floor. The telephone exchange can be seen east of the headquarters. Earl Wright, in charge of all transportation for the cavalry post, resisted using the motorcycle and preferred his sturdy black stallion, Attaboy. (NARA.)

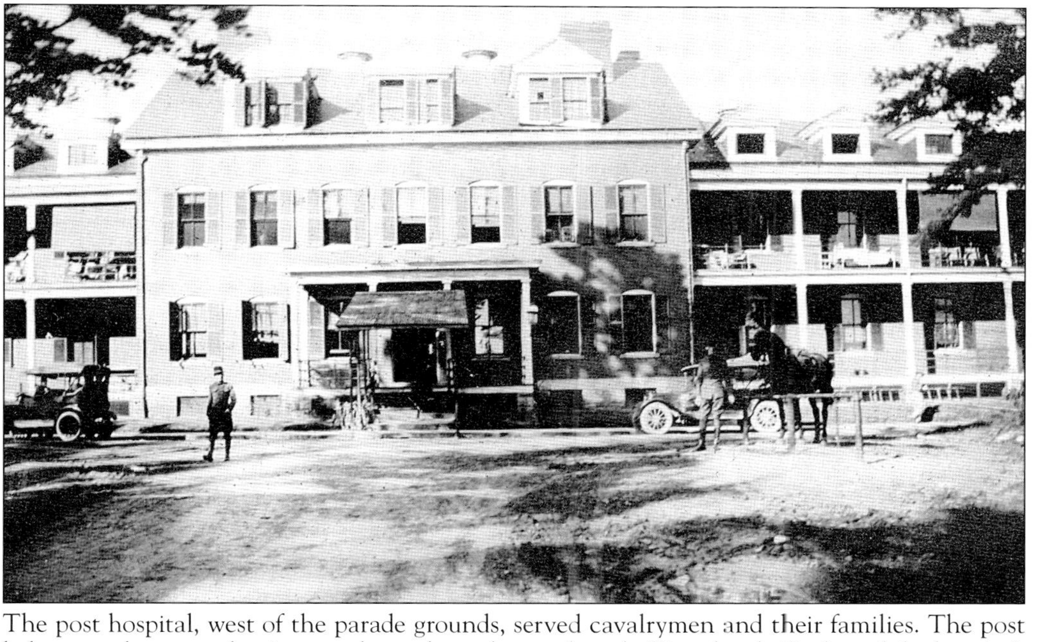

The post hospital, west of the parade grounds, served cavalrymen and their families. The post bakery was between the six troop barracks at the north end of Barnhardt Circle and the hospital, making delivery of the daily goods convenient. The services of the military doctors and civilian nurses were critical to fighting the influenza of 1918, which severely attacked the troops and prisoners of war at Fort Oglethorpe. (SCM.)

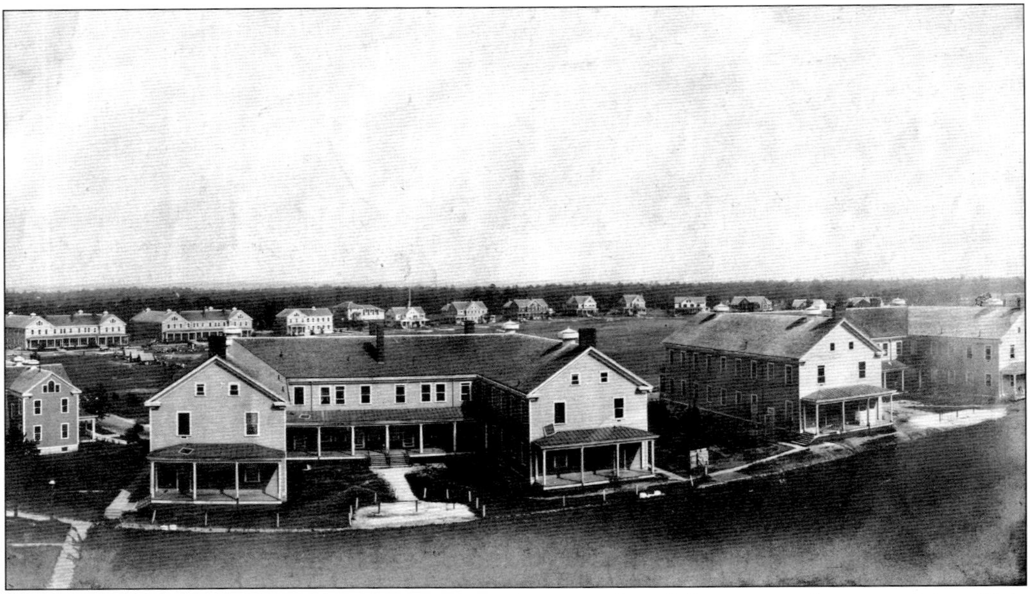

The Signal Corps produced long, composite photographs of the post and its activities. This center of a 54-inch photograph shows the rear of a troop barrack, which housed two troops and almost 200 men. The Band Barracks, to the left, which housed 26 band members, appears quite small compared to its neighbor. This view only suggests the size of the post around the parade grounds. (SCM.)

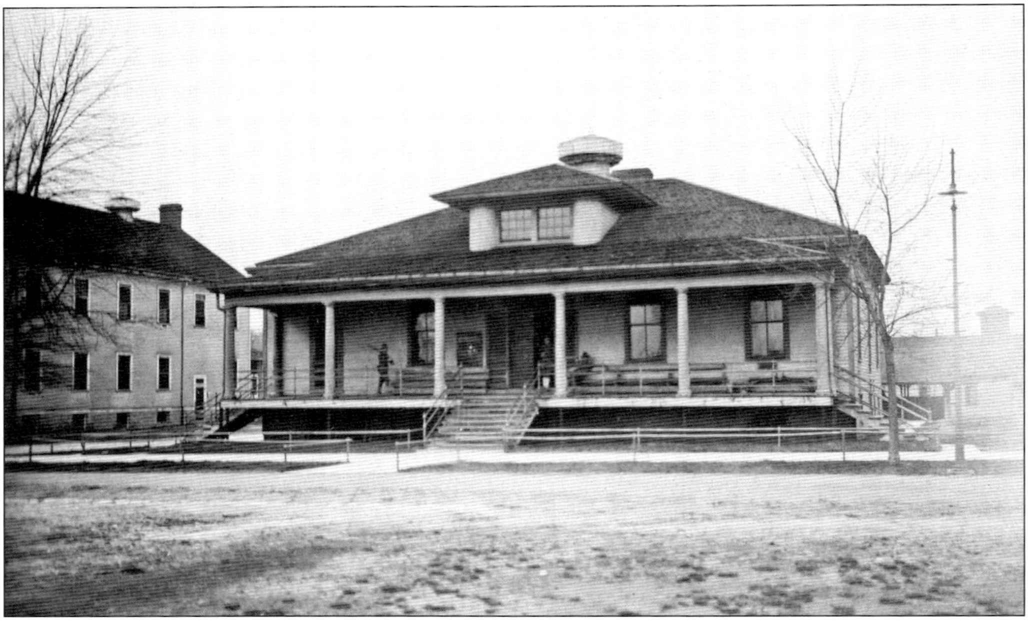

The guardhouse/stockade, located at the north end of the parade grounds in the center of the six troop barracks, had offices and sleeping quarters in the front of the building. The rear portion was the stockade. Two large holding cells contained men who were charged with normal discipline problems such as fighting and drinking. Several individual cells housed men who had committed more serious offenses and were held longer than overnight. (NARA.)

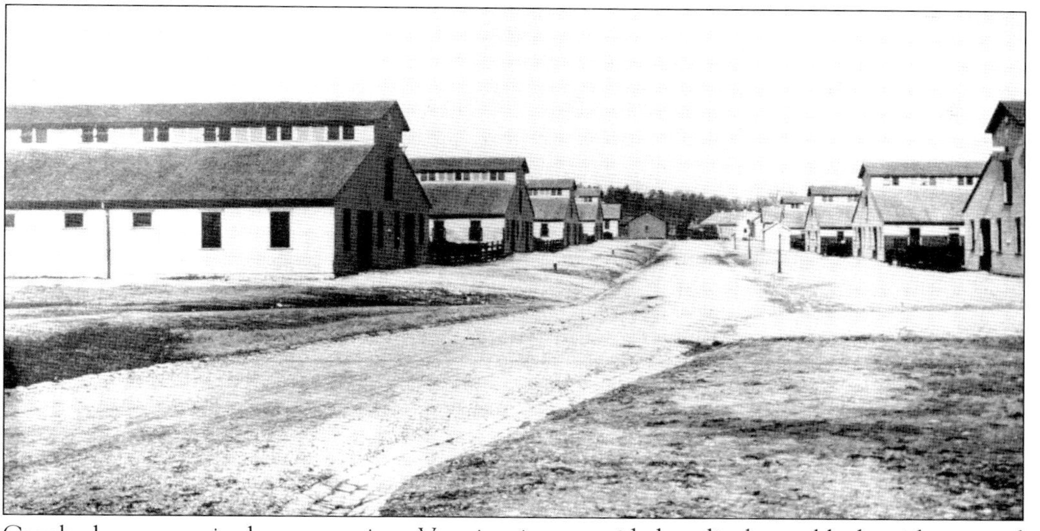

Cavalry horses required many services. Veterinarians provided medical care, blacksmiths created horseshoes, and the quartermaster ordered and maintained feed supplies. Approximately 1,500 head of horses arrived with the 6th Cavalry in 1919. Additional stables were located east and north of the post proper. A stable fire in 1940 resulted in the death of several horses, including Duke the Wonder Horse. (NARA.)

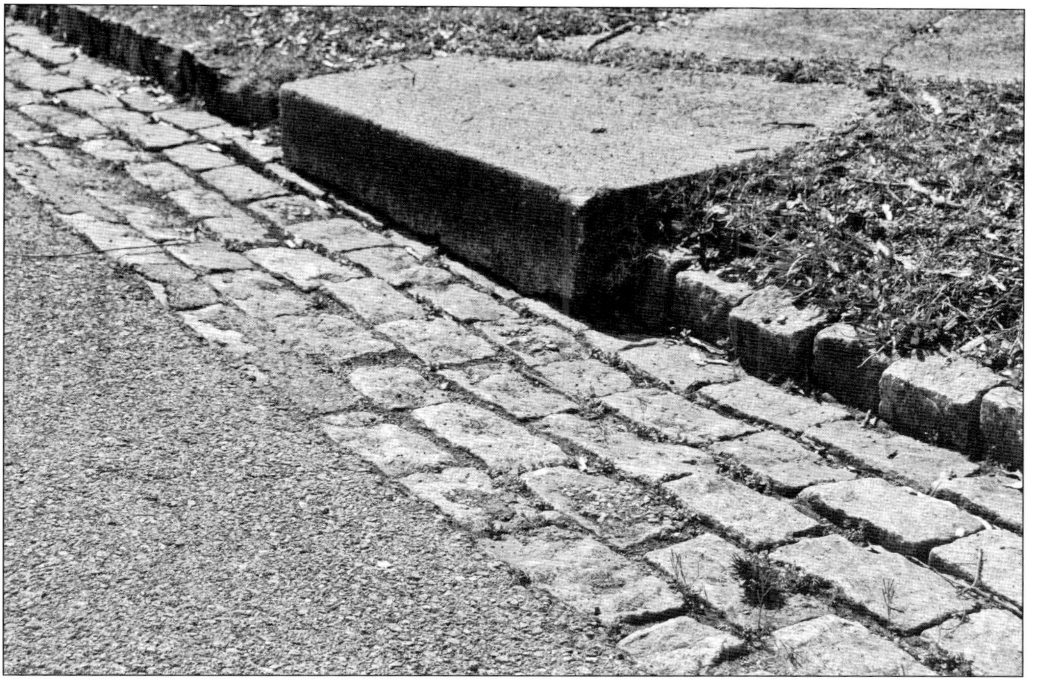

Stone gutters are throughout the post. The stones, cut from nearby quarries, remain in service to this day. The steps from the curb linked the road to the sidewalks. Sidewalks in front of the residences were 5 feet wide. Sidewalks on the north end were 10 feet wide to accommodate the needs of the troops as they assembled for roll call and moved in groups of several men. (LP.)

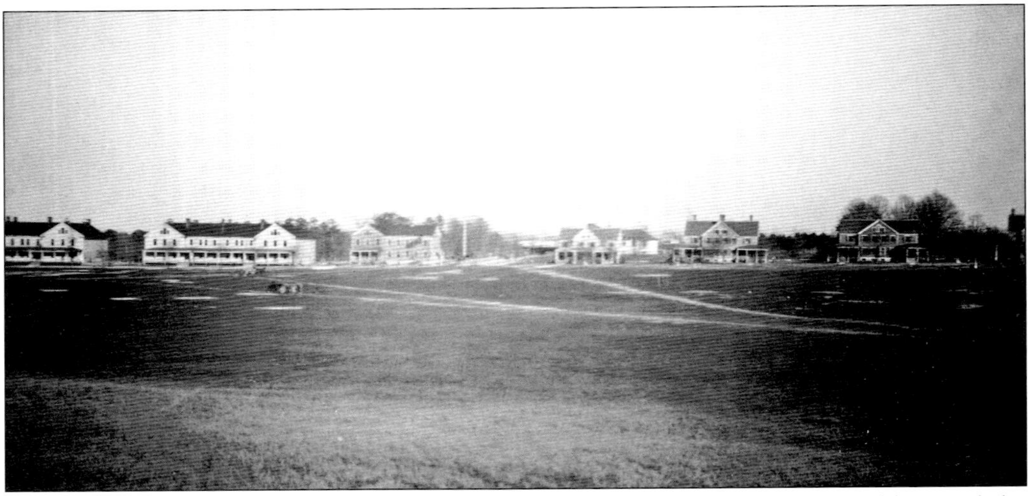

The parade grounds in 1920 are crisscrossed with paths to the headquarters building and the troop barracks. The landscaping has not developed near the houses or around the flagpole. Polo fences and horse jumps will not appear for almost a decade. A lieutenant's house and two captains' houses, seen to the right of the flagpole, are three of the 18 houses for officers and their families constituting Officers Row. (NARA.)

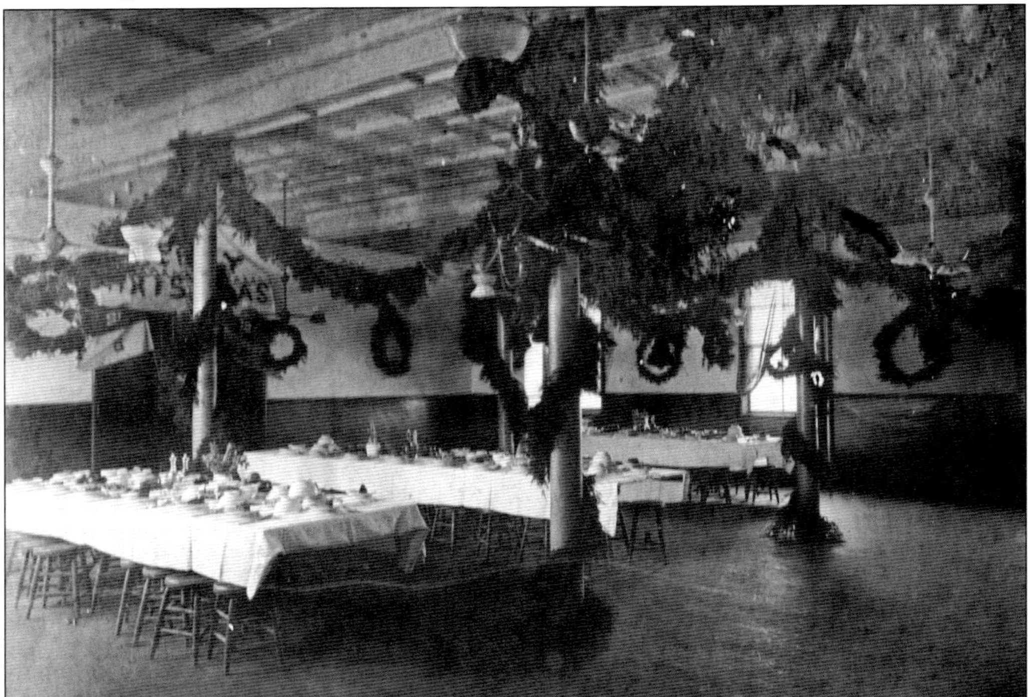

Individual troops celebrated the holidays. A program was provided that gave the menu as well as a complete list of all troop members with their ranks. The accomplishments of the troops for that year were also given. Horse show ribbons, sports championships, and expertise in shooting all were recognized. Here at Christmas 1906 is the dining hall of Troop D, 12th Cavalry, festooned with wreaths, garlands, and a banner. (SCM.)

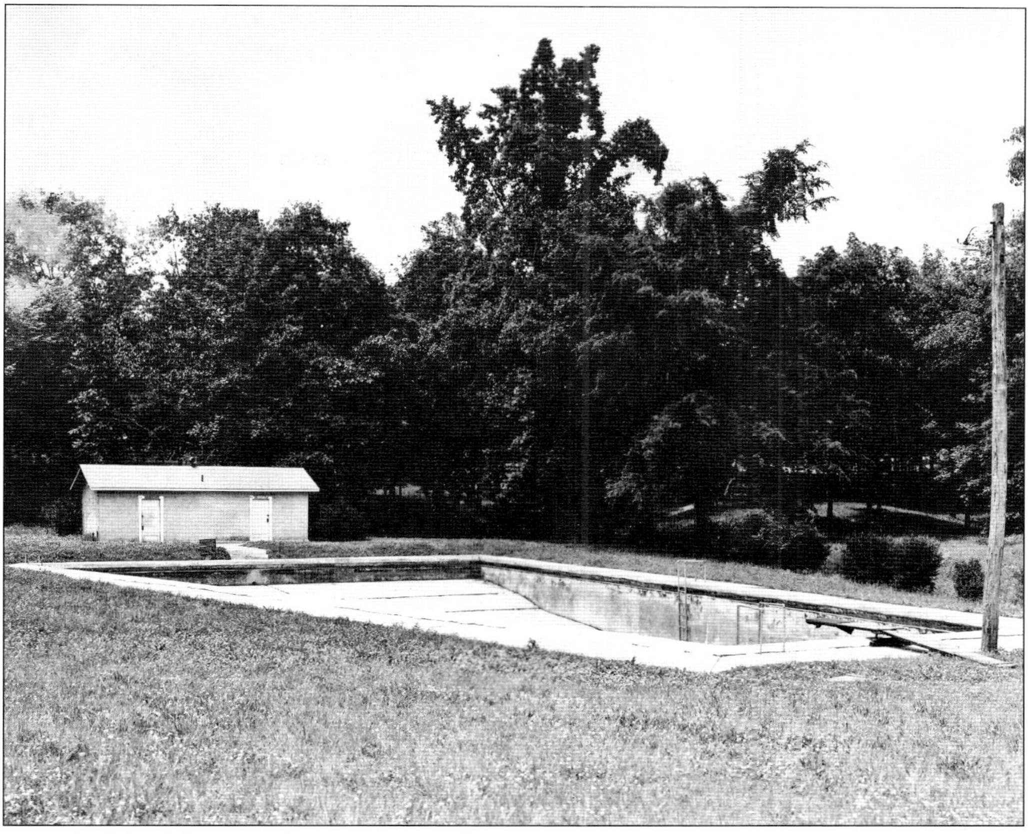

Over the life of the post, there were several swimming pools. The most popular were the one at the Officers Club and the one at the enlisted men's club. This pool has been unused for several seasons. The Officers Club with its pool was later purchased by St. Gerard's Roman Catholic Church. The club was converted into an elementary school, and the pool was used during summer camp for local children. (SCM.)

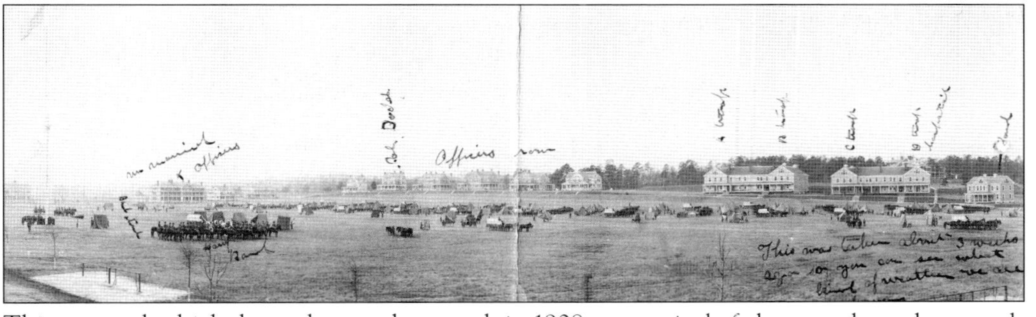

This postcard, which shows the parade grounds in 1908, was typical of photographs and postcards troopers send home to family and friends. A trooper sent this double postcard home, and he labeled various buildings, including the unmarried officers' quarters, Officers Row, troop barracks, the bandstand, hospital, and the band in the left of the picture. On the parade grounds are wagons and their teams, mounted cavalry, and tents. (CHCBL.)

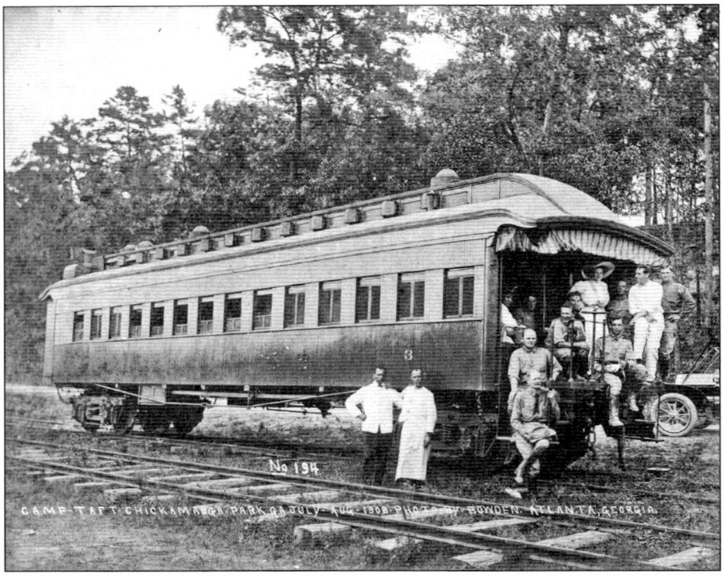

National Guard units from Georgia, Tennessee, and Alabama used the battlefield for training. Troops were stationed at Camp Taft in July and August 1908. Two ladies and a gentleman appear to be visiting troops at the battlefield. Two men standing beside the railroad car appear to be waiters to serve the visitors and their friends. (CHCBL.)

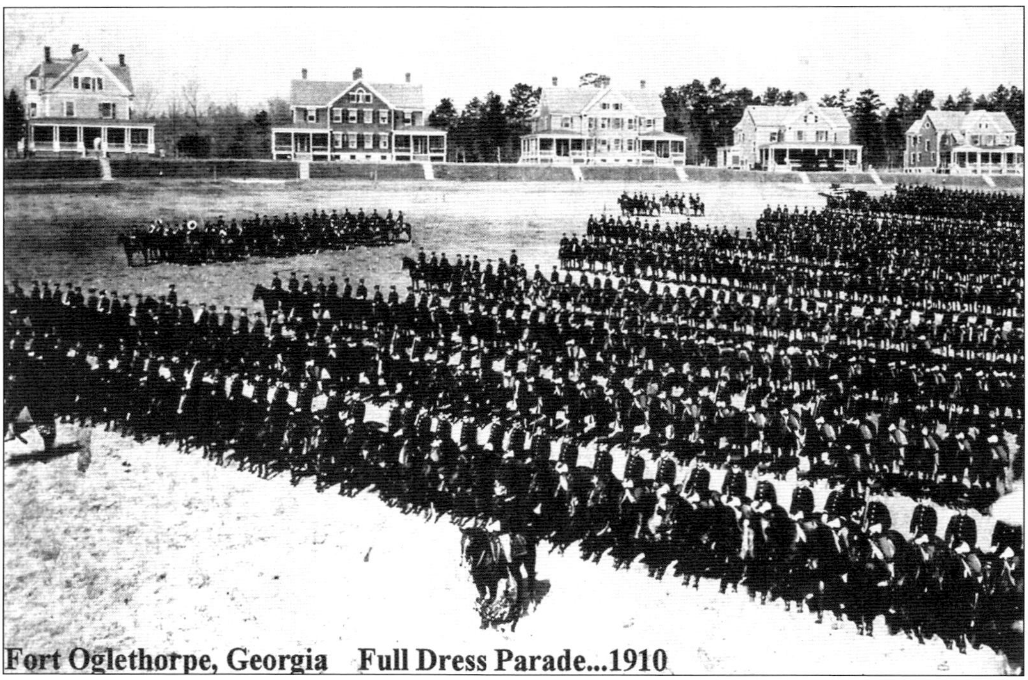

A full dress parade at Fort Oglethorpe was an impressive sight. The band (rear left) often played while mounted. The public traveled from Chattanooga and as far south as Atlanta to enjoy the precision and glamour of these events. The 11th Cavalry, shown here in 1910, was stationed at Fort Oglethorpe from 1908 to 1919, when it left for the Presidio, California, and the 6th Cavalry arrived. (CHCBL.)

Two

Training for War

During the early 1900s, small groups of men in the northwest Georgia area informally trained together in warfare. When Pres. Woodrow Wilson announced the United States was at war, many of these men quickly enlisted in the army. They became the core of troops training at Fort Oglethorpe. Medics and doctors were trained at Camp Greenleaf in Chickamauga and Chattanooga National Military Park. The medics learned how to treat the wounded in trenches as well as on the battlefield; the ambulance corps was trained to transport the injured soldiers from the front to rear area hospitals.

From September 20 through December 20, 1917, Capt. Dwight D. Eisenhower taught trench warfare at Camp Forrest in Chickamauga and Chattanooga Military Park. Both the north and south sides of Snodgrass Hill were used for trench-digging exercises. Although the government permitted expansion into the military park for training during times of emergency, the park was quite concerned over damage to the property.

The World War I Signal Corps training camp was located at the present corner of Battlefield Parkway and Lafayette Road in Fort Oglethorpe, Georgia. A contingent of Signal Corps graduates went overseas with General Pershing's Expeditionary Force.

The Red Cross Volunteer Canteen Service was directed by Mrs. T. H. McClure during World War I. Local women volunteered at the canteens, where the soldiers could come to rest and relax, have refreshments, write letters home, and relieve the loneliness of being away from their families and friends.

Armistice Day was celebrated on November 11, 1918, and the streets of downtown Chattanooga were crowded with parades and civilians and soldiers all celebrating together. Flags waved, and spectators crowded the sidewalks and hung out of windows as they joined in the gaiety.

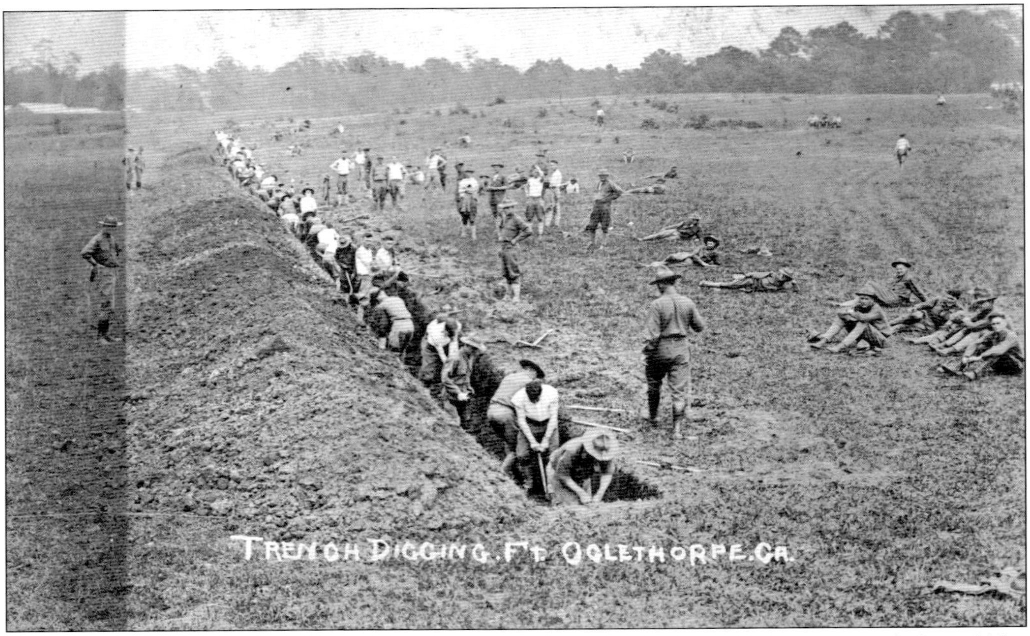

At Camp Forrest, soldiers learned to dig trenches and dugout areas where wounded could be treated and communication stations sheltered. The shovel and pickax were the tools most commonly used. On September 20, 1863, at Chickamauga, Gen. George Thomas, the "Rock of Chickamauga," made his stand at Snodgrass Hill, holding off pursuing Confederates until the Union troops were safely toward Chattanooga. Both the north and south sides of Snodgrass Hill were used for trench construction. (NARA.)

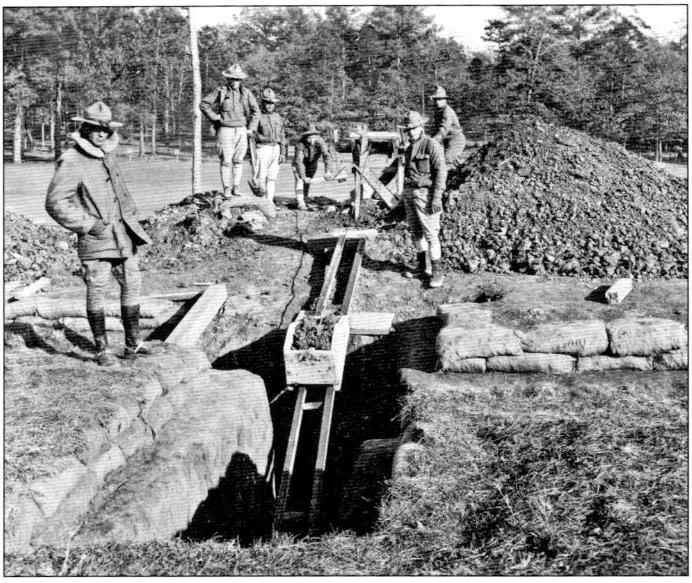

Trenches were also built with the assistance of machines. Both ways were taught by instructors, among them Capt. Dwight David Eisenhower, stationed at the post from September 20 to December 20, 1917. Eisenhower was considered such a valuable instructor that he was assigned stateside during the entire war. As a professional soldier, Eisenhower worried his lack of command experience during World War I would hinder his remaining army career. (NARA.)

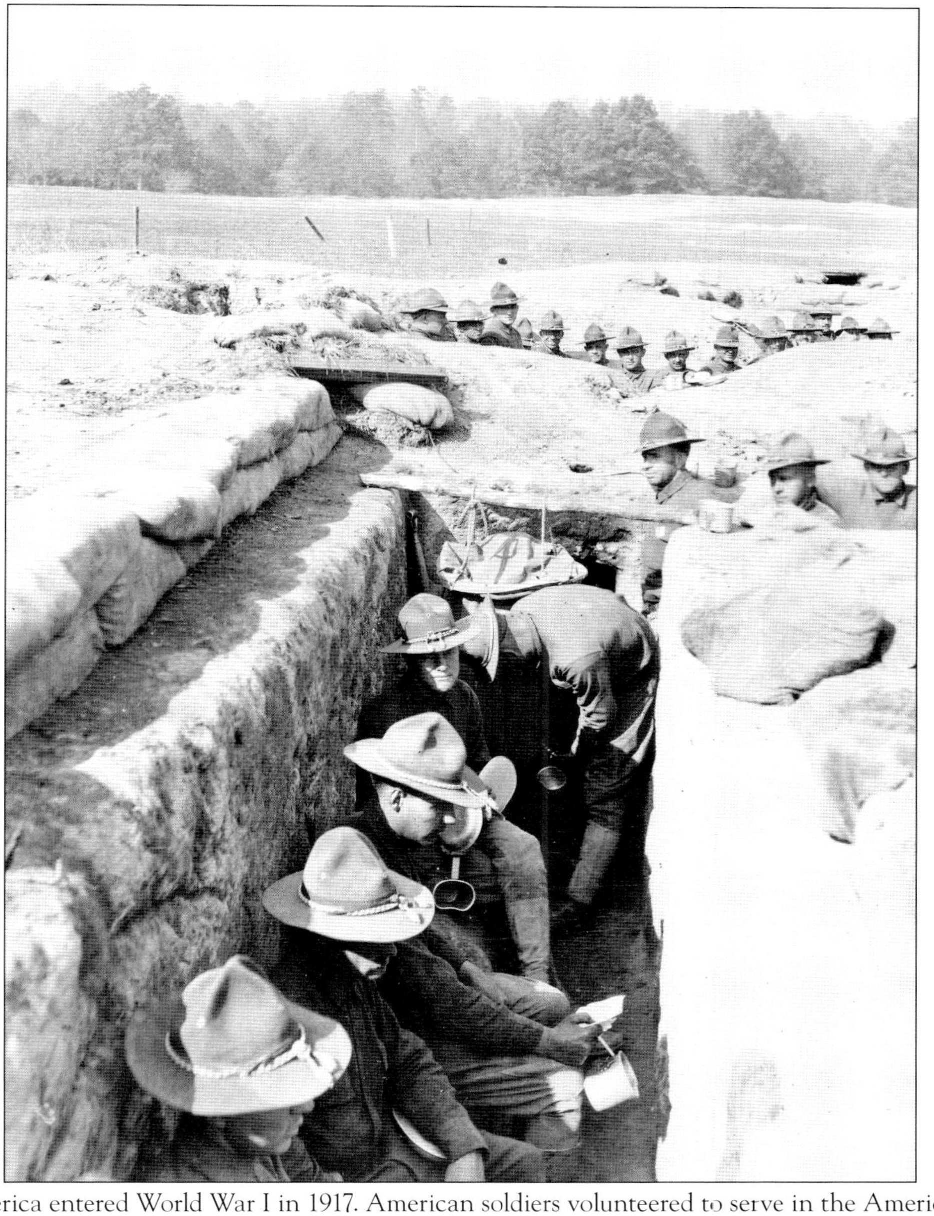

America entered World War I in 1917. American soldiers volunteered to serve in the American Expeditionary Force under Gen. John J. Pershing. At the front, soldiers from both sides faced each other across an open area called "No Man's Land." Their trenches were a maze of interconnecting ditches and intersections that were confusing, especially at night. Some trenches had steps built into their sides, and others provided some protection for a single shooter. The safety of the Chickamauga battlefield in the sunlight belies the constant danger in which the men served. Poisonous gas such as mustard gas was fatal to many soldiers, and they all sought trench protection during such gas attacks. The men shown in the front of this picture have protection as long as they remain sitting. The other men are standing and are susceptible to enemy fire. These men at Fort Oglethorpe casually sit with water cups ready. A water bag hanging from an improvised rod can be seen in the center and a bunker opening is in the right rear of the photograph. (NARA.)

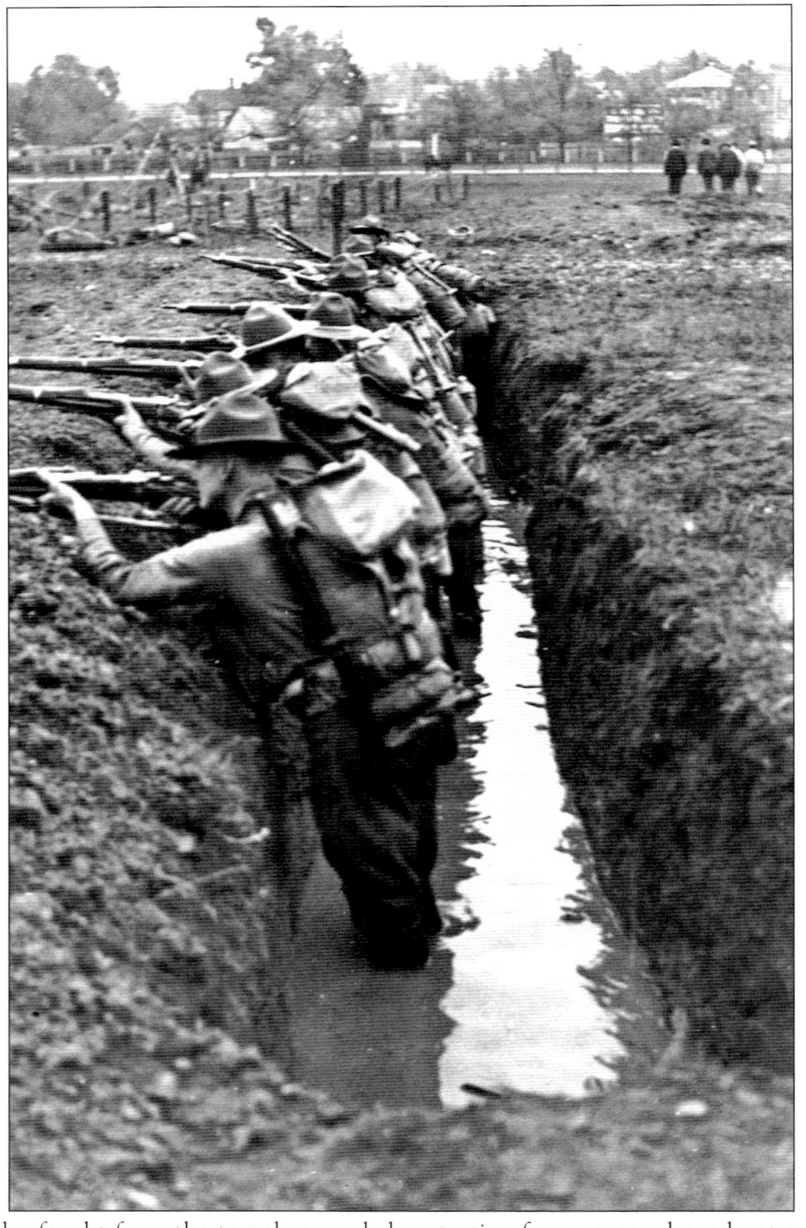

Soldiers who fought from the trenches needed protection from enemy sharpshooters. Bursting bombs lit the night sky and showed where the enemy was located. To protect a standing soldier, trenches were dug from 8 feet to 12 feet deep. These soldiers show another aspect of trench warfare: standing in water for long period of time. The programs at Camp Greenleaf addressed training to ensure the soldiers left the post in the best health possible and that they sustained a minimum of discomfort and illness from such exposure. Trench training was held in open fields, but the proximity of the houses in the background would indicate that much of the park land was in use in some way for all training needs. The national military parks in the United States were under the Department of the Army until 1933, when the National Park Service was created and placed under the Department of the Interior. (CHCBL.)

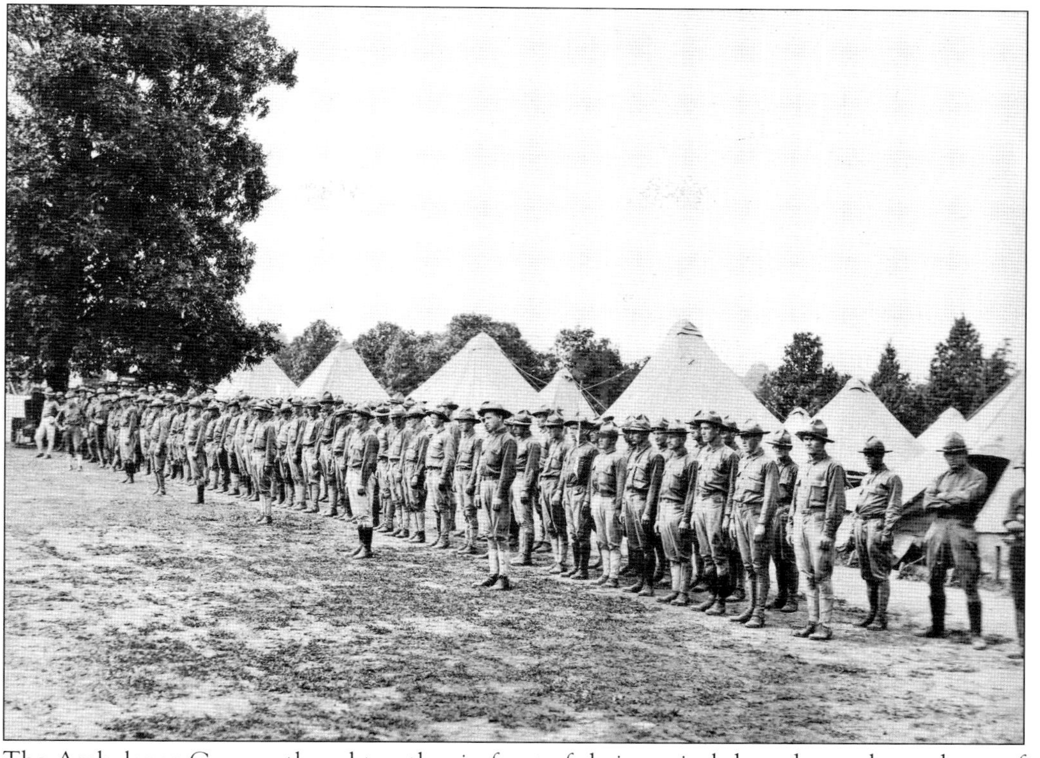

The Ambulance Corps gathered together in front of their conical-shaped tents located east of the post. Their training included first aid and transportation of wounded. Through their efforts, men were successfully transported from the battlefields of Europe to the skilled hands of dental surgeons at Fort Oglethorpe who reconstructed destroyed jaws. Many a grateful soldier remembered these surgeons in Christmas cards sent over the years. (NARA.)

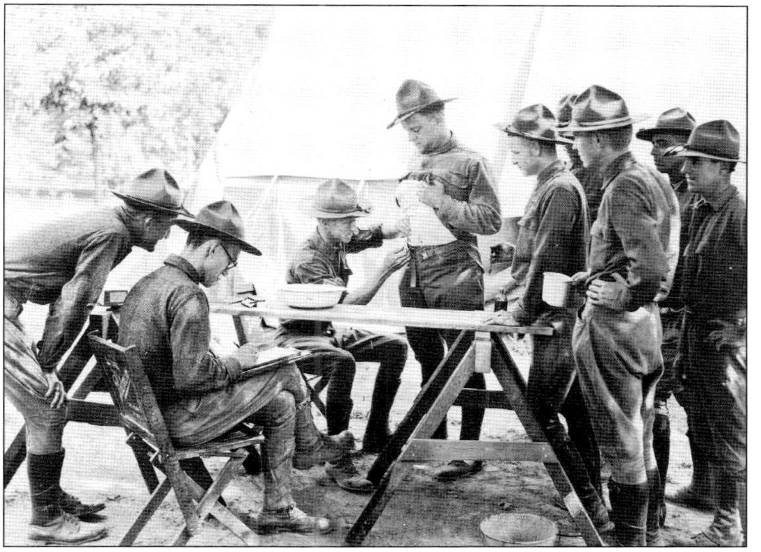

Camp Greenleaf, one of three camps at Fort Oglethorpe, earned the nickname "the West Point of Medicine." The staff was concerned with the health of troops going to war as well as with the medical treatment provided the troops at the front line. Here the Ambulance Corps receive their vaccinations. As they wait, these medical men do not appear to be nervous. (NARA.)

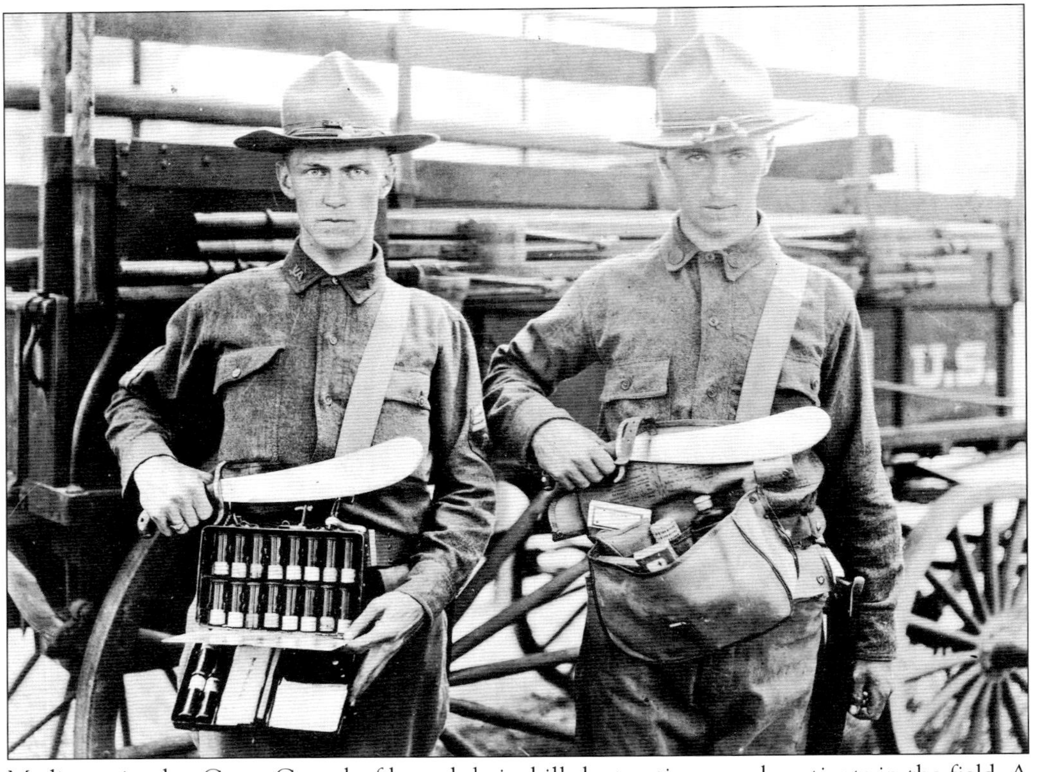

Medics trained at Camp Greenleaf honed their skills by treating sample patients in the field. A machete was one tool that every medic carried. Broken bones, head wounds, and severe cuts were common injuries. Training photographs captured correct and incorrect ways of stabilizing men until they were transported behind lines. (NARA.)

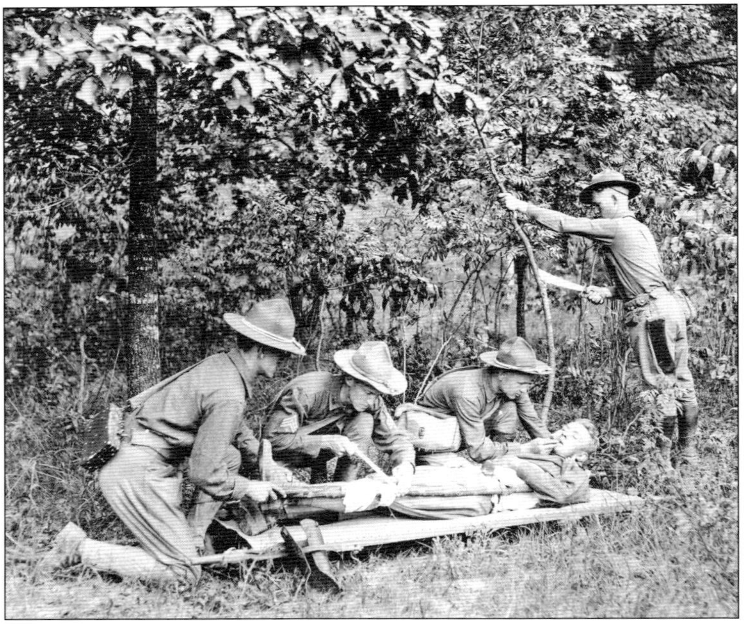

One medic uses his machete to cut down a stick to stabilize the "wounded" soldier's leg. The four medics have divided responsibilities, one cutting a splint to stabilize the soldier's leg and the other three medics attending to his leg. He will be transported on a stretcher made of canvas tied to the wooden sides. (NARA.)

Medical attention was just the first step. Once stabilized, the wounded soldiers were carried back to safety. One man is carried by two medics, and another medic carries a soldier slung over his back. The medics then sought the safety of a friendly trench or an ambulance. The medics could not rest until a doctor and a field hospital were reached. (NARA.)

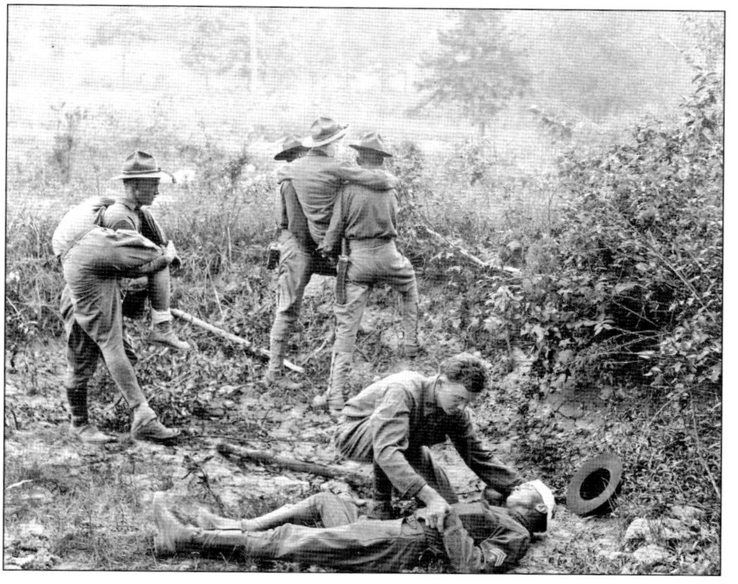

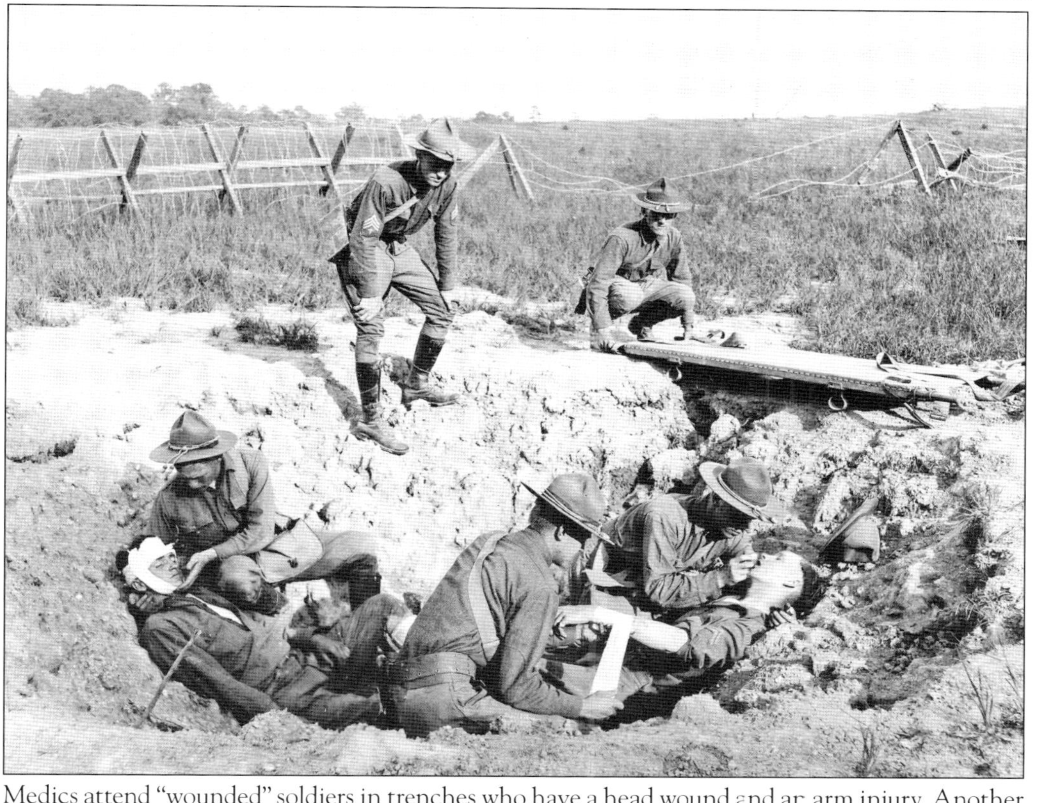

Medics attend "wounded" soldiers in trenches who have a head wound and an arm injury. Another medic awaits directions for the stretcher. This trench area is surrounded by barbed-wire wrapped around fence works. Attacking forces had to force their way through or over such barbed wire in order to reach the enemy. Medics trained to work under such conditions and were well prepared for their service overseas. (NARA.)

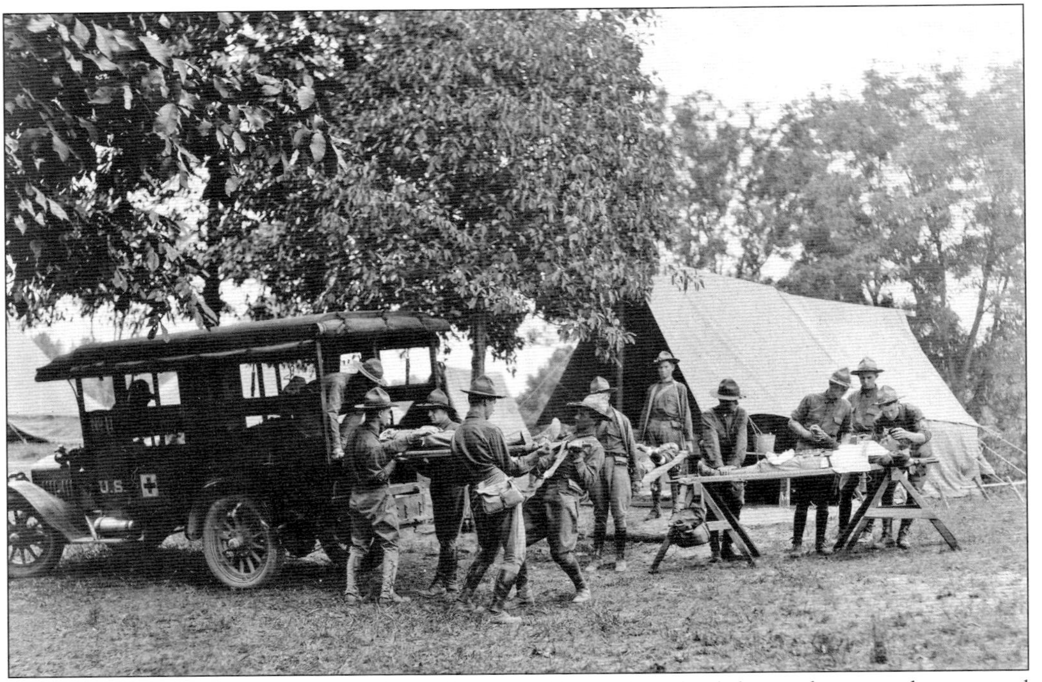

The Ambulance Corps trained at Camp Greenleaf learned on both horse-drawn and motorized ambulances. The ambulances were identified with the initials "U.S." and a red cross on a white square. Doctors as well as medics were trained for work done under less than preferred conditions. Two "wounded" soldiers are moved from the ambulance as a third is already on the operating table set up on sawhorses. (NARA.)

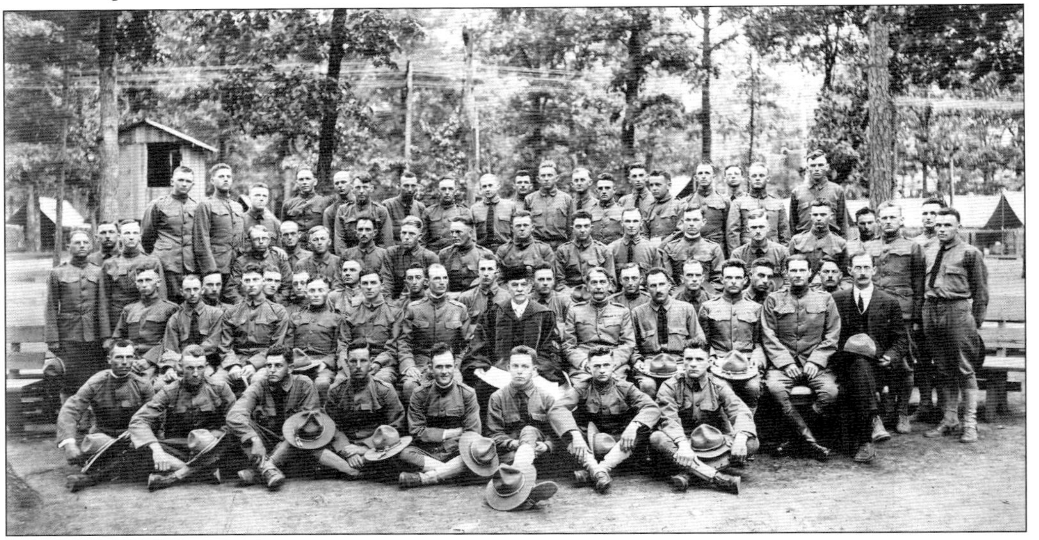

Graduating seniors from the University of South Carolina reported to Fort Oglethorpe before graduation exercises. The post commandant and the university president conversed about the situation, and the commandant agreed that the president was welcome to come to the post and present to the seniors their diplomas. University of South Carolina president William S. Carroll posed with the graduating seniors. (Courtesy of the University of South Carolina Archives.)

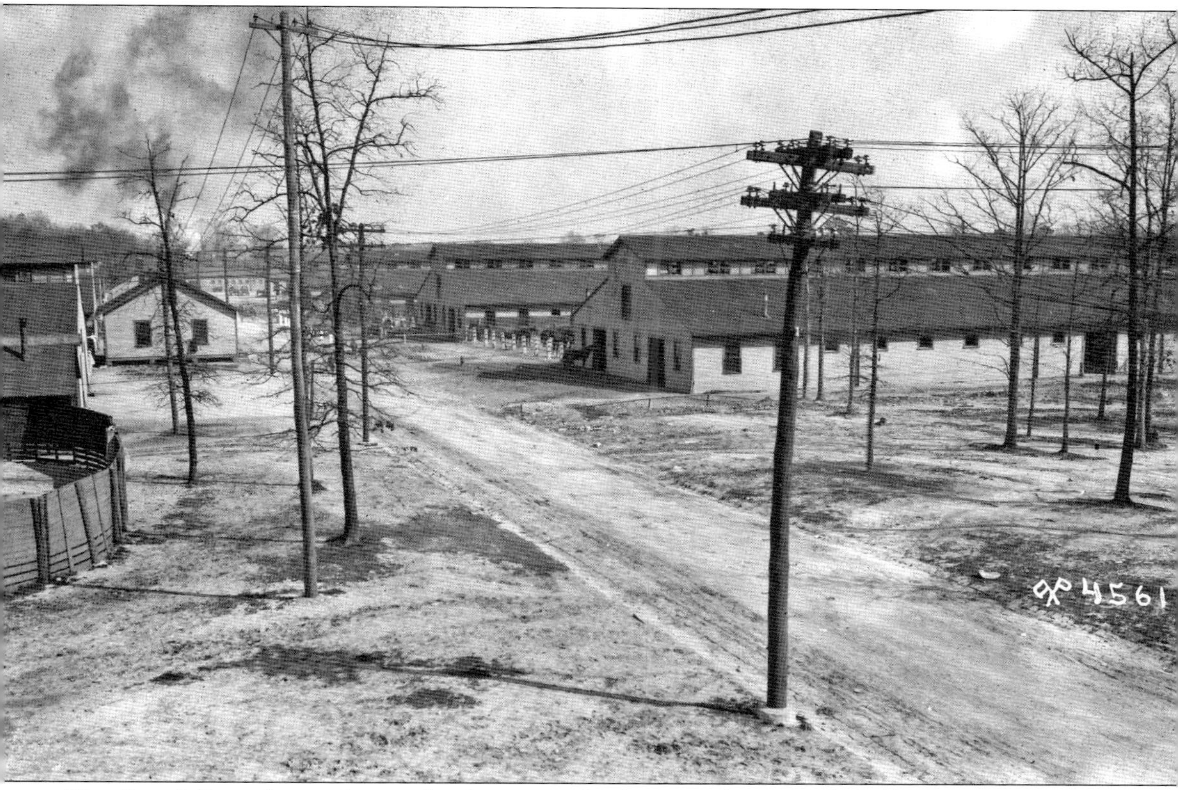

The Signal Corps began during the American Civil War and even included balloons for aerial surveillance. As technology advanced and the nature of battles changed, the corps developed more modern ways to communicate. A Signal Corps Training Camp was located at Battlefield Parkway and Lafayette Road. (If one asked 6th Cavalry troopers, they would say that stables indicated these were men who were cavalrymen who happened to be in the Signal Corps.) Their training interfaced with the trench training. Some of the bunkers were built specifically to shelter communication centers. Wires had to be strung and radios made operational under battle conditions. A contingent of Signal Corps graduates went overseas with Pershing's American Expeditionary Force. All official Signal Corps photographs are complete with captions identifying subject, date, location, and names. These photographs have one of two corps emblems with an identifying number. (NARA.)

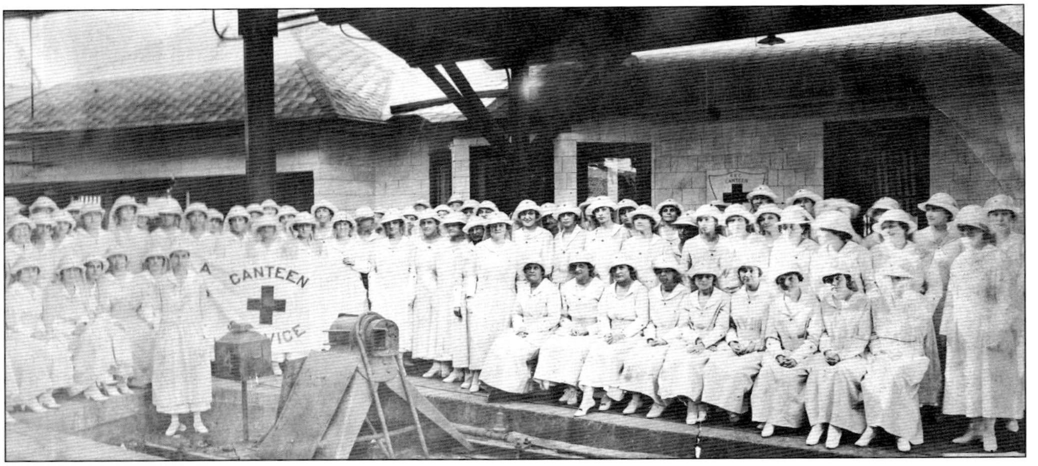

Local women helped on the home front by volunteering for Red Cross Canteen Service. These ladies manned area canteens where soldiers could rest, get refreshments, write letters home, and satisfy their loneliness away from home. These ladies pose at a station on the trolley line or train line. Mrs. T. H. McClure served as the general chairman of the Chattanooga canteens. (CHCBL.)

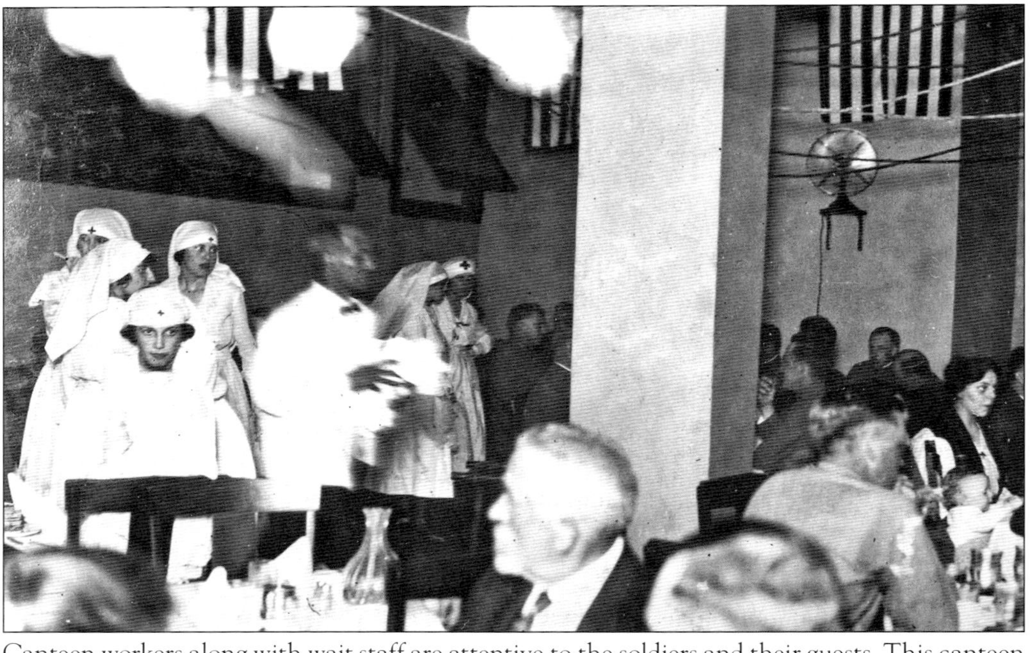

Canteen workers along with wait staff are attentive to the soldiers and their guests. This canteen was located in the Park Hotel at East Seventh Street in Chattanooga. The crowd suggests this was a popular site for relaxation and fellowship. The city of Chattanooga served its military family well. During peace time, the city held dances and entertained officers and their wives at various community club luncheons. (CHCBL.)

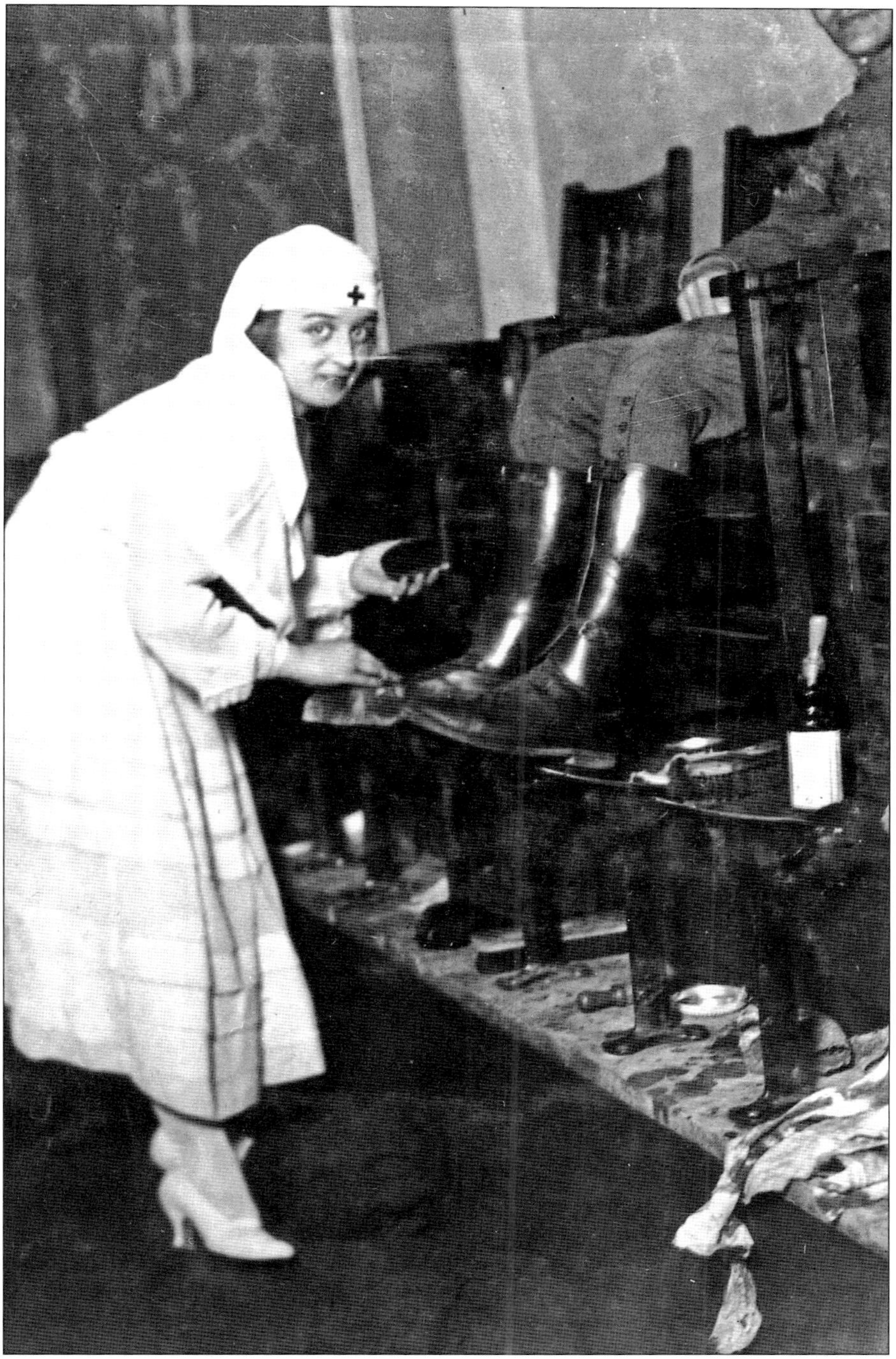

Dorris Carter poses in 1918 in her white canteen uniform and her graceful white pumps as she polishes a soldier's boots at the Park Hotel. One might think that the conversation with a young lady was as welcomed as the free boot shine. The young matrons of the local "Godmothers" chapter helped troops with letters and packages. A women's committee oversaw the activities of all relief groups. (CHCBL.)

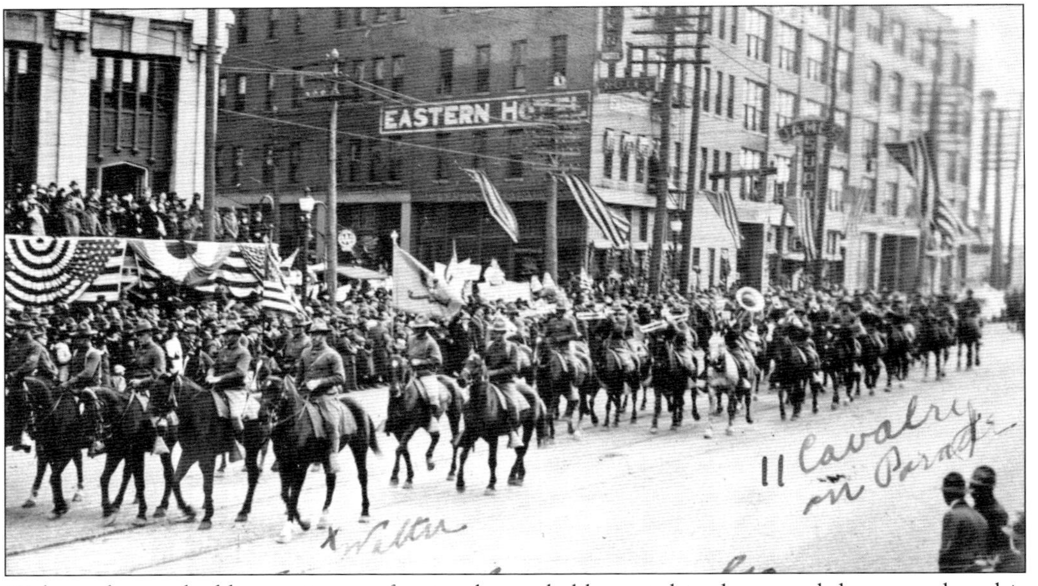

Walter, who marked his position at front right, probably sent this photograph home to show his family that the 11th Cavalry participated in this Liberty Loan Parade on April 6, 1918. Members of the Medical Officers Training Corps also participated in these local parades for the war effort. The reviewing stand is in front of the Patten Hotel. The Eastern Hotel advertises AAA service. (CHCBL.)

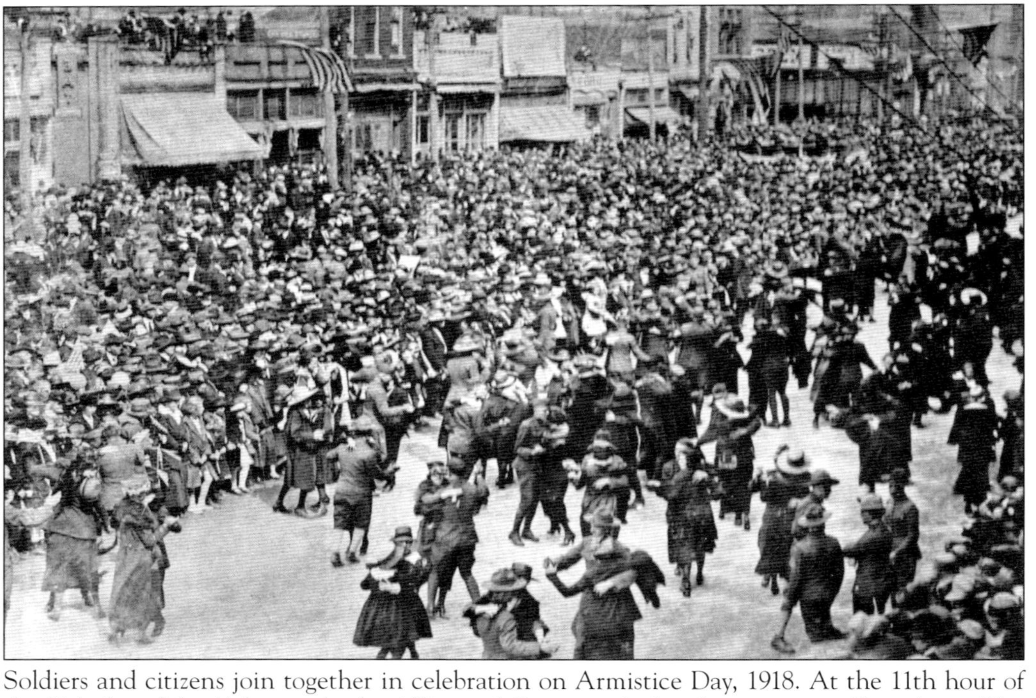

Soldiers and citizens join together in celebration on Armistice Day, 1918. At the 11th hour of the 11th day of the 11th month, the Allies and Germany declared a cessation of hostilities. The war officially continued in other areas of the world, but the news of the armistice drew many to downtown Chattanooga. (CHCBL.)

Three

INTERNING PRISONERS OF WAR

Dr. Karl Muck, conductor of the Boston Symphony Orchestra, and Earnest Kunwald, former conductor of the Cincinnati Symphony Orchestra, were both members of the Millionaire's Club at Fort Oglethorpe. The Millionaire's Club was a nickname for a group of enemy alien civilians detained at Fort Oglethorpe during World War I who were wealthy and lived in a separate compound from the other enemy aliens. They paid for their own upkeep and were not required to do any labor.

Dr. Muck was reportedly imprisoned because he was born in Bavaria, Germany, and because he refused to play the "Star-Spangled Banner" at a concert. He was at Fort Oglethorpe until a year after the war ended, when he was deported to Germany.

Twenty-nine members of the Boston Symphony were also imprisoned at Fort Oglethorpe. While Dr. Muck was there, William Taft sent him music and a piano. An orchestra was formed, and cars from Chattanooga often lined the streets outside the compound as citizens listened to the music.

A total of 3,400 people were confined at Fort Oglethorpe over the four years of World War I. Some of these were from German and Austrian ships that had been seized in American ports. Others lived in the United States, but because they were of German or Austrian descent, they were considered a threat to the country. Because of the disparity of the enemy aliens and the prisoners of war, the POWs were eventually shipped to another camp at Fort McPherson in Atlanta, Georgia, and the enemy aliens remained at Fort Oglethorpe.

Although they did no labor, the members of the Millionaire's Club did enjoy gardening and growing their own vegetables. Fresh vegetables were provided for the entire post. This helped contribute to the good health of the troops at Fort Oglethorpe. It also meant the prisoners could eat many of their favorite native foods, such as sauerkraut. Some of the men baked delicious bread. To occupy their time, the enemy aliens enjoyed reading, playing cards, keeping pets, and playing volleyball and basketball.

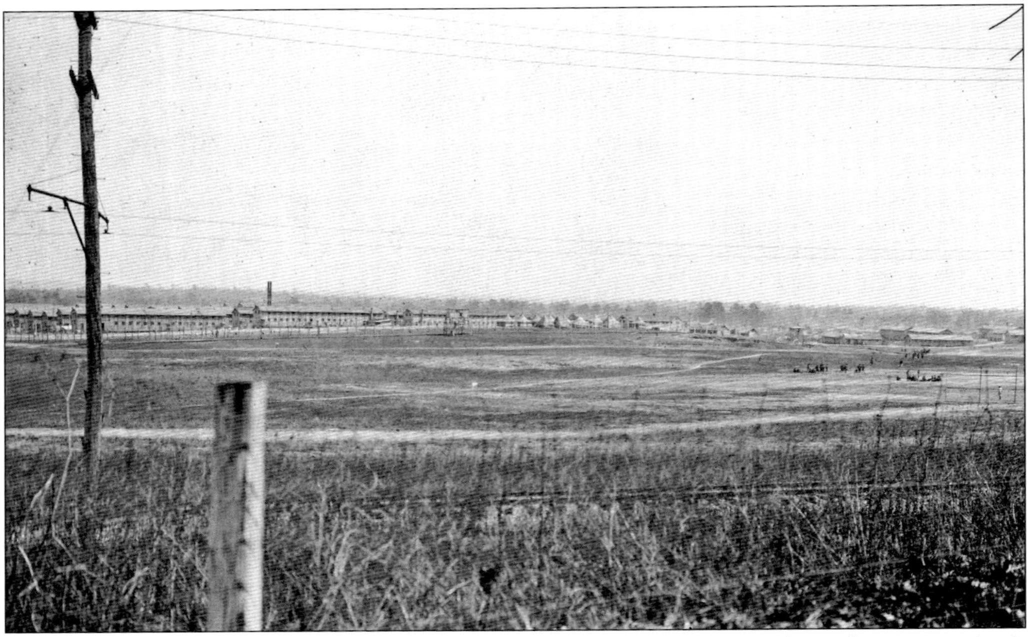

The United States entered World War I in 1917, and the prisoner of war (POW) camp was built in 1918. Administrative buildings and guard barracks are to the right. A hospital unit, identified by its familiar conical tents, was just outside the camp area. The prison camp was at the present site of the Gilbert-Stephenson City Park on Van Cleave Street, extending north across Battlefield Parkway to Patterson Street. (CHCBL.)

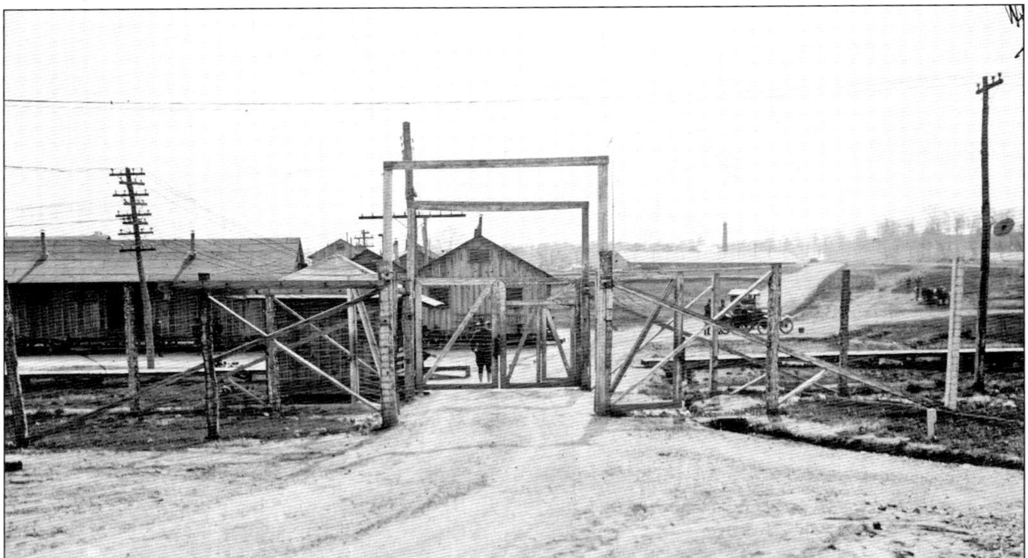

Fort Oglethorpe was one of three POW camps in America during World War I. After a few months, only enemy aliens and a few Bolsheviks who were kept separate from the others were confined at Barracks No. 2, Fort Oglethorpe. The military prisoners were kept at Barracks No. 1, Fort McPherson, Atlanta. All military prisoners taken west of the Mississippi were kept at Barracks No. 3, Fort Douglas, Utah. (NARA.)

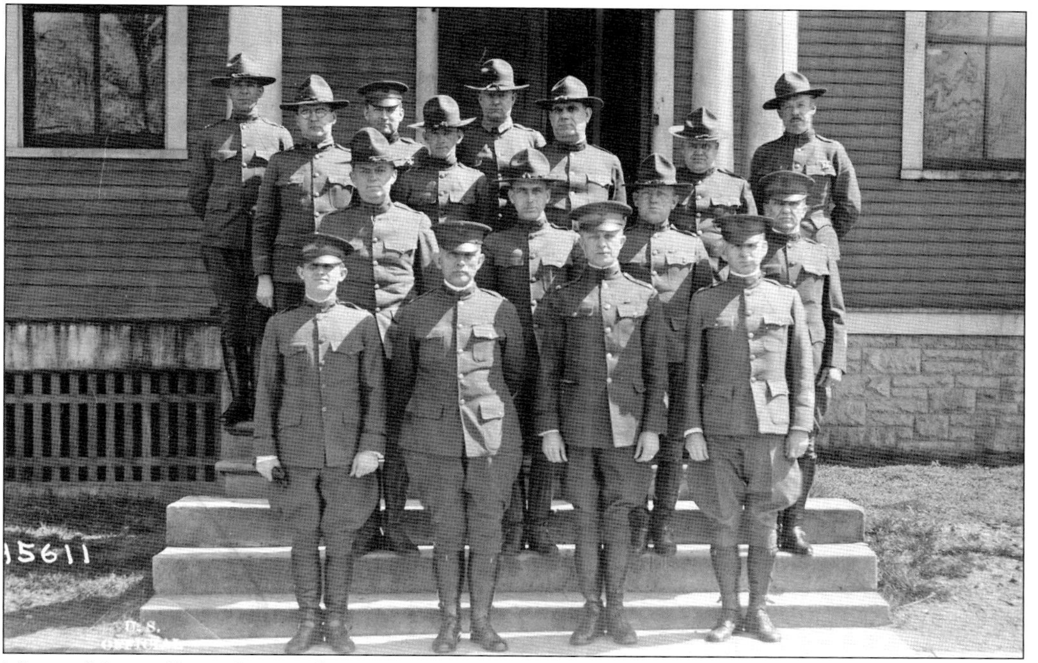

Many of the staff members at the POW camp were retired army veterans. Their age and experience made them better suited to handle the over 3,000 POWs held at Barracks No. 2, Fort Oglethorpe. Thirty-two commissioned officers and 452 enlisted men guarded the POW camp. As a result, there were few attempted escapes, with only three successful. (SCM.)

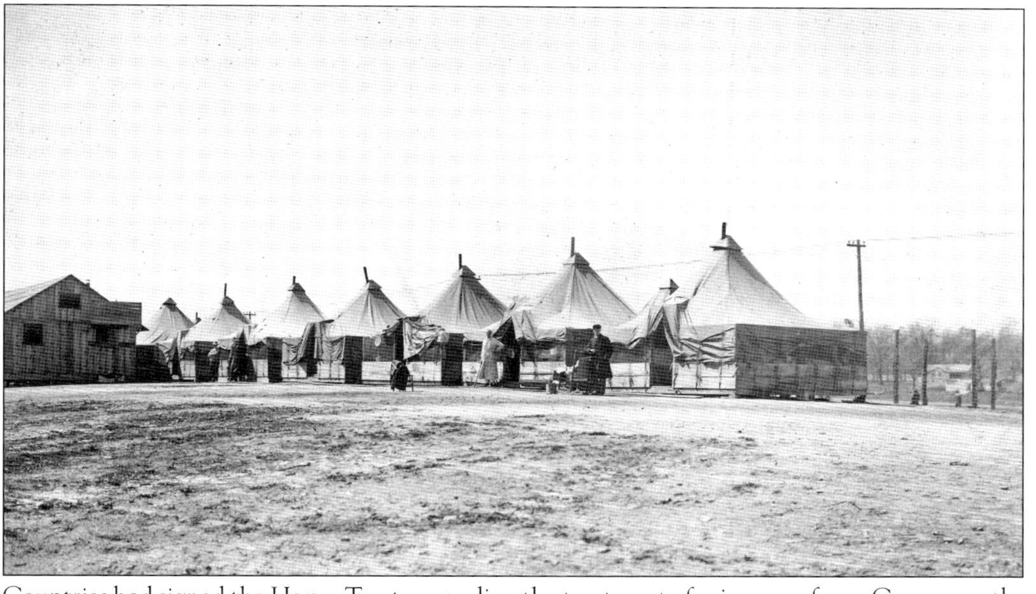

Countries had signed the Hague Treaty regarding the treatment of prisoners of war. Consequently, the internees at Fort Oglethorpe had shelter, clothing, a good diet, and exercise. All countries agreed to have medical services available at the prison camps. Here are shown the conical-shaped tents, familiar to the Ambulance Corps. Swiss observers visited the camp and verified the quality of food and services provided the prisoners. (NARA.)

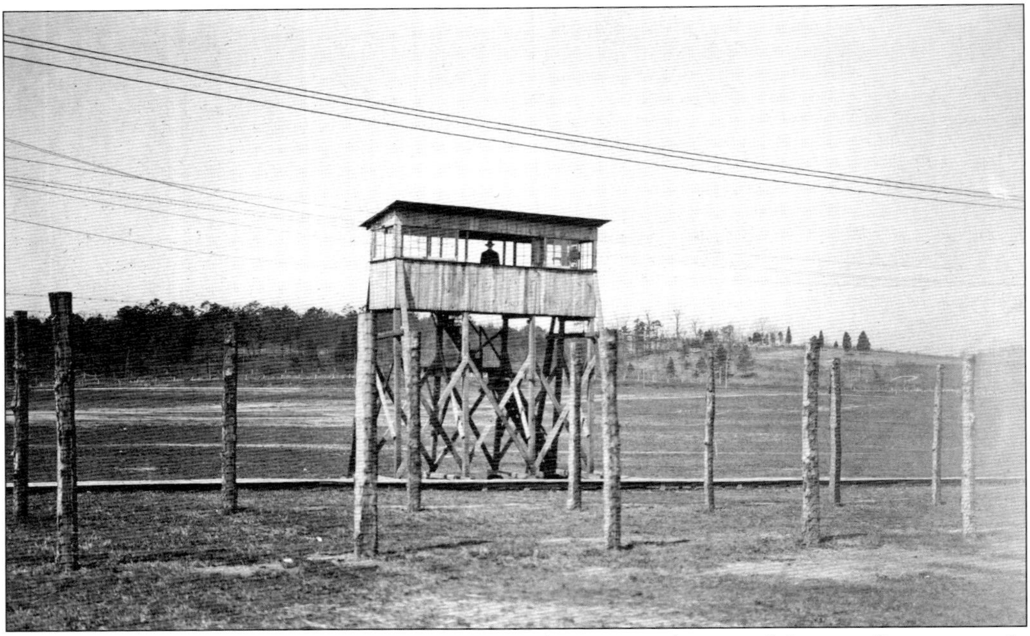

A guard observes his area of the POW camp. Wooden steps at the rear of the guardhouse provide access. A sidewalk encompassed the outside perimeter of the camp. When the camp was originally opened, the sentry made his inspection around the perimeter of the camp in 20 minutes. After more prisoners came and the camp had been enlarged, his inspection required one hour. (NARA.)

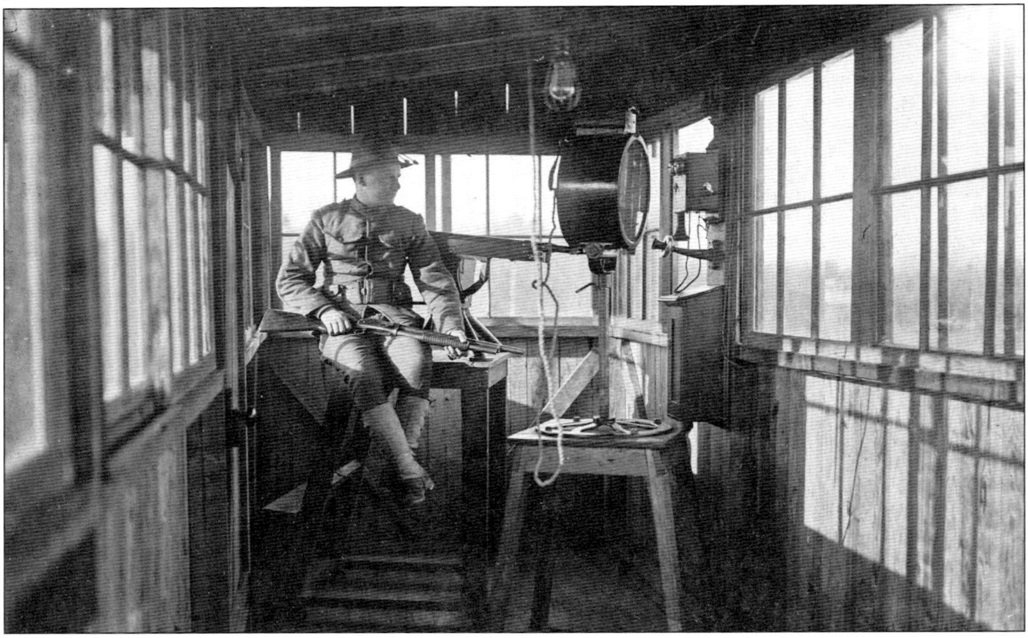

In the guard towers, each guard was armed with a rifle and, in case of an escape attempt with more than one prisoner, the machine gun mounted on a tripod stood ready at his side. The tower was equipped with lights, a telephone, and a spotlight. The towers were located around the perimeter of the camp. (NARA.)

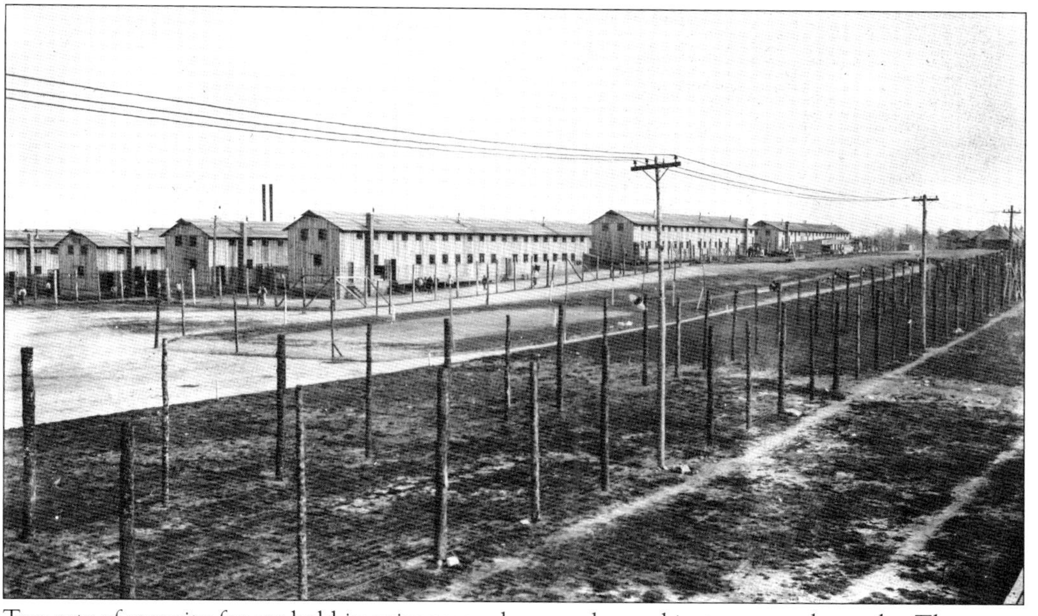

Two sets of security fences held in prisoners, who were housed in two-story barracks. The camp had electricity and lights. The hospital unit can be seen to the right side of the photograph. An activity field can be seen in this Signal Corps photograph taken from a guard tower. (NARA.)

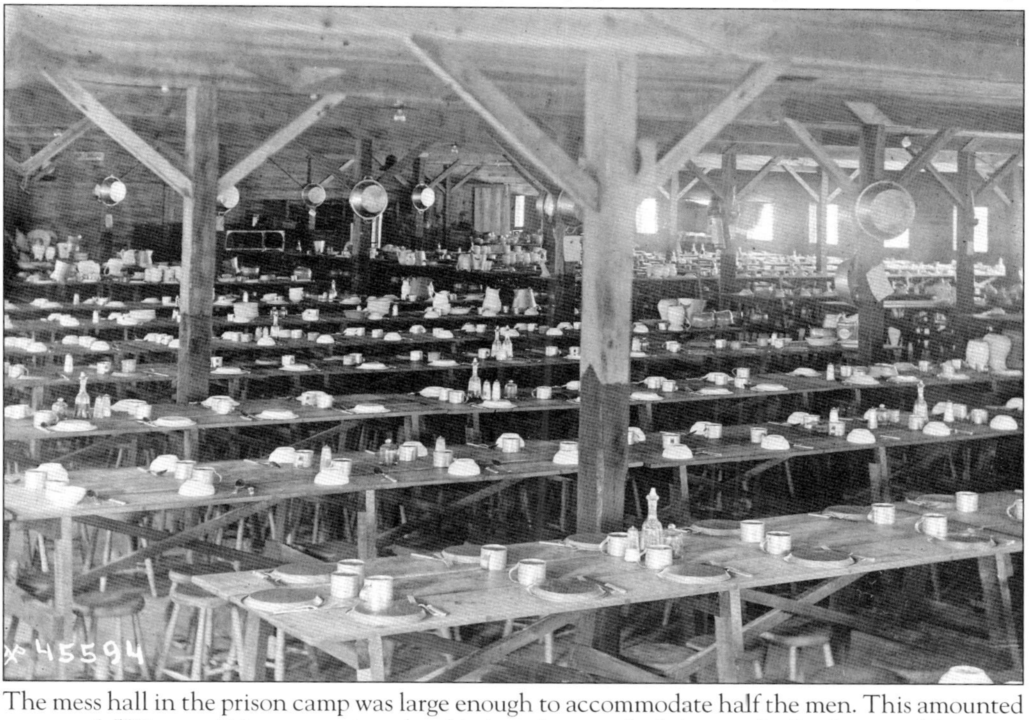

The mess hall in the prison camp was large enough to accommodate half the men. This amounted to some 1,500 men. Prisoners assigned to kitchen duty cooked the meals. Fresh vegetables came from gardens located throughout the camp. The prison mess halls looked familiarly like the mess halls in the troop barracks at the post. (NARA.)

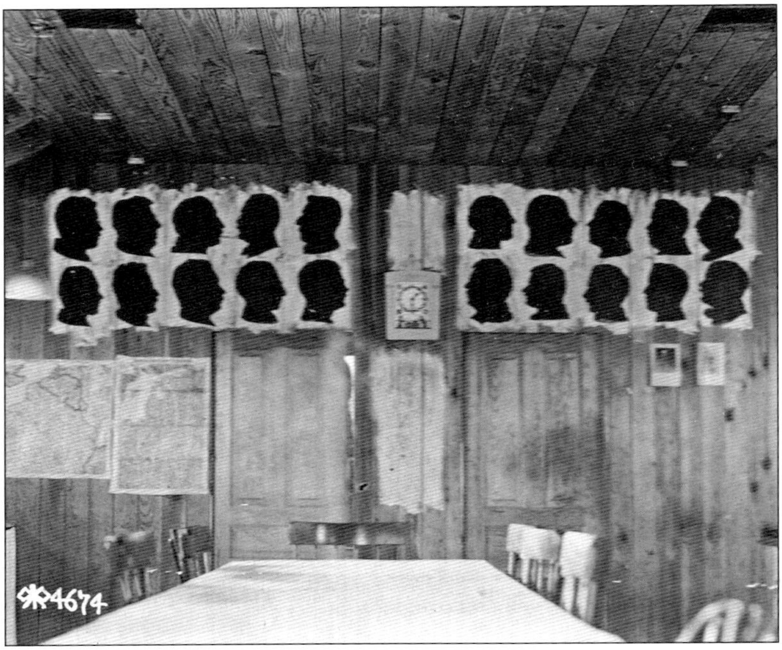

Silhouettes of the more prominent German alien POWs in Section A of the camp were painted on the wall of the "Millionaires" mess hall by F. Baumgarten of Cleveland, Ohio. There were many highly educated aliens in this camp. They taught classes for those who could not read or write and printed a camp newspaper, which contained skilled woodcuts in each issue. (NARA.)

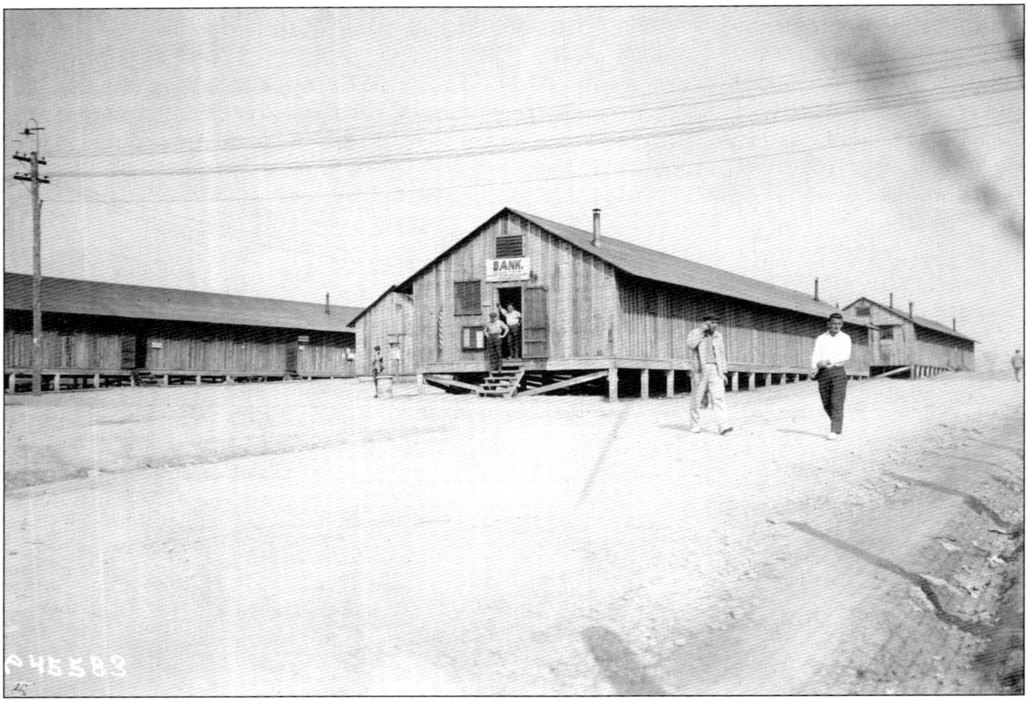

Wealthy prisoners deposited funds from friends and family in the camp bank, which provided them with a higher standard of living than most prisoners. Sale of camp newspapers and monies raised from theatrical presentations provided funds for other activities. Upon release, a prisoner was given the balance of his account. For those who chose not to work, release found them without funds for their life as free men. (NARA.)

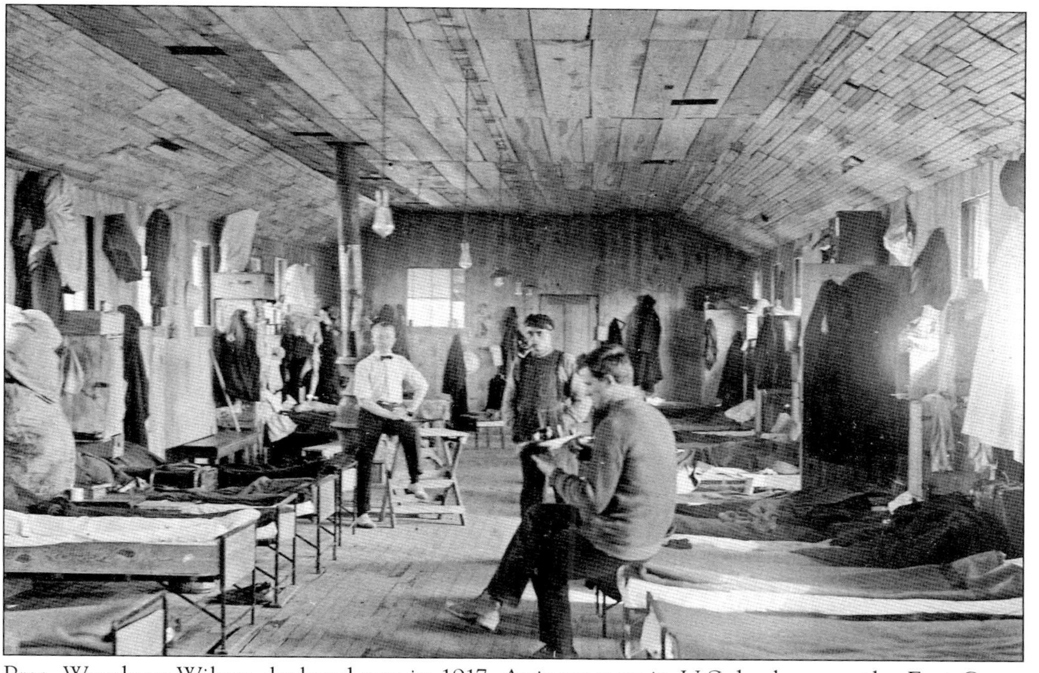

Pres. Woodrow Wilson declared war in 1917. Axis seamen in U.S. harbors on the East Coast became prisoners of war. People identified as enemy aliens and suspected of un-American activities were arrested and imprisoned. Animosity between the educated aliens and the military prisoners ended with the military POWs being confined at Fort McPherson and all enemy aliens at Fort Oglethorpe. Additionally, the Russian Bolsheviks at Fort Oglethorpe were kept separate from the educated German and Austrians in the main camp. In August 1918, the seamen interred at Hot Springs, North Carolina, were transferred to Fort Oglethorpe. The last prisoner at Fort Oglethorpe was released in 1920. These interior photographs show the rough-hewn construction of the barracks and the prisoners' living conditions. The seamen are shown using their time making models of the ships they served on. (Both, NARA.)

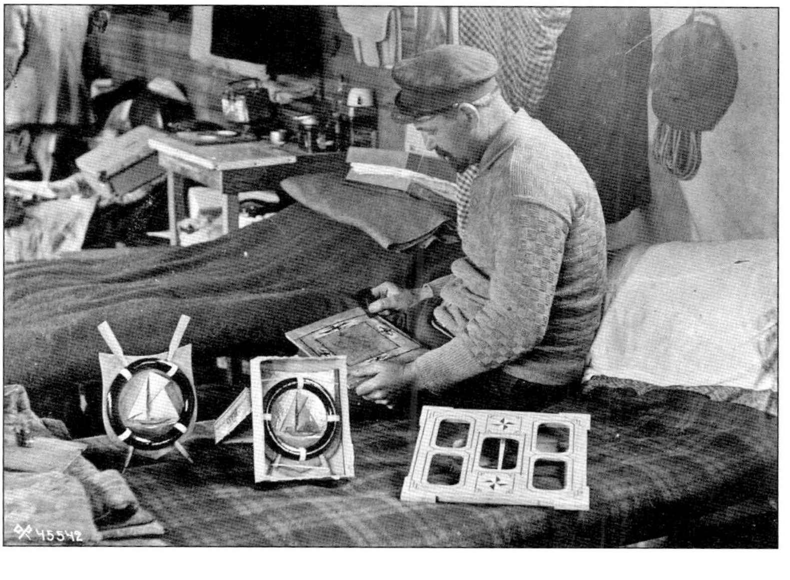

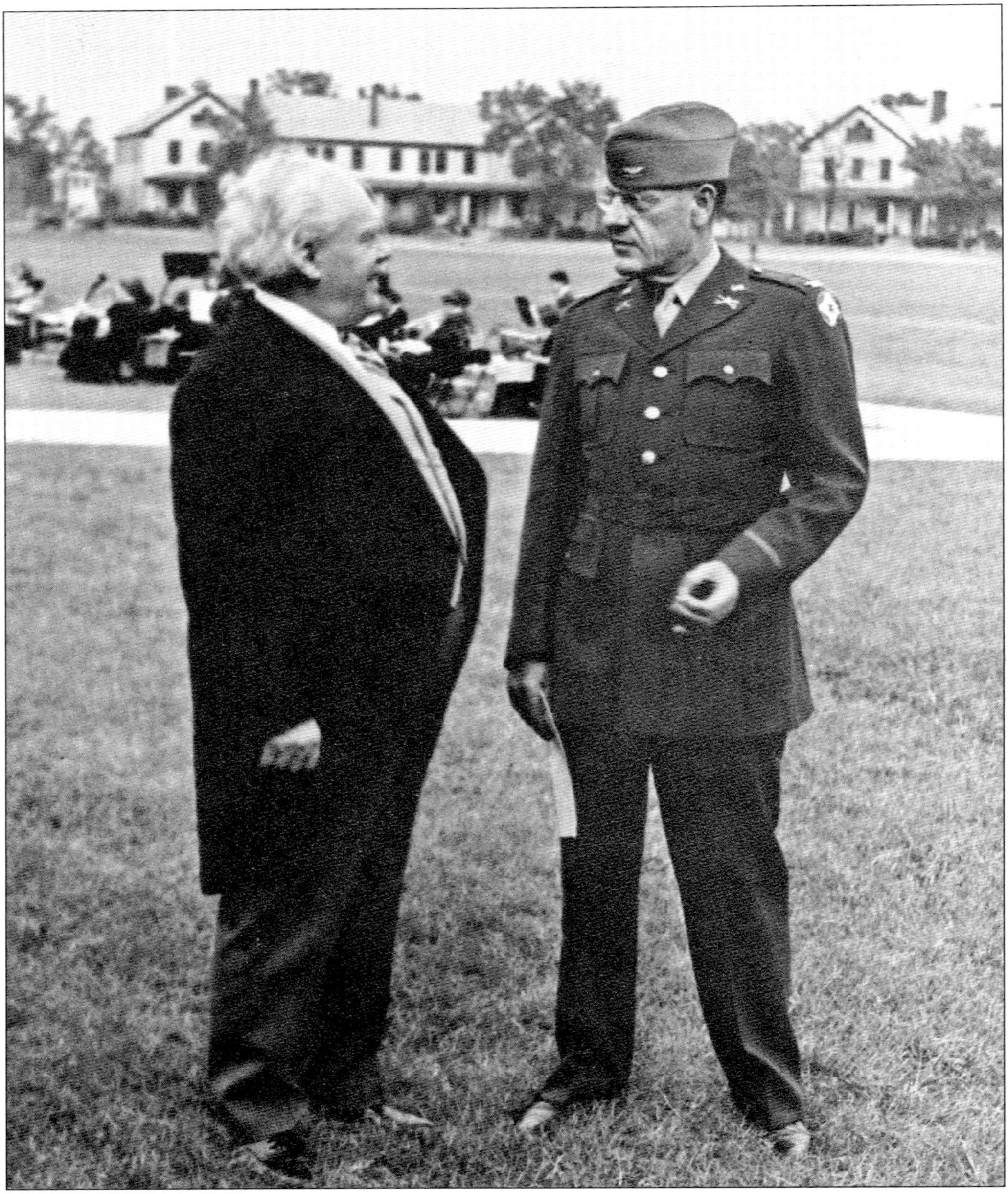

Dr. Karl Muck, director of the Boston Symphony, and the former conductor of the Cincinnati Symphony were arrested and sent to Fort Oglethorpe. Dr. Muck (left) is shown speaking with Col. Duncan Richart, commandant of the post. They are on the parade grounds. Muck's orchestra, composed of members from several large city orchestras, can be seen behind the two men. Dr. Muck conducted Sunday afternoon concerts on the parade grounds, and many people from the area drove out to the post to enjoy the music. He was arrested in May 1918 and released in 1920 to return to his native Germany. He continued his musical career and conducted before Adolph Hitler but was not a supporter of him or his Third Reich. In March 1921, he later reportedly said that he simply conducted German music, and he denied any disloyal actions. Many innocent people were caught in the wartime concerns of American citizens. (Julie Powell.)

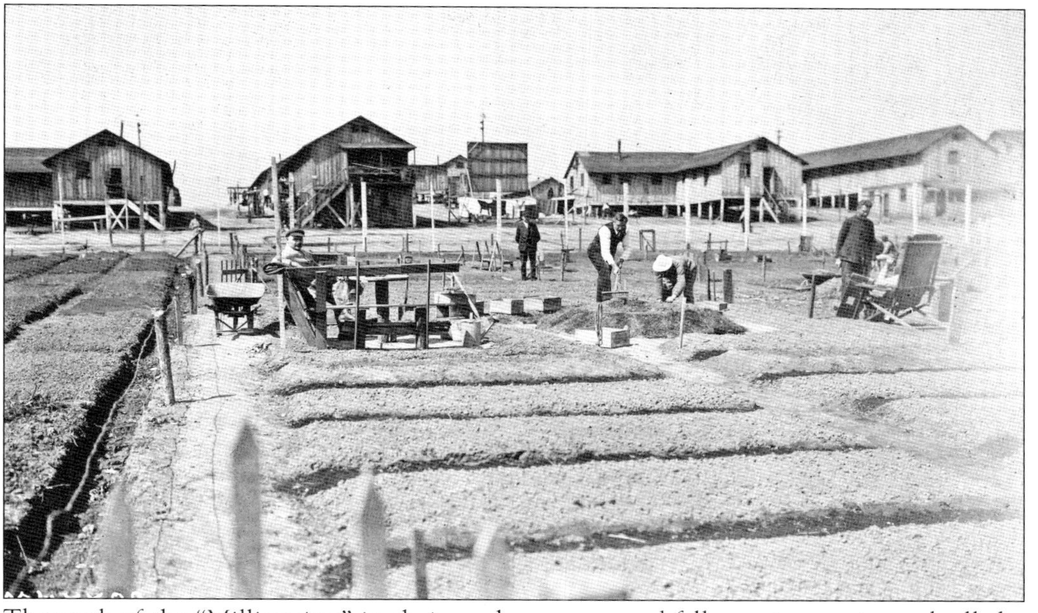

The work of the "Millionaires" in their garden encouraged fellow prisoners to work all the spare space at the camp to grow vegetables for a more healthy diet. A favorite German dish was sauerkraut. The prisoners used various supplies, including garden tools and a wheelbarrow. The wealthy prisoners rested in the garden area, and one can be seen in a lounge chair. (NARA.)

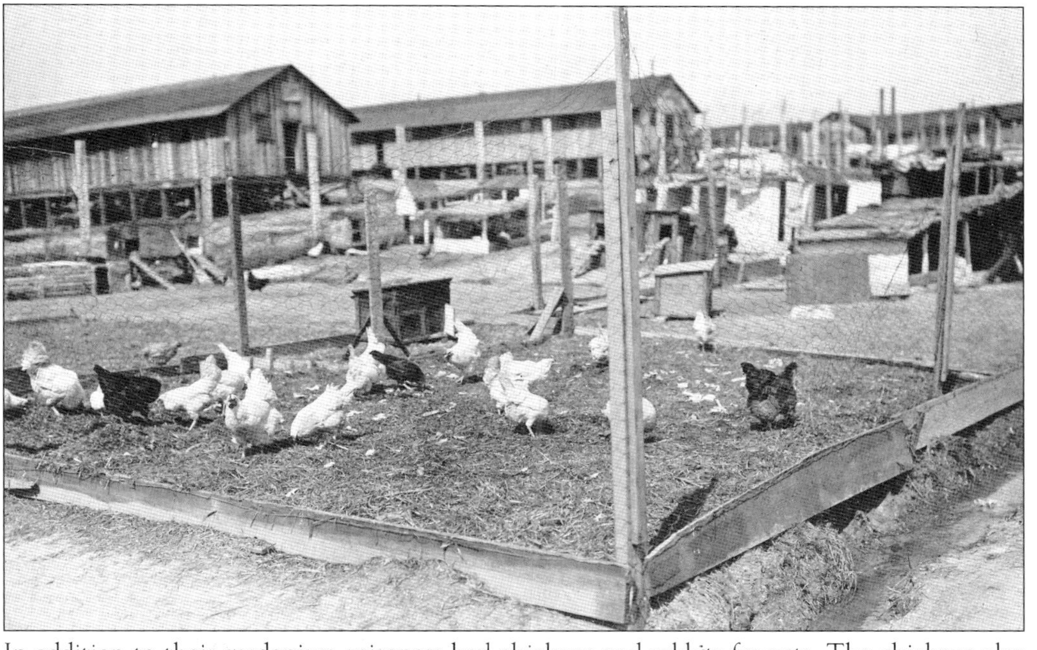

In addition to their gardening, prisoners had chickens and rabbits for pets. The chickens also provided eggs, which added protein to the diets of the prisoners. The roughness of the construction of this chicken yard suggests that the materials used were either surplus or taken from other structures. The prisoners did not have to walk far to perform their daily tasks of gardening and maintaining the chickens. (NARA.)

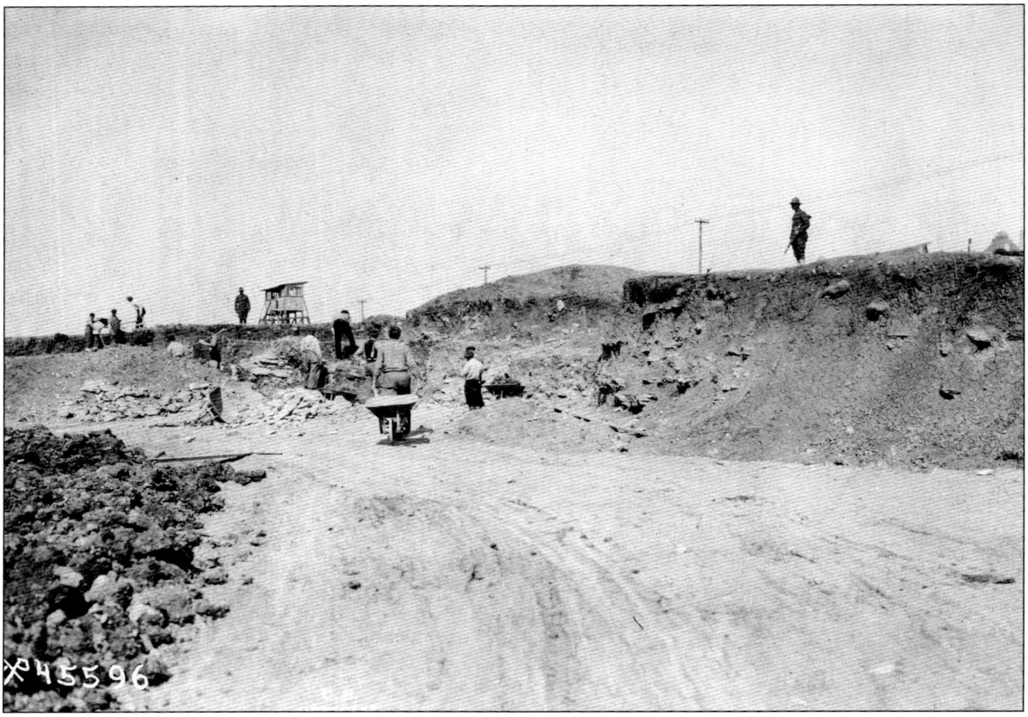

East of the camp, a quarry was worked to provide stone for the post. This stone was used in projects similar to the walls around the hospital and the quartermaster's buildings. Armed guards watched the prisoners, and a watch tower was located on the hilltop. These workers were paid a daily allowance for their work. (NARA.)

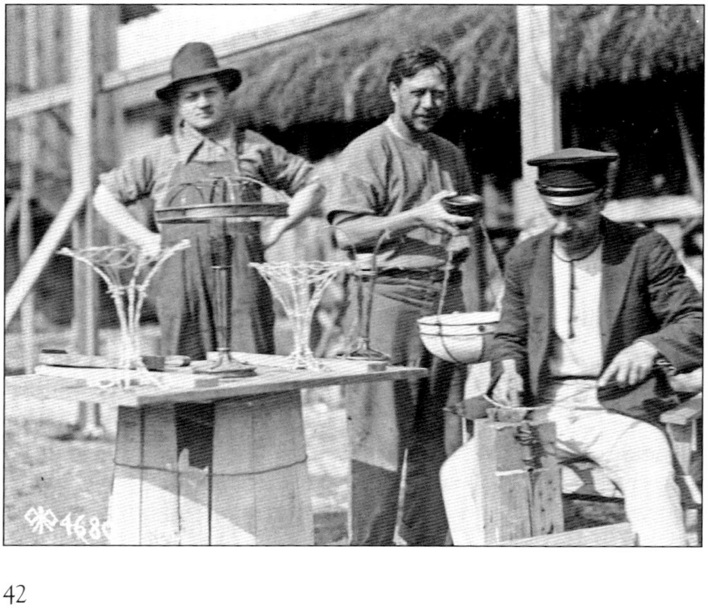

From left to right, Herr Post, Herr Peterson, and a third prisoner are shown with lamps, fruit dishes, ashtrays, and similar novelties they made from bits of barbwire used to fence them in and bits of copper and small accessories, which they were permitted to purchase at the Prison Camp Exchange. They sold these to the "Millionaires," who had the extra funds to purchase them. (NARA.)

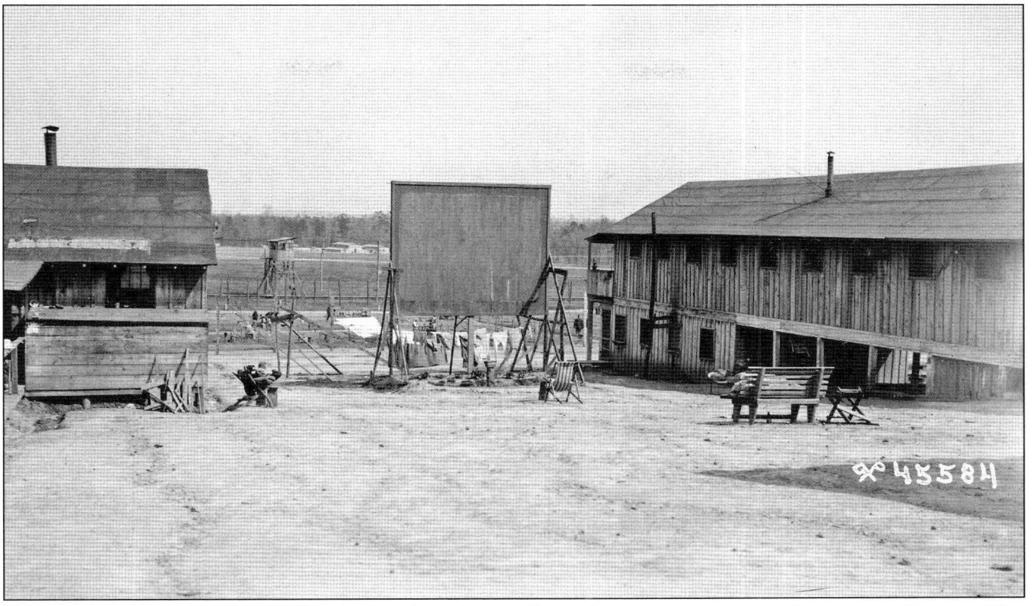

An open-air theater screen has been placed in a cleared area to accommodate an audience. The funds collected from various camp activities such as the newspaper and theatrical performances were used to purchase a moving picture projector. Additional funds were used to rent American motion pictures. They watched silent movies because sound and "talkies" did not appear until the 1920s. (NARA.)

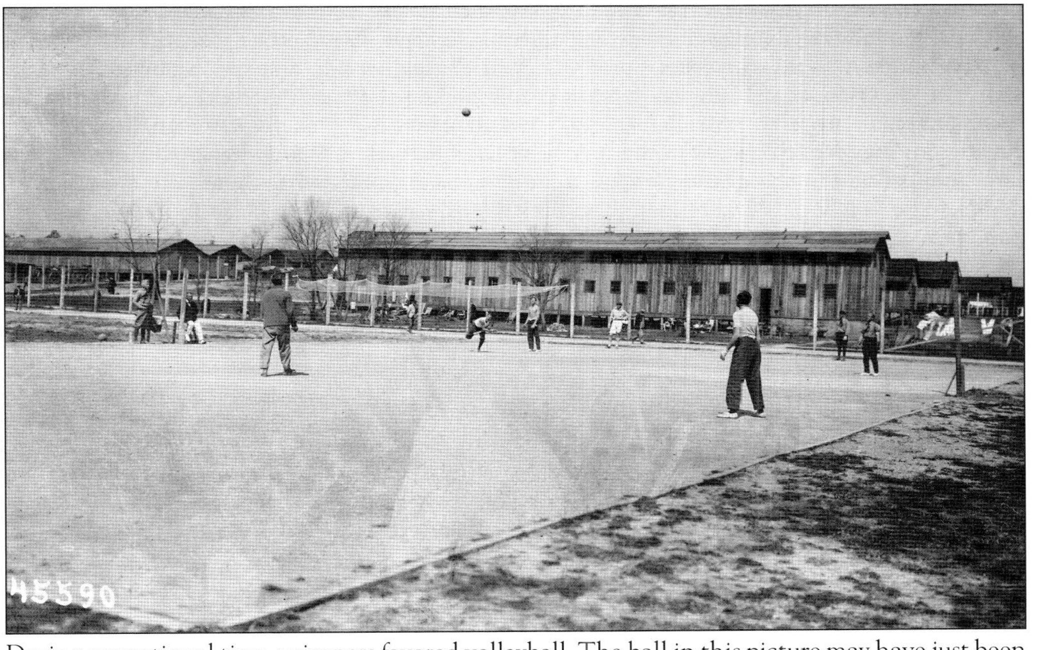

During recreational time, prisoners favored volleyball. The ball in this picture may have just been successfully served, and the man in the forefront awaits its downturn. Some prisoners wrote plays for performances, took educational classes, and played cards. Each prisoner was allowed to send out two letters and one postcard per week and was allowed visitors one day a week. (NARA.)

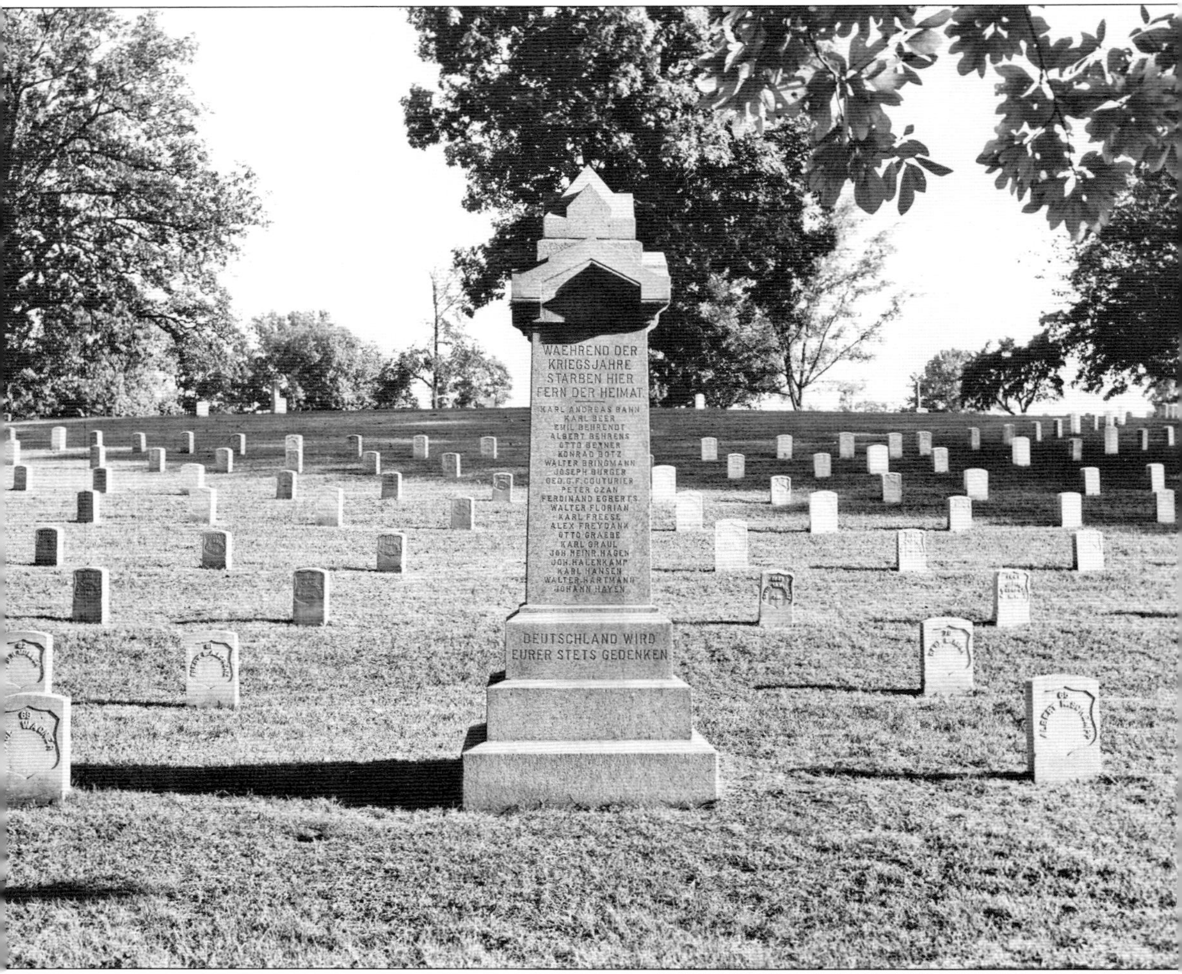

Each November 6, the Day of National Mourning in Germany, the German Consulate office places a wreath on this monument in the Chattanooga National Cemetery dedicated in 1935 to the German prisoners of war who died in this country. This is the only national cemetery in the United States that contains the graves of German prisoners of war from both world wars. (Chattanooga National Cemetery.)

Four

Enjoying Peacetime

The 6th Cavalry was permanently assigned to the Fort Oglethorpe military post on July 4, 1919. This was considered an elite posting. The 6th Cavalry was given a respite from wartime duty and performed peacetime activities. The dashing young soldiers took part in polo matches, horse shows, and other competitions. Fox hunting was another popular sport at the time, and many hunts originated from the post.

The soldiers escorted young ladies to dances and intermingled with the social scene in Chattanooga. Dances were held at the gymnasium at the post. Groups of carefully chaperoned young ladies from Chattanooga would often come to the post by bus to enjoy an evening of fun and dancing with the enlisted soldiers.

Polo games were quite an exciting attraction. The teams traveled as far as Atlanta and Birmingham to take part in army competitions. They also played against civilian teams at Bendabout Farms in McDonald, Tennessee, and against the University of Georgia. As a young officer, Gen. George Patton visited the post and played in several polo matches here.

Baseball and basketball games were popular, and Fort Oglethorpe was proud to have several championship teams. Basketball was played in the post gymnasium on Lafayette Road, and the bowling team hosted tournaments on the lower level of the gym.

During the 1930s, the 6th Cavalry began to experiment with mechanized vehicles at the post. They field tested the bantam car (forerunner of the jeep), the scout car, and the motorcycle. Parts of the Chickamauga and Chattanooga National Military Park and Chickamauga Lake were used as testing grounds for military vehicles. By the time the 6th Cavalry left for the World War II battlefields, it was fully mechanized, and the horses were left behind.

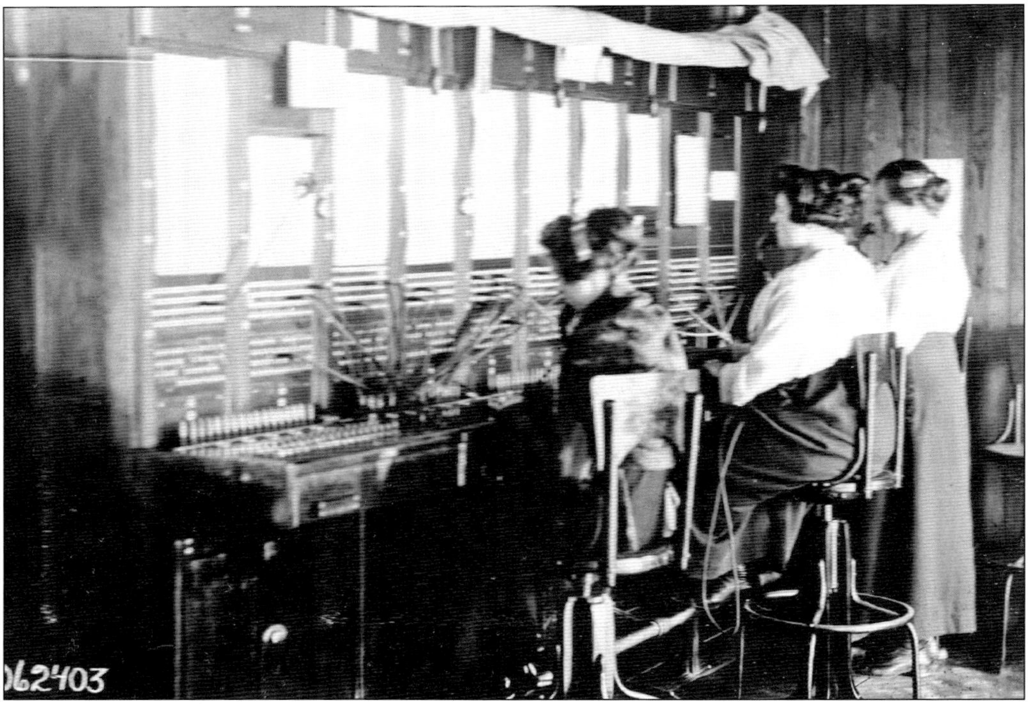

With electrification came the telephone. The above photograph was taken in 1919 and shows the inside of the telephone exchange. This building was erected to the east of the Post Headquarters on Lafayette Road. These women operators were civil service contractors. They were employed by the federal government and were not military. The operators were among a number of civil servant contractors who worked at the post and were paid by the government. Some, like master plumbers and electricians, received off-post housing for themselves and their families. The photograph below, taken in 1930, shows a more modern facility that still uses the switchboard with its cords and plugs. Women continued to serve in this capacity at the post. (Both, NARA.)

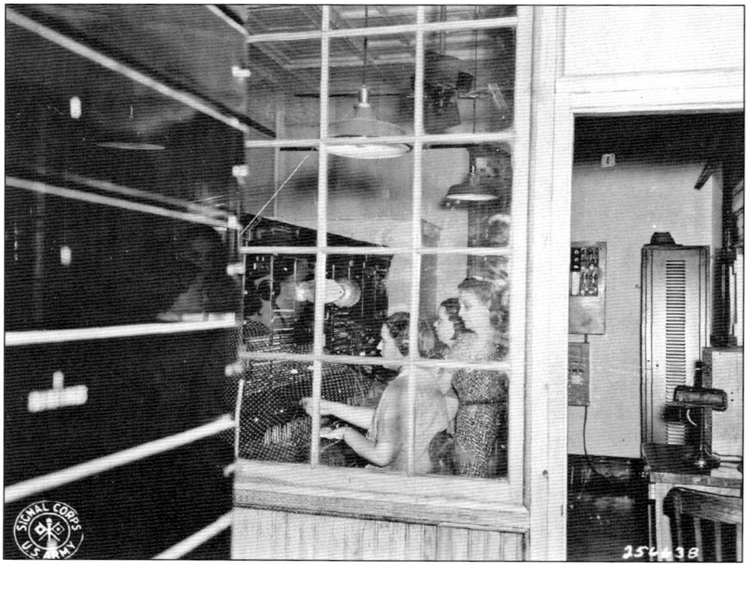

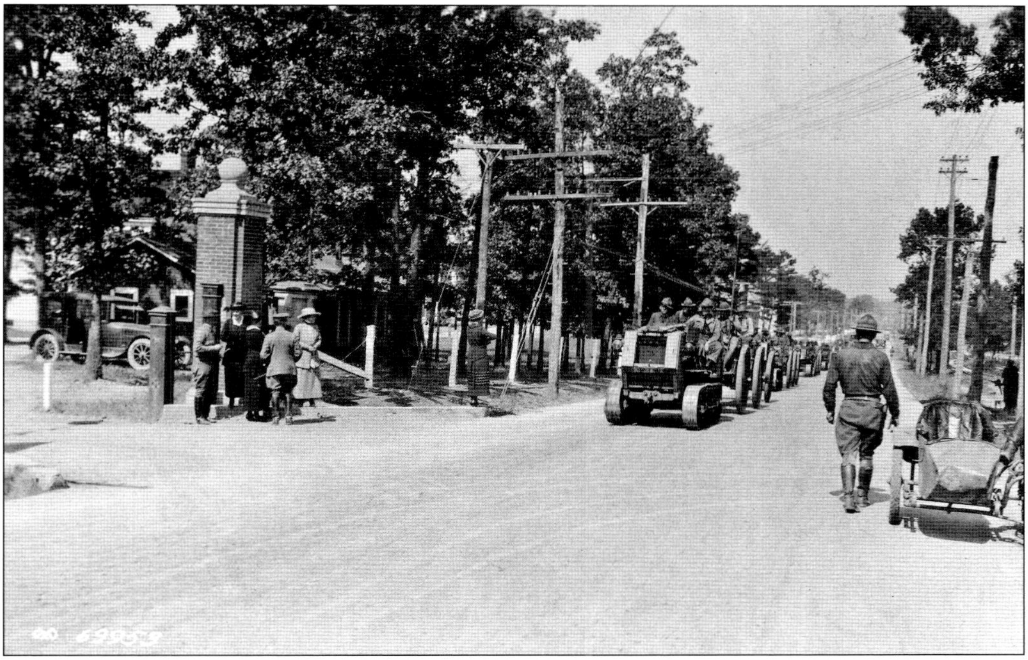

In 1920, the 83rd Field Artillery, Motorized, on maneuvers from Camp Knox, Kentucky, to Camp Benning, Georgia, approached the main gates of the post on Lafayette Road. Women civilians and various cavalrymen watched the approach of tanks, trucks, and other mechanized vehicles. A 6th Cavalry trooper and his motorcycle show that the cavalry was utilizing mechanized vehicles, and even in the 1920s, the day of the "horse" soldier was numbered. (NARA.)

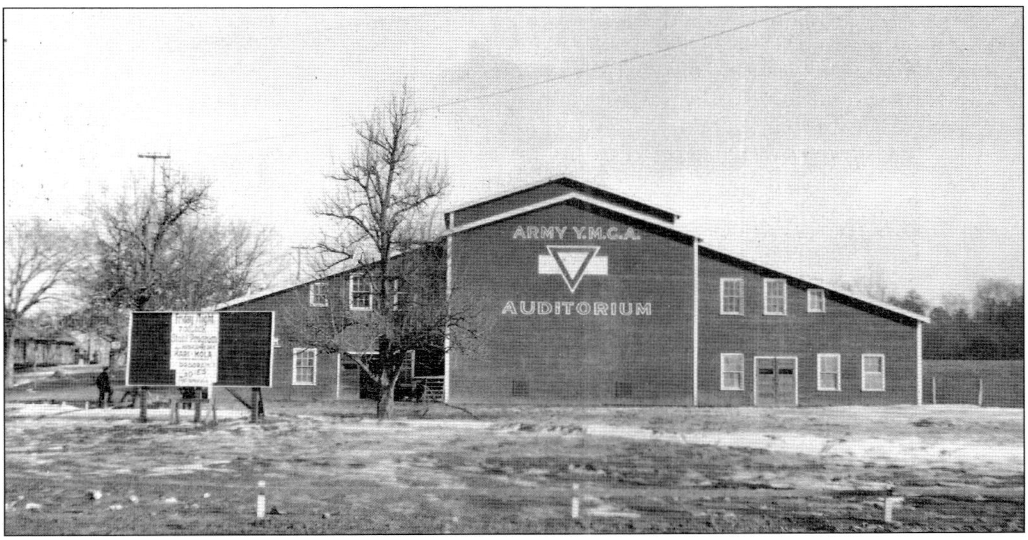

Local community groups from Chattanooga worked together to meet the social needs of the soldiers at the post during World War I and continued their presence at Fort Oglethorpe into the peacetime years. The YMCA Auditorium, pictured here, was located directly across Lafayette Road from the main gates at Harker Road. The YMCA, at one time, had more than a dozen buildings scattered throughout the greater post area. (NARA.)

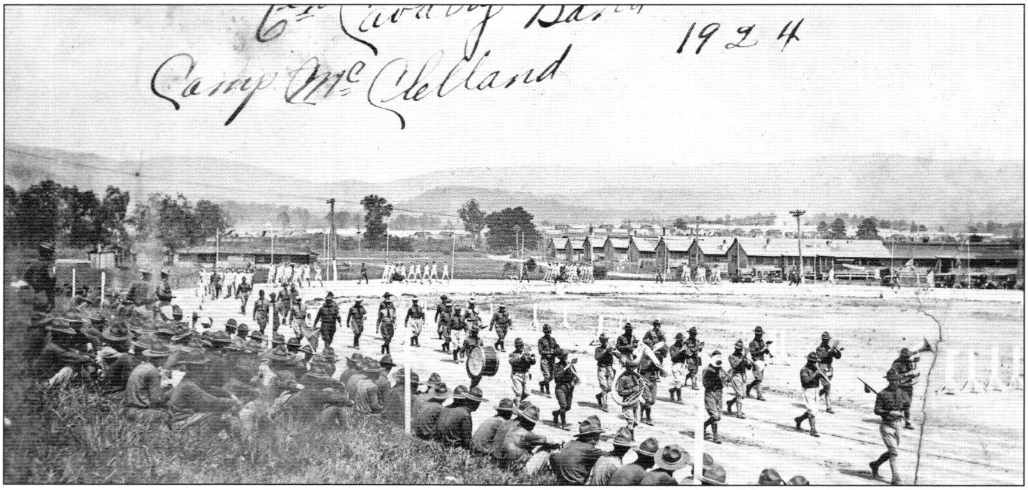

During the years between the world wars, the soldiers continued their military duties. Units of the 6th Cavalry performed detached duty for both Civilian Conservation Corps (CCC) camps and Civilian Military Training Camps (CMTC) in Georgia and neighboring states, training high school and college students. Here the 6th Cavalry band adds to the review of the CMTC Cavalry unit at Camp McClellan, Alabama, in 1924. (SCM.)

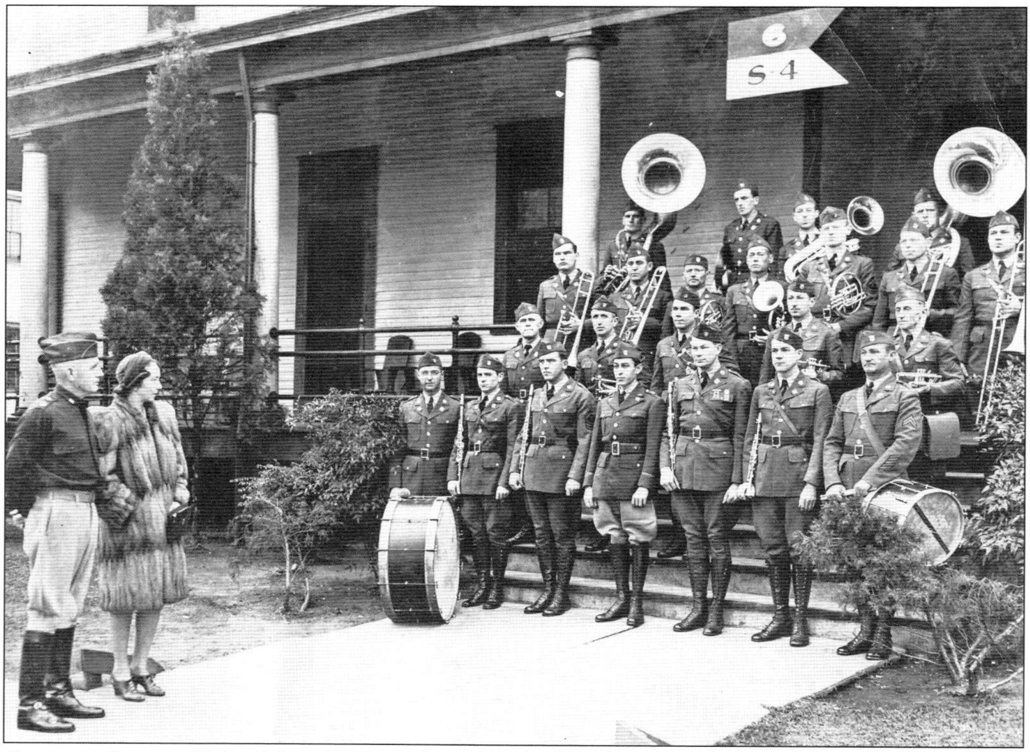

Commandant and Mrs. John A. Considine visit the band at their barracks. The band, consisting of 26 members, played both mounted and dismounted. The Band Barracks had a large open room on the main floor in which the entire band could practice. Dormitory-style cots were located upstairs, and downstairs were lockers, storage, and laundry facilities. (SCM.)

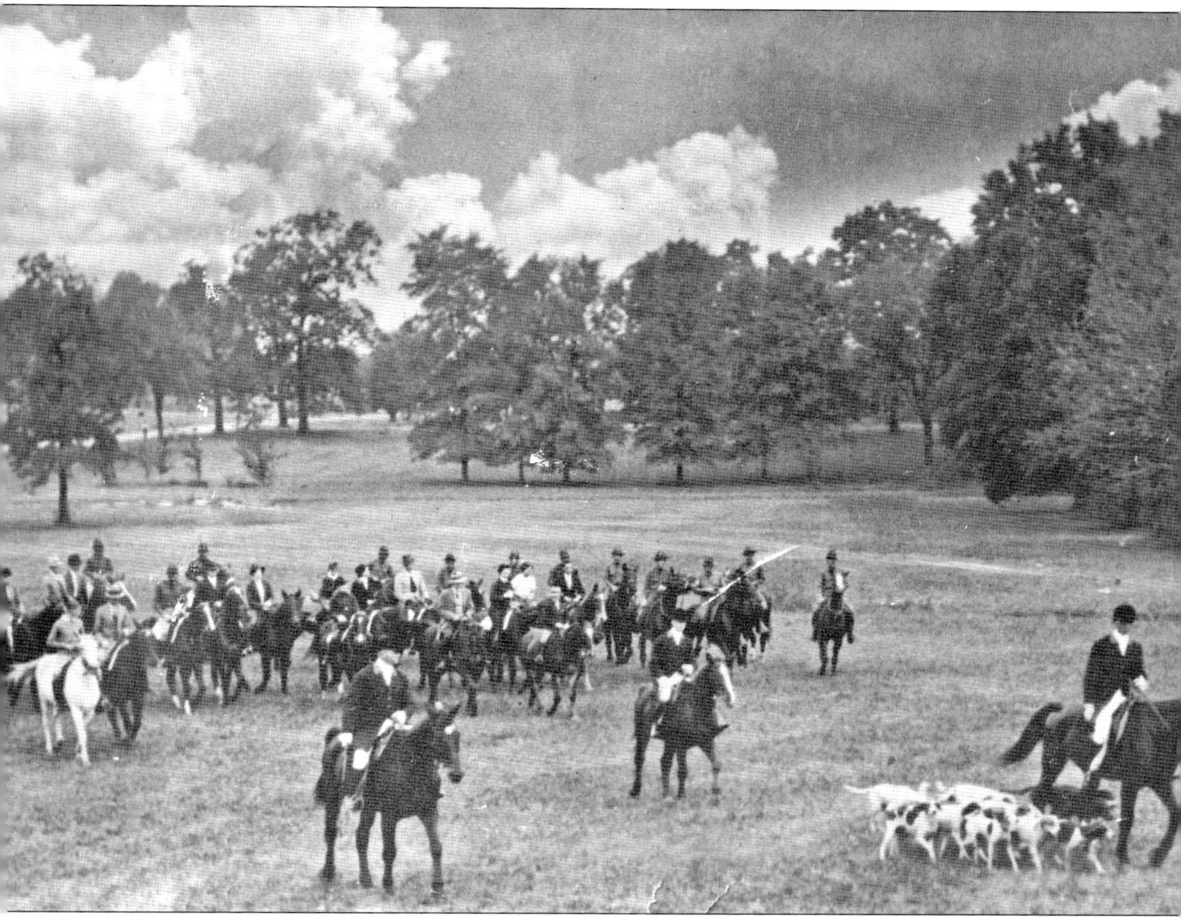

Peacetime between the world wars allowed troopers a more relaxed routine while maintaining their exercises and fighting techniques. During the 1920s and 1930s, social events included riding teams, hunt clubs, horse shows and dances. Many activities involved women who lived on the post as well as civilian friends. Civilian men and women joined in this hunt through Chickamauga Park. The hounds master maintained the dogs at the post and led the group. At the annual horse shows, these same civilians participated in riding competitions, including distance riding and jumping, for silver cups and ribbons. All these social activities served to keep the men and the horses in shape. (SCM.)

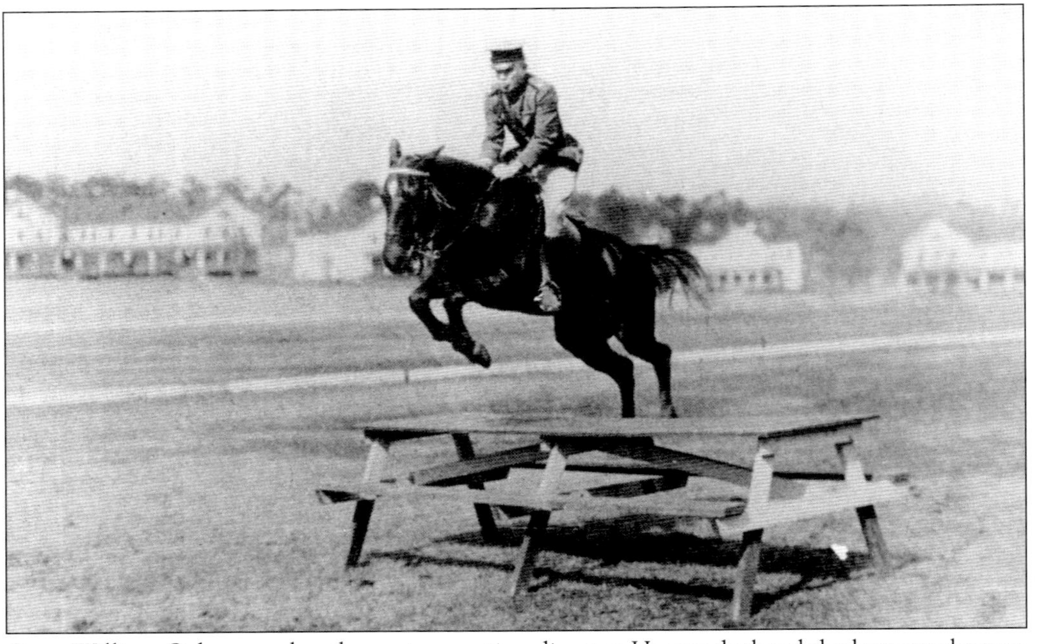

Capt. William Ochs served as the post recreation director. He was declared the best cavalryman jumper for several years. His horse, Snooks, for several years was declared the best cavalry horse in the 6th Cavalry. Their reputation spread through the U.S. Cavalry. Here they practice by jumping over a picnic table on the parade grounds. (SCM.)

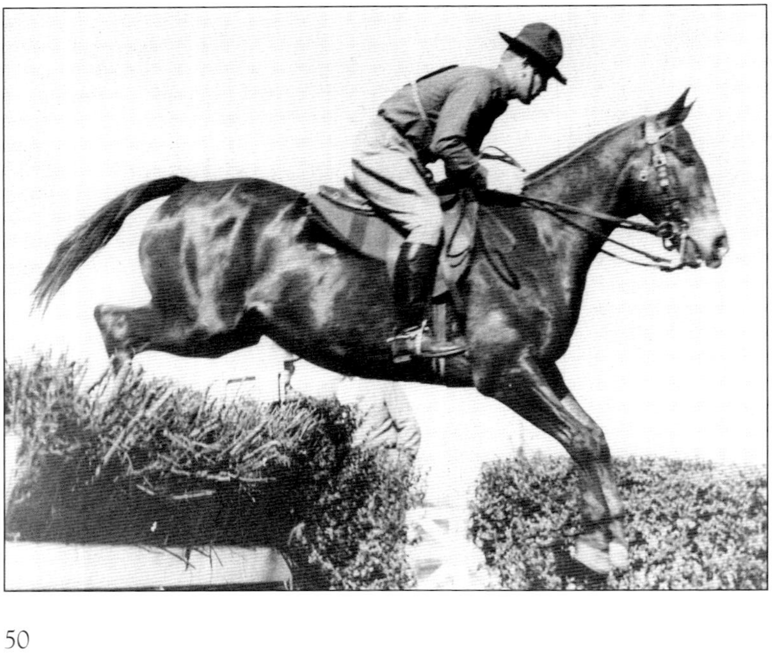

Dr. Robert C. Robertson, U.S. Medical Corps, is jumping a split jump, similar to those in a steeplechase race. One such jump remains on the west side of the parade grounds. The men of the 6th Cavalry who trained the medical officers insisted the outcome would be a cavalryman who could do surgery and not a surgeon who could ride a horse. (SCM.)

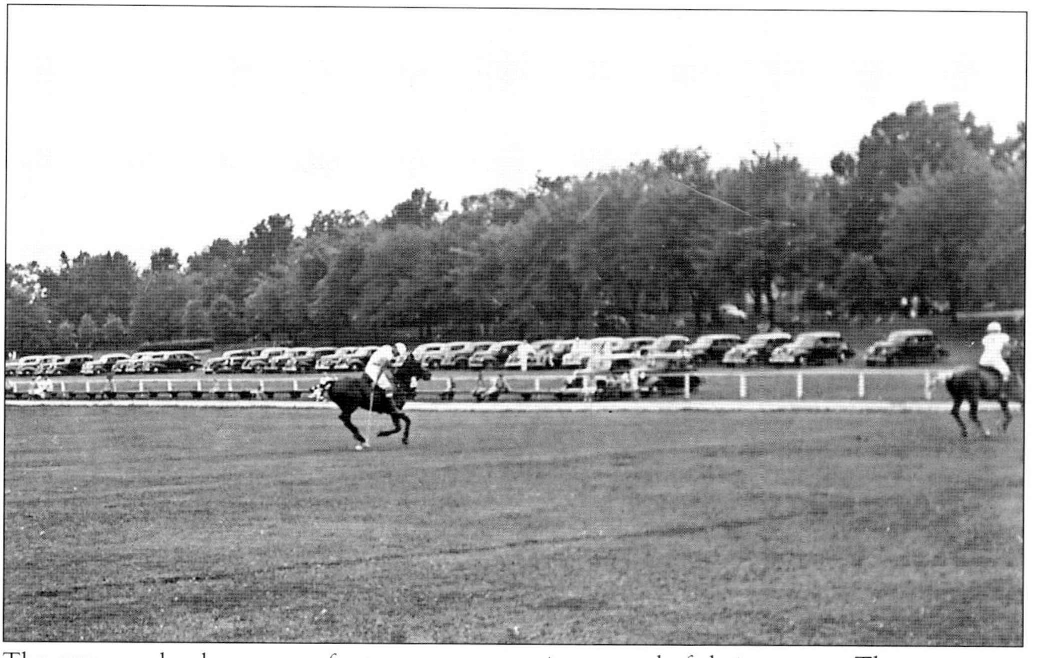

The army used polo as a way for troopers to practice control of their mounts. The post teams played other army teams, as well as Bendabout Farms in McDonald, Tennessee, and the University of Georgia team. The $15 seasonal parking fee went into a fund to assist officers in purchasing their riding supplies. (SCM.)

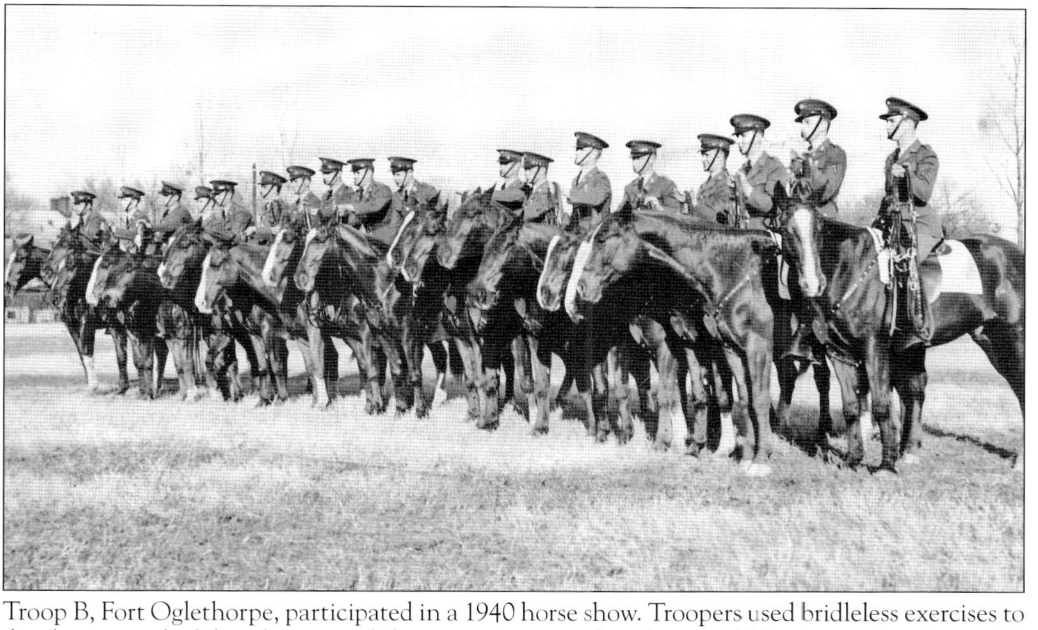

Troop B, Fort Oglethorpe, participated in a 1940 horse show. Troopers used bridleless exercises to develop control of their horses with leg movements so that they would be free to fire their rifles and engage in battle. Shown here, the bridles have been removed from the horses and are being held by the riders. This practice exercise was incorporated into competitions in horse shows at the post. (CHCBL.)

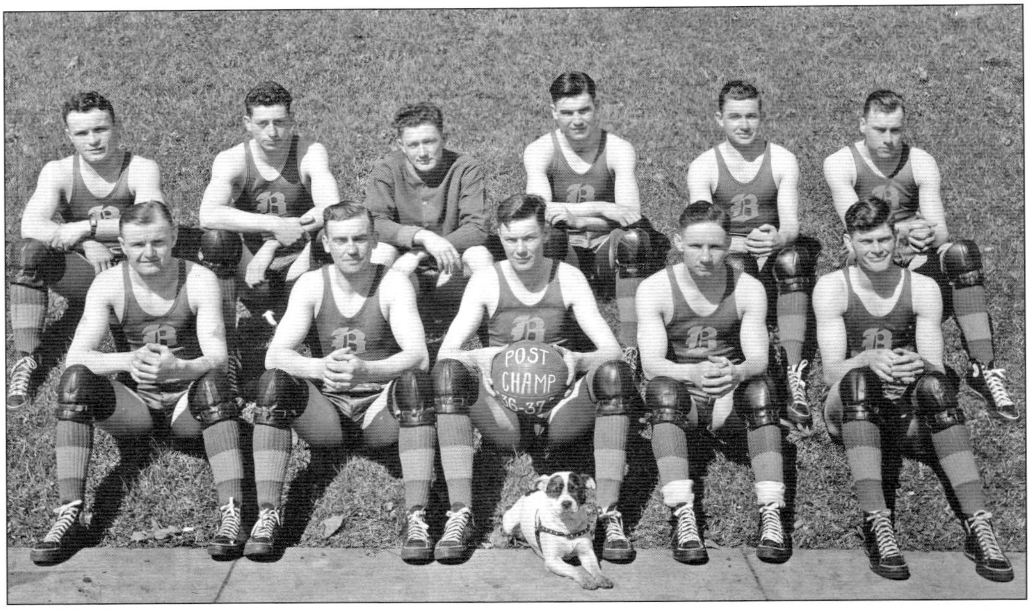

Soldiers at Fort Oglethorpe had many opportunities to participate in sports. Championships were commemorated in photographs, silver trophies, and banners. Troop B was post champion in basketball in 1936, 1937, and 1938. They are shown in the above photograph in uniform and knee pads, holding a basketball proclaiming their success. Below, Troop B poses as the 1937 post champions in baseball. Troop B also was post champion in 1935 and regimental champions in 1938. A different mascot owes allegiance to the baseball team. A close look shows the baseball players to be an older group of men. (Both, SCM.)

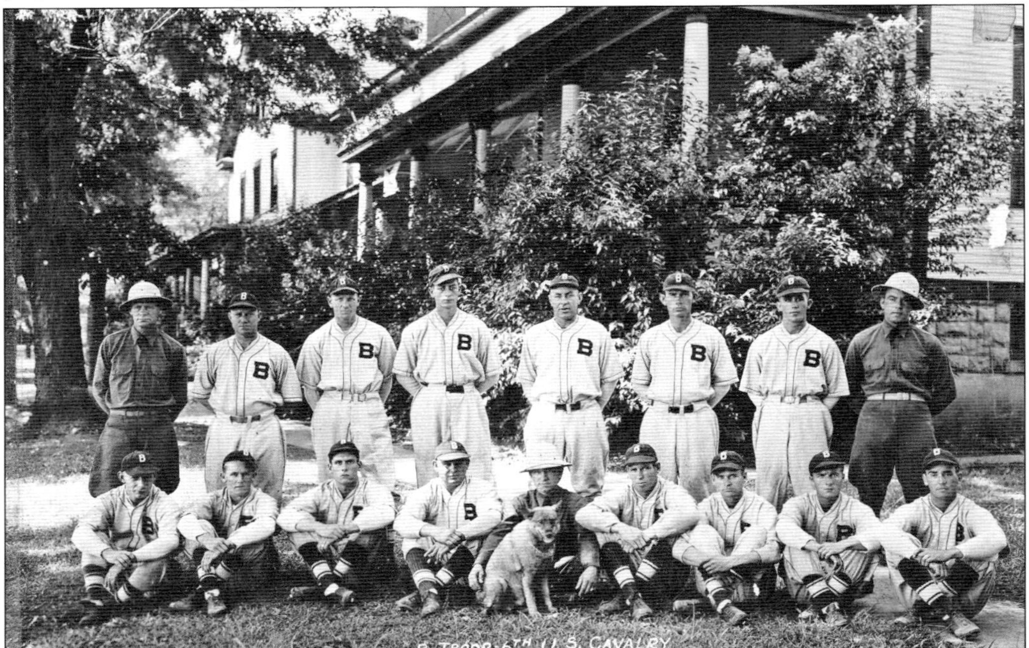

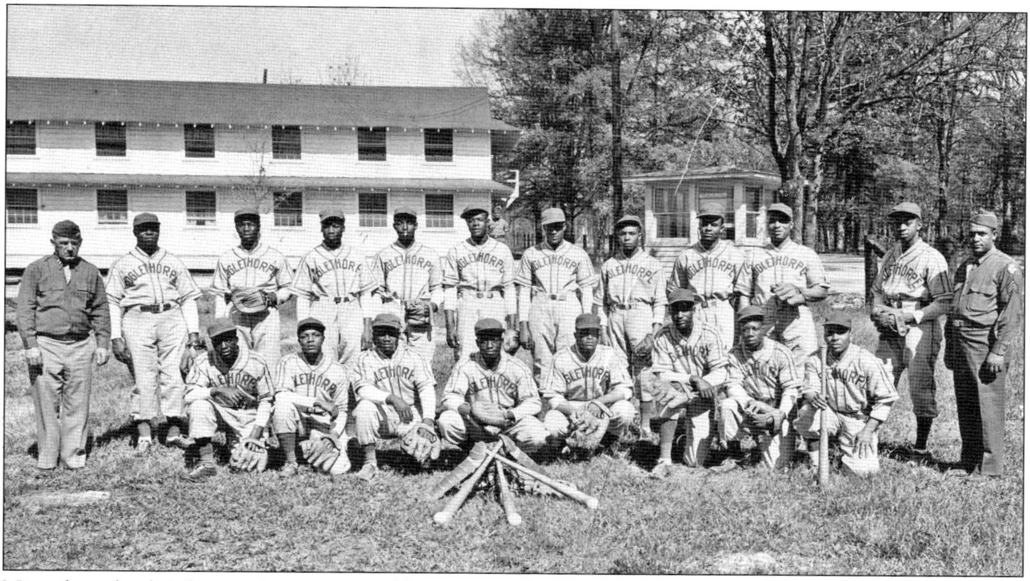

Nine hundred African American soldiers arrived at the post and were housed in the old CCC buildings east of the post. Col. Duncan Richart, commandant, related he had "nine hundred men who had never seen a horse and eleven hundred horses who had never seen a man, but by the end of training, they were near-perfect." The 1942 Labor Day activities included a baseball game between two units of this detachment. (SCM.)

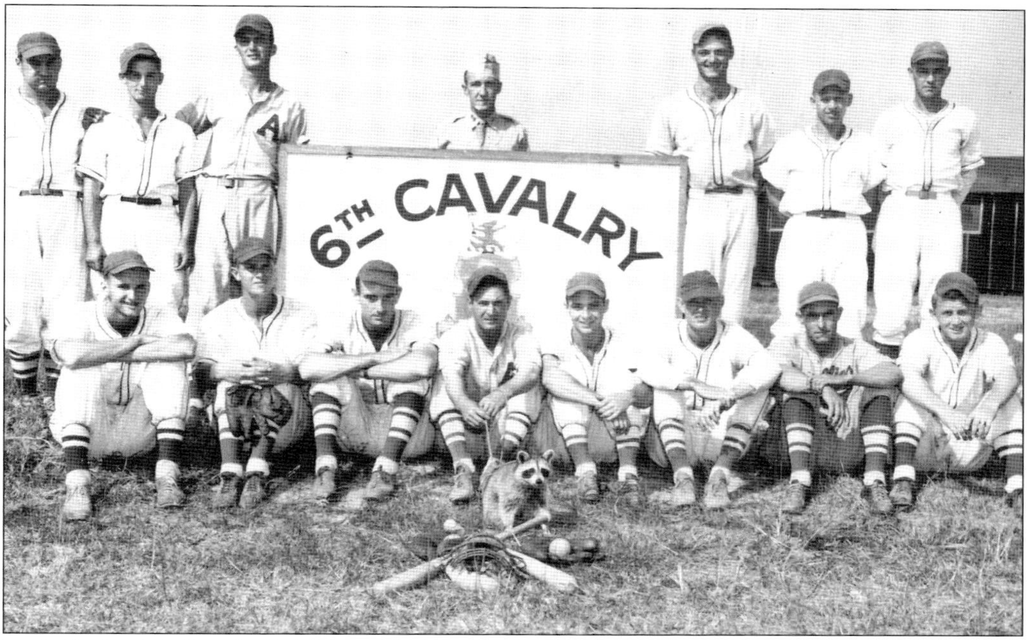

In 1942, the 6th Cavalry left Fort Oglethorpe. Their ship and all their supplies needed for action in North Africa were sunk by a German submarine off the Atlantic Coast. They were sent to Fort Jackson in Columbia, South Carolina, to await re-equipping. The 6th Cavalry continued to beat their competition in baseball. "Preacher," their new mascot, shares the limelight in this September 25, 1943, photograph. (SCM.)

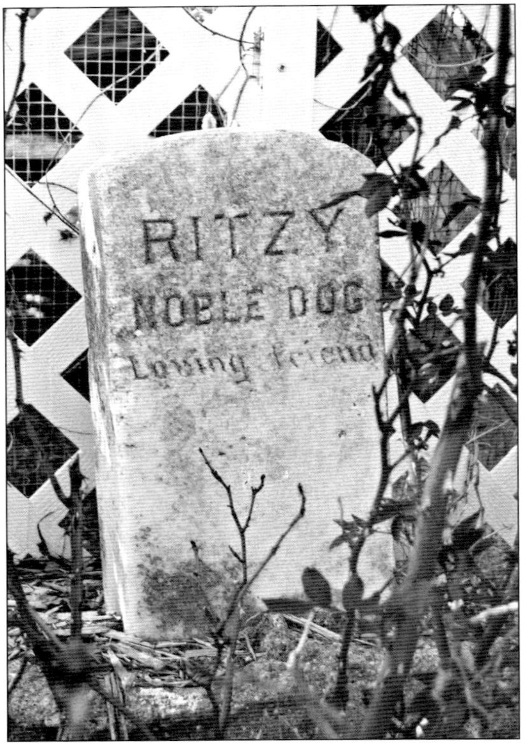

Horses shared the post with other animals. One of the troopers' favorites was Ritzy. His headstone reads, "Noble Dog, Loving friend," and is now located at the Sixth Cavalry Museum. Sancho, another dog, is buried on the post grounds. According to Steven Mosman, local historian, Sancho's headstone reads, "Surely, if the Heavenly Father notices the fall of a sparrow, then this good and faithful friend, though but a dog, will long be remembered." (LP.)

The post had a Master of Hounds who supervised the care and training of hounds used during hunts. Local women joined the Riding Club at the post and rode in the hunts. A grand Hunt Ball was held at the post. The dogs watch the chickens inside the coop. (SCM.)

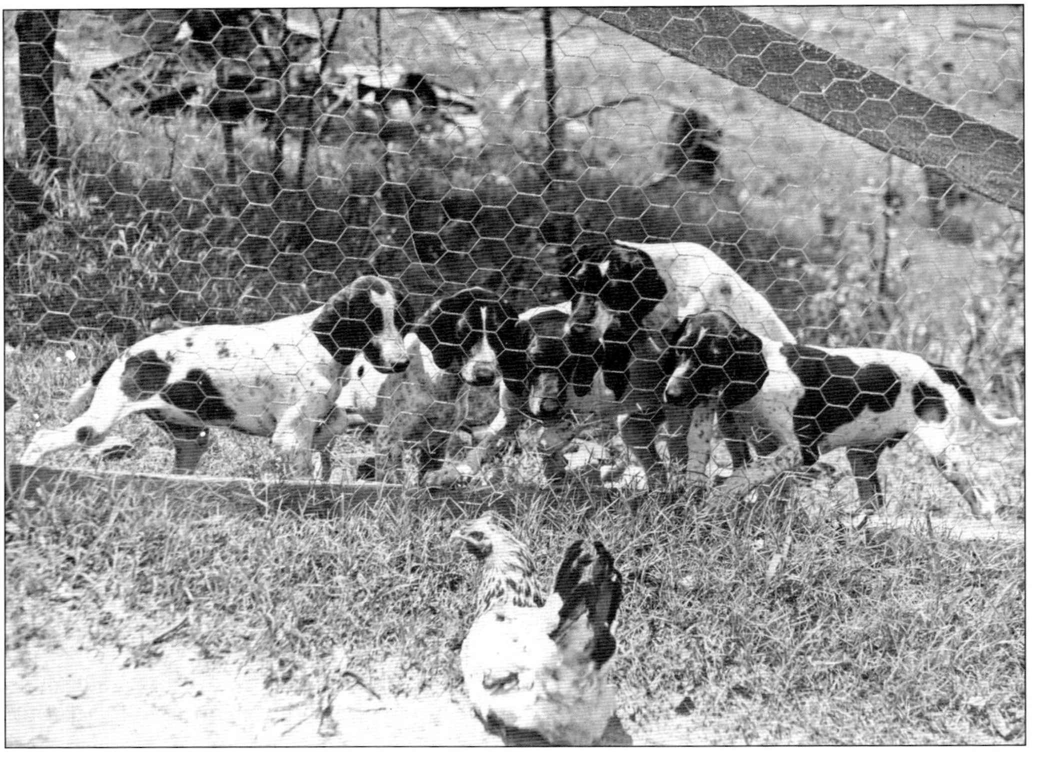

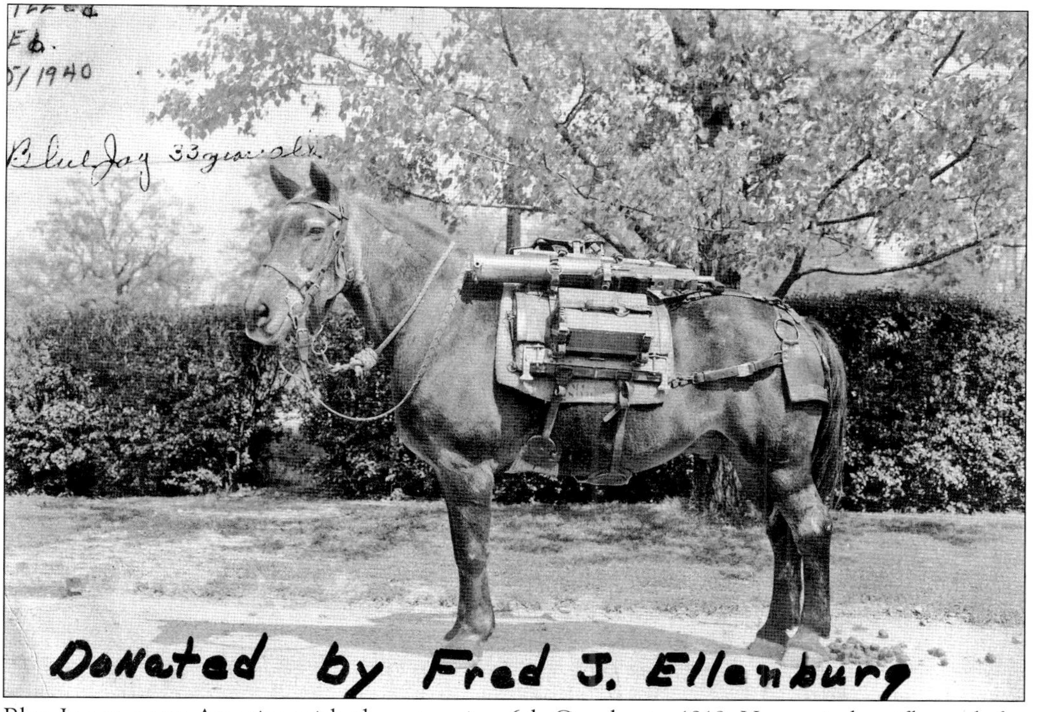

Blue Jay came to America with the returning 6th Cavalry in 1919. He carried a rifle pack for almost 5,000 miles before being retired. When he became quarrelsome and no one would put him down, he was taken out to the firing range. After a few more years there, he began biting troopers. Finally, a post veterinarian put him down February 14, 1940. He was 33 years old. (SCM.)

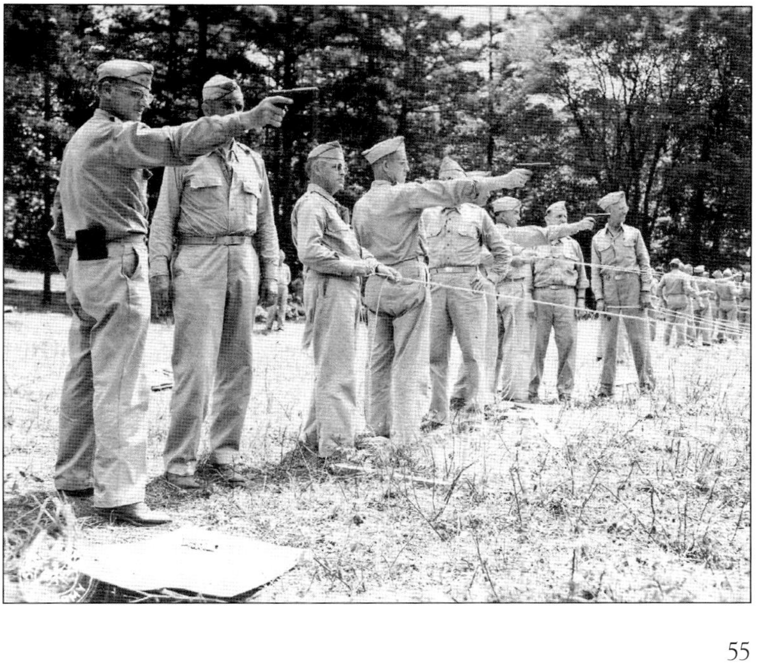

Officers practice firing their handguns. The targets are pulled forward by the string held by others. The rifle range was located 13 miles east of the post, near Ringgold, Georgia. Cavalrymen rode there to practice firing their rifles and to practice with their artillery pieces. The land is still owned by the federal government and is used as a military training center for the area. (SCM.)

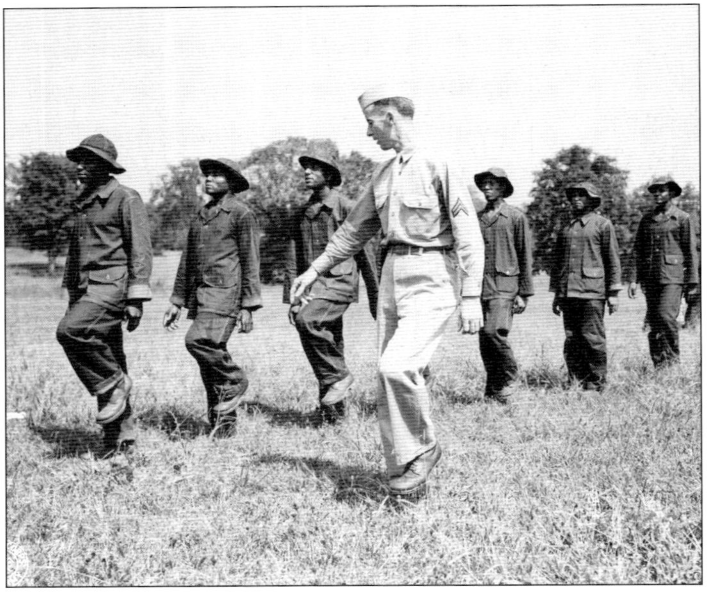

The African American troops at the post followed in the steps of at least two previous groups. During Spanish-American War preparations, the Buffalo Soldiers, 10th Cavalry, were here. During the 1930s Depression, African Americans composed the George Washington Carver CCC Camp east of the main gate. While these men and their unit have not been identified, the presence of African Americans at Fort Oglethorpe is part of the post's history. (SCM.)

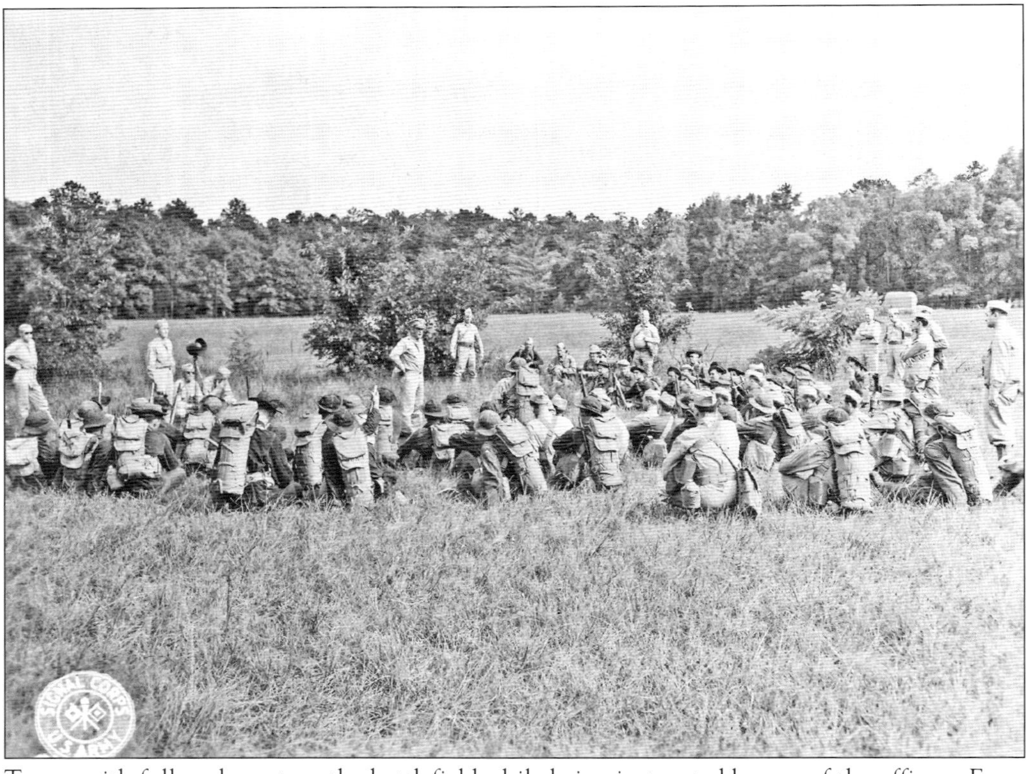

Troops with full packs rest on the battlefield while being instructed by one of the officers. From 1936 to 1941, horses were a part of training and yearly maneuvers. The 1940 and 1941 maneuvers proved that horses would not be the primary source of transportation. Although the 6th Cavalry left for Europe without its horses, the nations of World War II used hundreds of thousands of horses. (NARA.)

An officer looks on as two enlisted men are walked through the workings of this jeep. The 6th Cavalry would be called "the eyes and ears of Patton's Third Army." The jeep enabled the 6th to scout ahead and provide Patton with reconnaissance information needed for his army's move through Europe. Like his horse, this "cavalryman" was responsible for the care and upkeep of his "horses" under the hood. (NARA.)

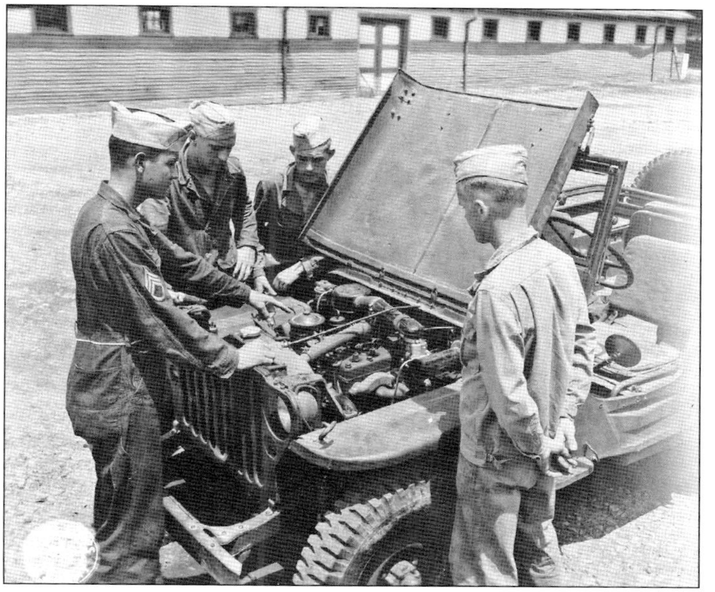

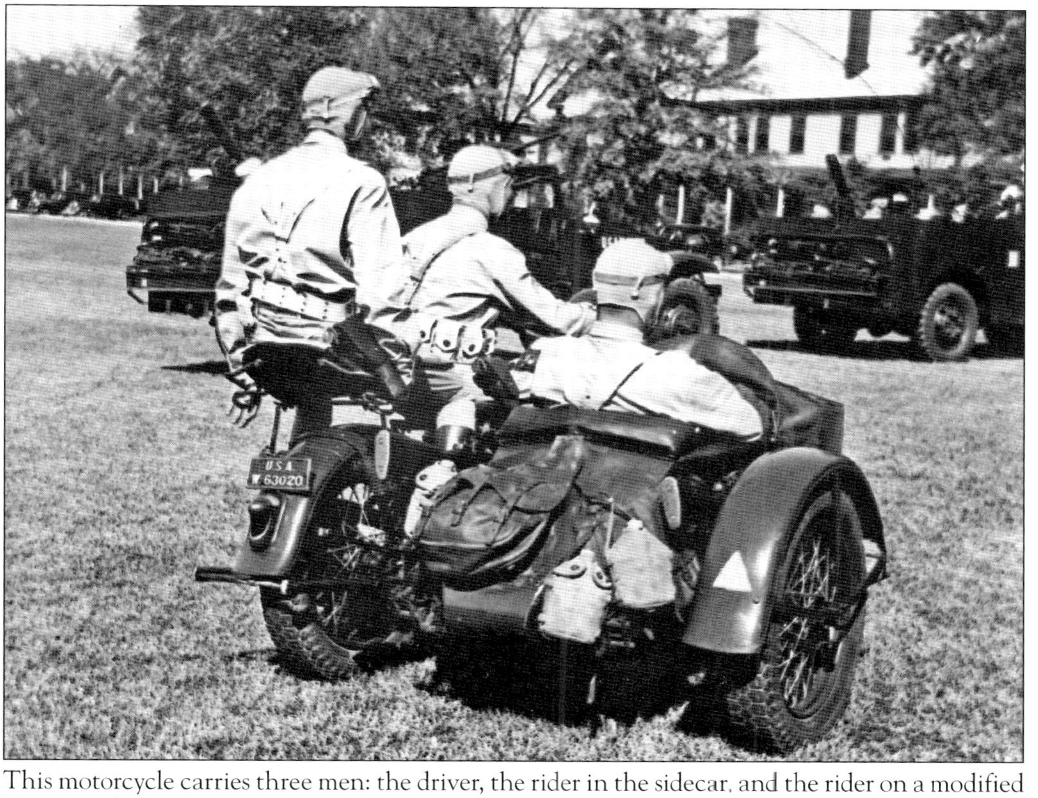

This motorcycle carries three men: the driver, the rider in the sidecar, and the rider on a modified jump seat behind the driver. The motorcycle has a U.S.A. license plate and carries three water bottles. Two rifles in their slings can be seen. The heavy treads will get them through mud and clay. This scout car section (the three vehicles seen in front of the motorcycle) is supported by the three-man Half Squad Motorcycle Troop, shown here in October 1940. (NARA.)

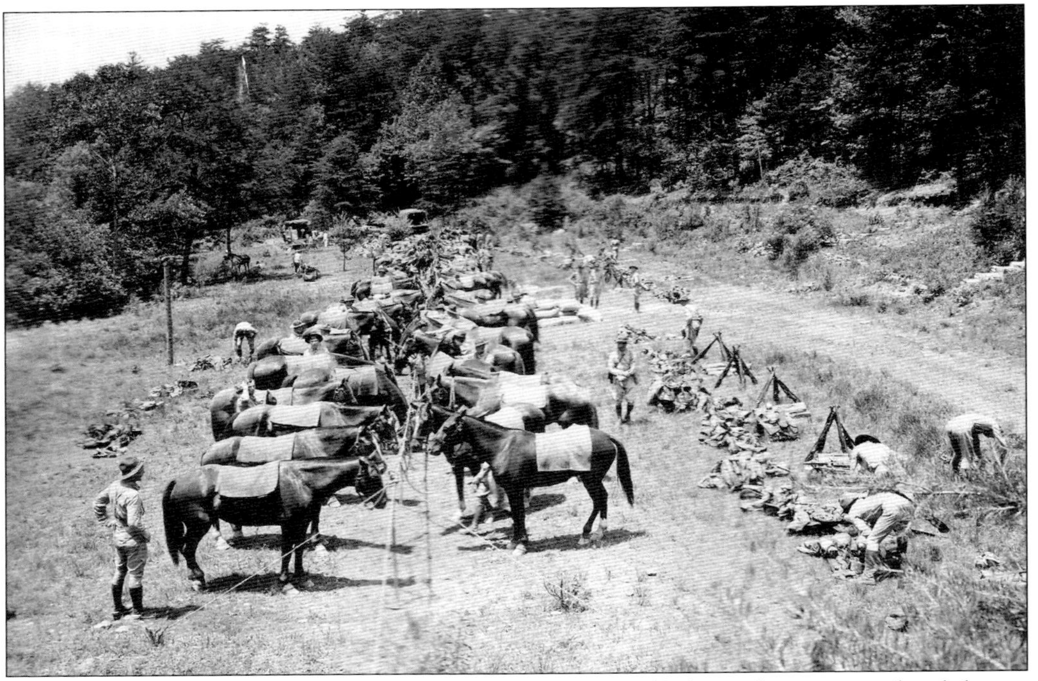

The army needed a good test to determine what role horses would play in the next war, already begun in Europe. During the 1941 maneuvers in the Cherokee National Forest in Georgia, the use of the horse was closely examined. Above, horse bridles and saddles are placed behind the horses and rifles are stacked for easy retrieval. Below, the horses are being loaded aboard "porties," trucks designed to carry horses to the next staging area. By the end of the maneuvers, the horses were exhausted and dehydrated. Shortly afterward, the 6th Cavalry became a completely mechanized regiment. When the 6th Cavalry left Fort Oglethorpe, they left their horses behind. (Both, NARA.)

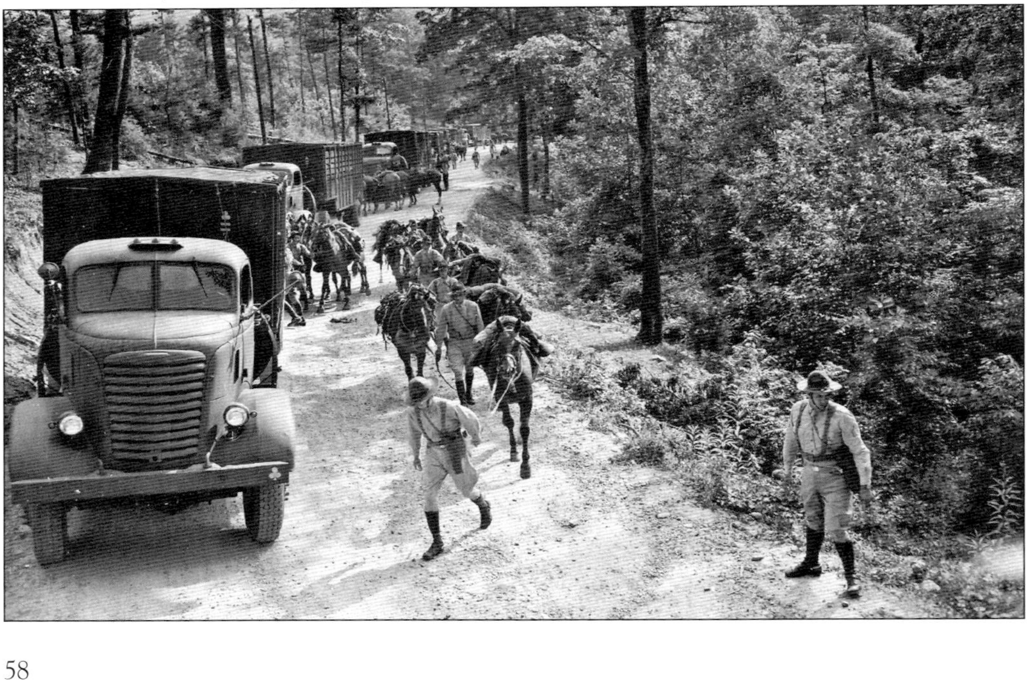

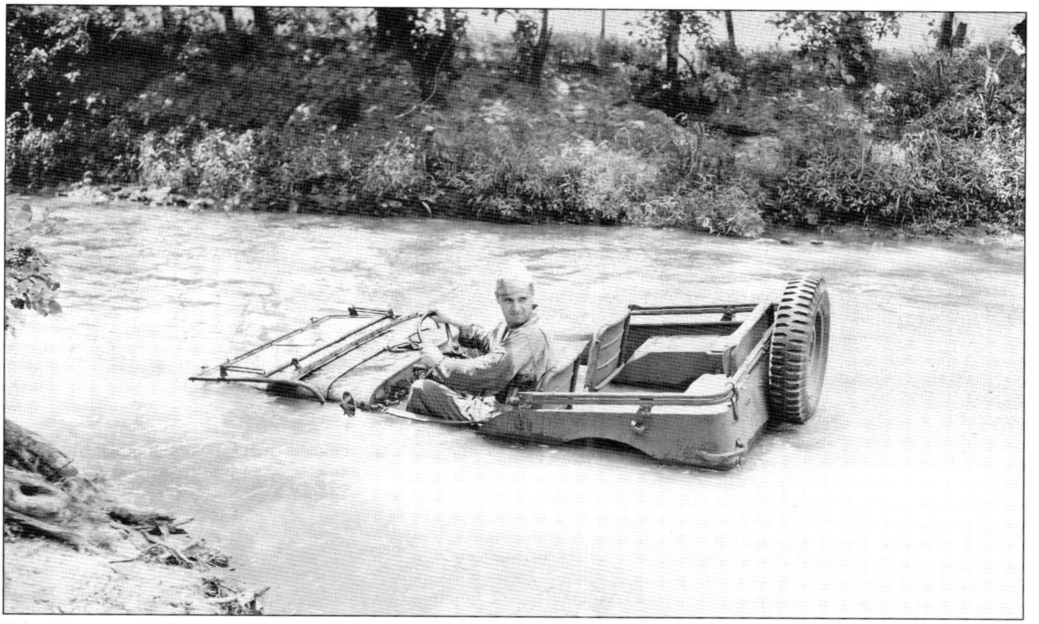

The Bantam, the jeep prototype, was tested on Harrison Bay at Chickamauga Lake and at Chickamauga Creek. Both sites provided water of various depths and the famous Georgia red clay to test the mettle of the vehicle. Here one can see that after crossing the creek successfully, the bantam encountered some problems going down the creek. Many G.I.s, as well as civilians, have found themselves in this situation: steering, pushing or, off camera, pulling a car out of a similar problem. The Bantam car proved worthy of the designing and testing it took and joined the army's pool of vehicles. Each vehicle of this kind was stenciled with GP (Government Property) and gained the nickname "jeep." (Both, NARA.)

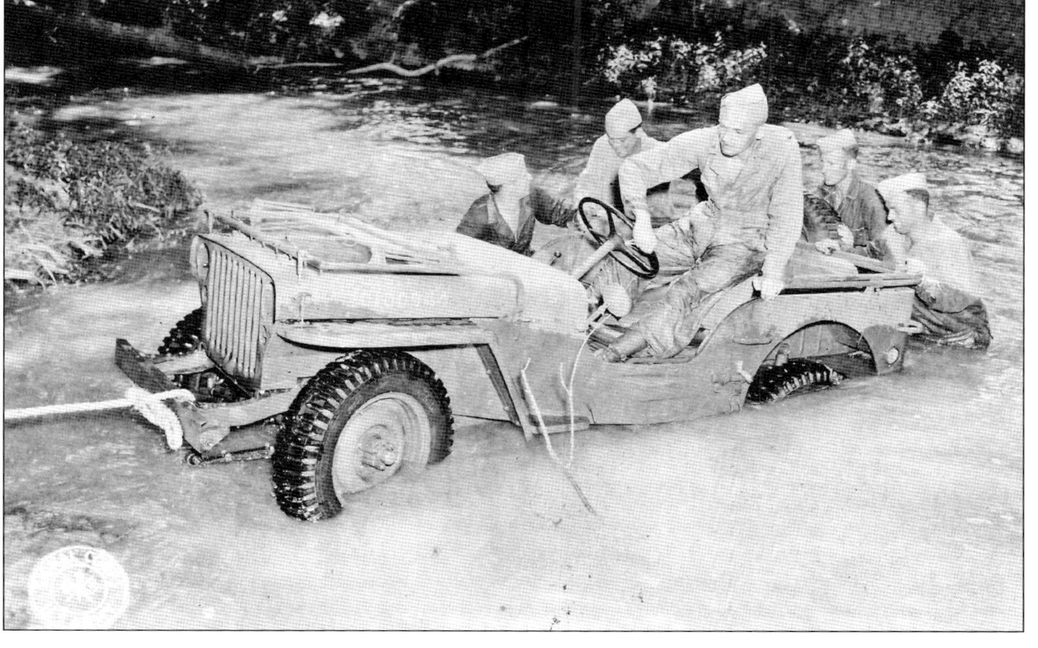

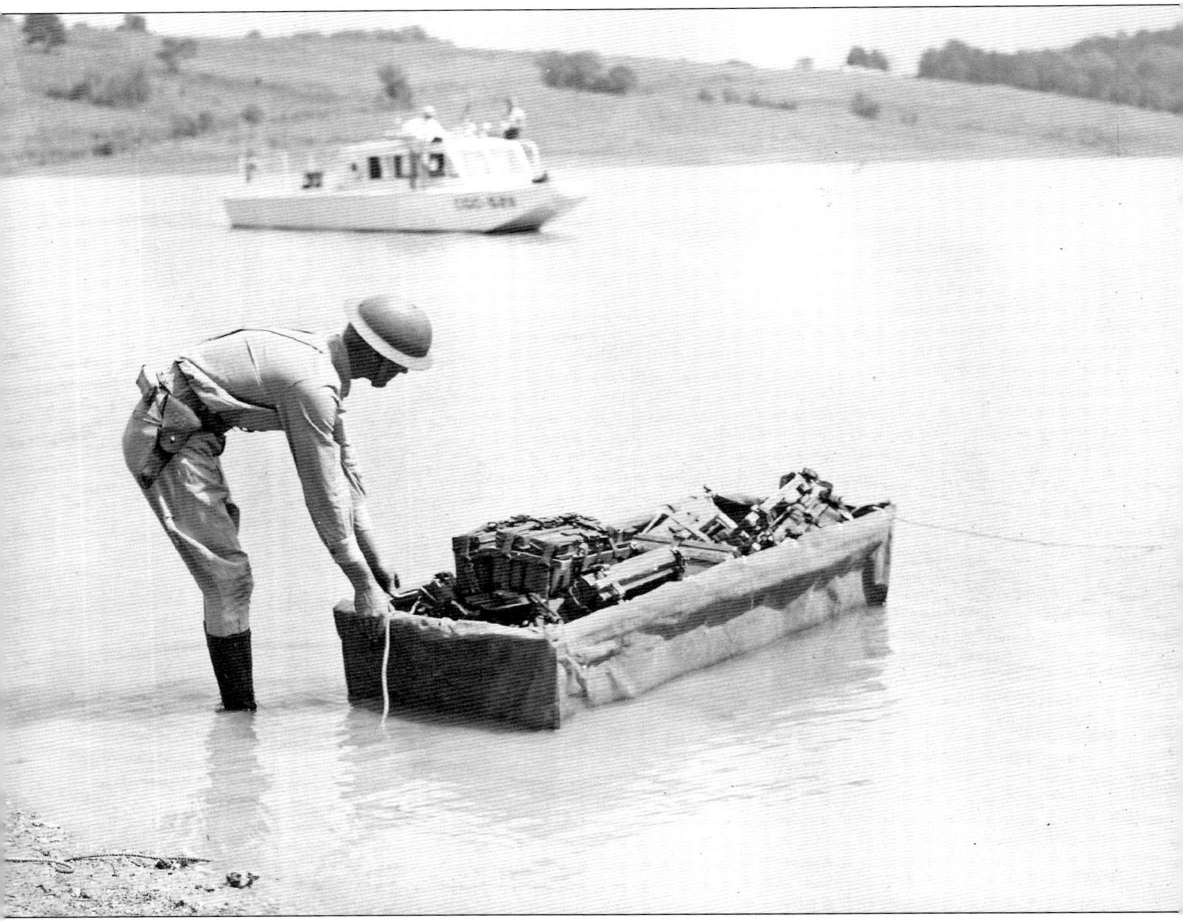

During the 1941 maneuvers, the army practiced floating materials such as radios and ammunition across streams in a waterproof craft designed by Col. John Considine of Fort Oglethorpe. The maneuvers ended December 6, 1941. Pearl Harbor was attacked on the next day, Sunday, December 7. In April 1942, the 6th Cavalry left Fort Oglethorpe after 23 years. (NARA.)

Five

Welcoming the Women

"When we heard the singing and marching, we hurried to put more food on the grills," said Adrian Rhodes of Lake Winnepesaukah Amusement Park. "We could tell the WACs were coming." The women marched in cadence whenever they came to the park. There they would enjoy a day of fun and relaxation.

Among the attractions at the park was the magician, but he had some concerns. With meat, silk (for parachutes), and metal rationed, what would he do if his rabbit died, or his silk kerchief wore out, or his metal props broke?

The WAAC came to Fort Oglethorpe in January 1943, and in July, Pres. Franklin Roosevelt signed legislation creating the WAC. The WACs were sworn into the army in August. The women were quite busy on base, with basic training, military regimentation, learning to march, and kitchen duty. Their quarters and uniforms had to be in inspection-ready condition. From Fort Oglethorpe, many of the WACs were sent to other posts for further training; some were sent to duty overseas. Over 50,000 WACs were processed through Fort Oglethorpe.

While the WACs were stationed at the base, Lana Turner visited Fort Oglethorpe to film part of the movie *Keep Your Powder Dry*.

Pres. Franklin Roosevelt visited the area several times while the WAAC was there. On April 7, 1943, he came to view a new Tennessee Valley Association project built near a railroad yard in Chattanooga. He was riding in a 1938 Cadillac convertible limousine, with the top down. One local resident remembers the day clearly. "I was a young lad," he said, "when Roosevelt came to town. There were some freight cars parked on one of the railroad spurs, and my buddies and I climbed on top of one of those cars. We had a splendid view of the president and all the proceedings."

While Roosevelt was in the area, he made an unannounced visit to Fort Oglethorpe to review the WAAC. The troops were told to assemble on the parade grounds for a dress review. Imagine their surprise when their "eyes right" saw the president in his limousine.

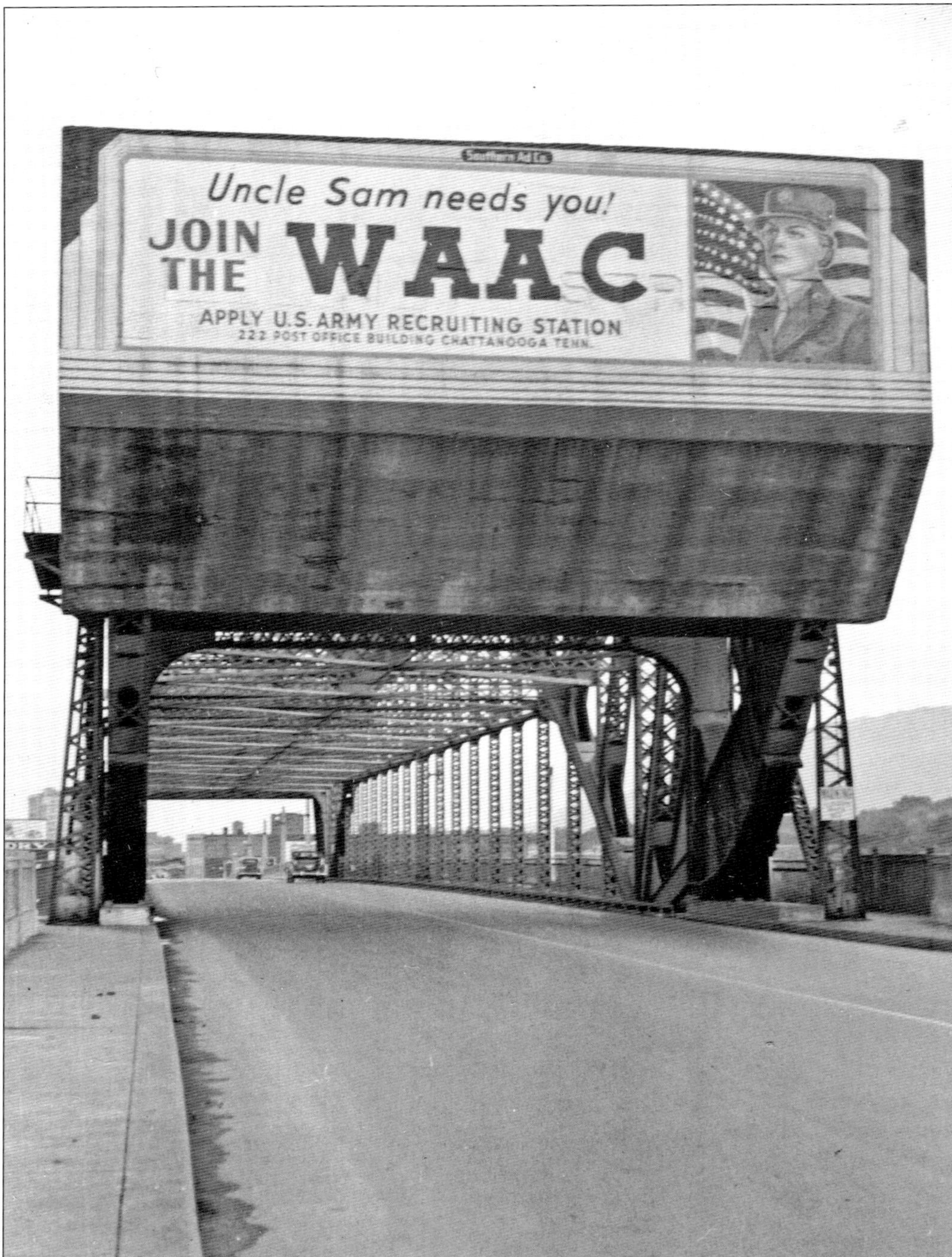

From January 1, 1943, through July 15, 1945, women trained at the post. Recruiting here, at home, Chattanooga advertises Uncle Sam's needs to his local nieces. Local women enlisted in Chattanooga, traveled by train to Nashville to be sworn in, and then returned by train to the post for their six weeks of training. This recruiting poster was painted on the north end of the Market Street bridge. (NARA.)

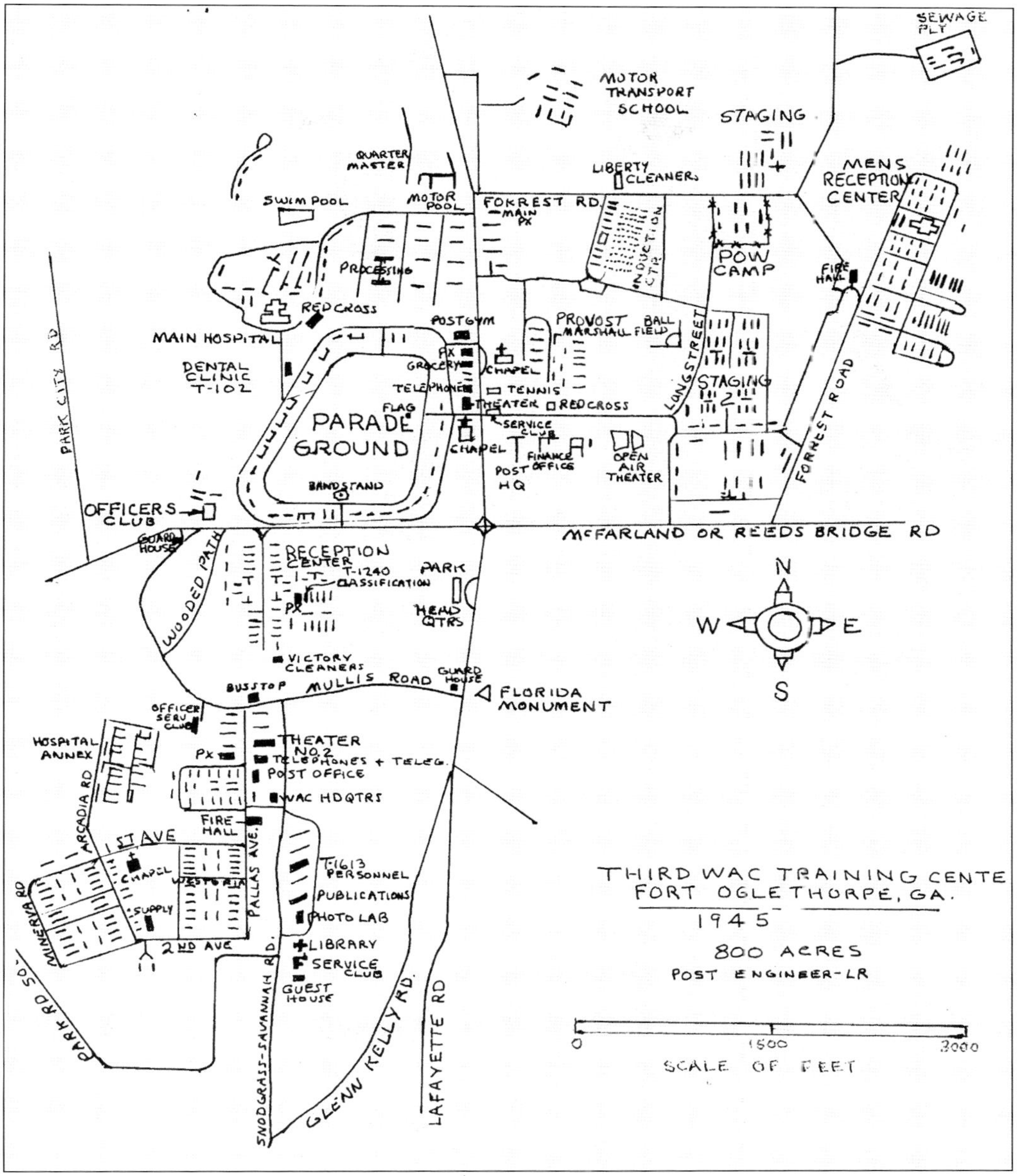

This map shows the park lands used by the Women's Army Corps in 1945. The original post is north of McFarland Road. Although the South Post was home to the women, they marched over the parade grounds each evening. Bus service to Chattanooga was available. A much smaller POW camp on Forrest Road is indicative of the smaller number of German POWs here. These men were Rommel's German soldiers from the North Africa campaign. Men were still enlisting at Fort Oglethorpe, and they used the Men's Reception Center on Forrest Road. Most activities concerning new recruits coming in or graduating WACs leaving were done east of the Main Post. The actual training of the WACs was done on the South Post. (NARA.)

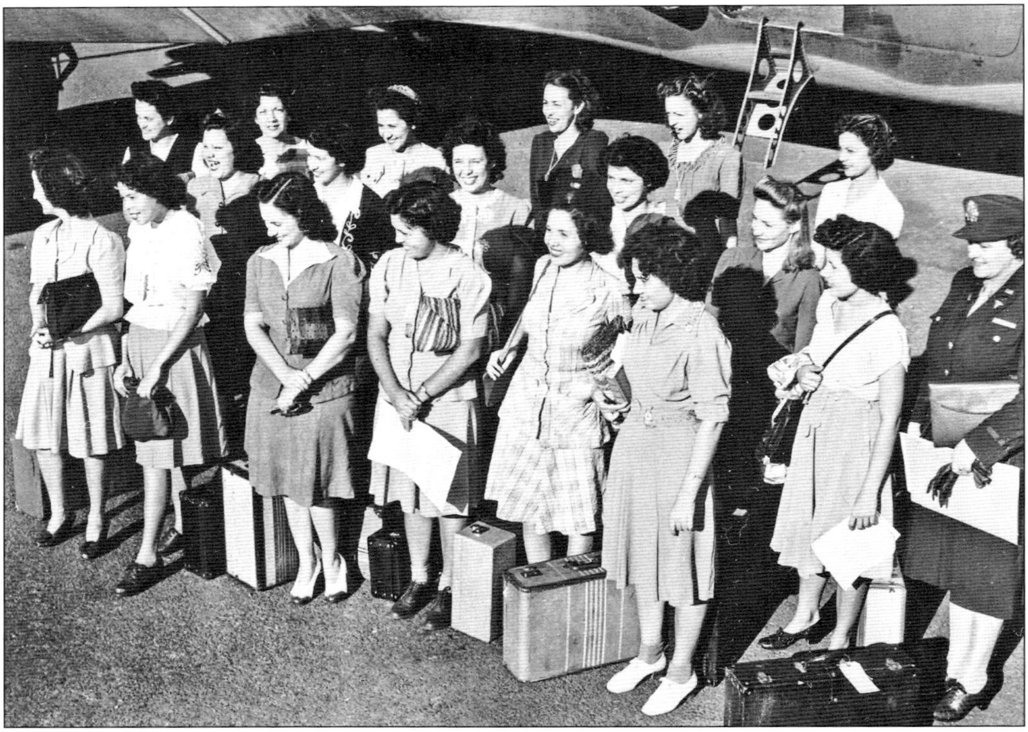

Most non-Americans who trained with the Women's Army Corps had either escaped from German prisons or fled their homelands as they became occupied by enemy troops. Women from Puerto Rico, above, are newly arrived at the post. After their training is completed, they will go to New York as a unit to work with the shipping needs of the army. Below, a Dutch group, at the post in 1944, practices their first lesson on how to salute. Women from Hawaii, the Netherlands, China, and Germany work hard. Once their training is completed, they will all return to their homelands to defend their countries against enemy forces. (Both, NARA.)

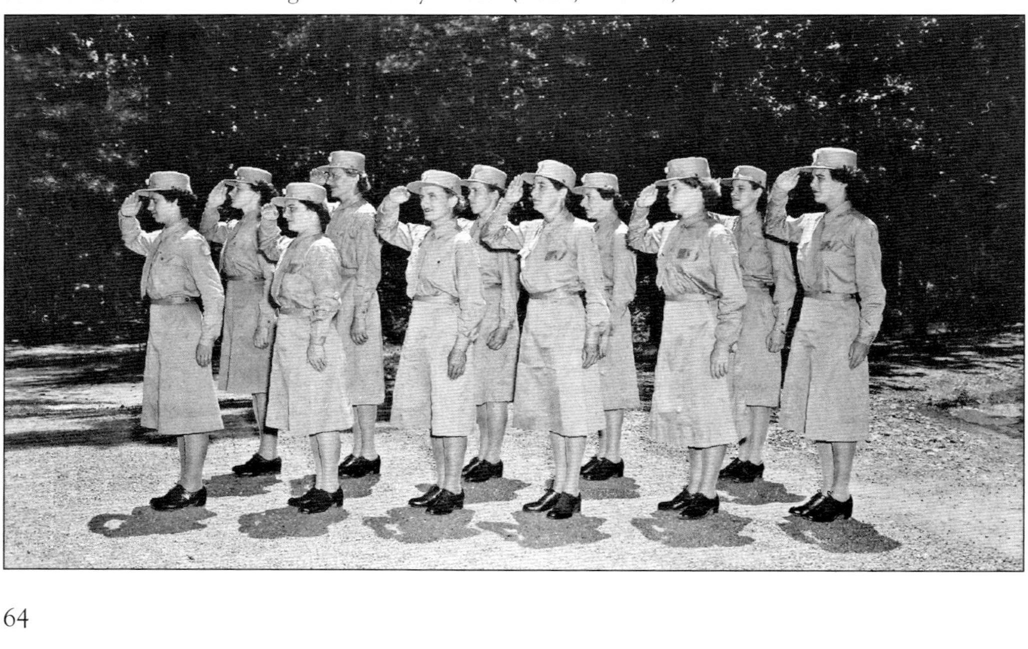

Many women who trained at Fort Oglethorpe never left the post during their six weeks training. Local girls like Mary Ruth Clinton of Chattanooga lived nearby and often went home. After finishing her basic training at Fort Oglethorpe, she went to Fort Monmouth, New Jersey, as a member of the Signal Corps. Mary Ruth is pictured here with, from left to right, her father, Lewis; her sister, Sarah; and her brother, Robert, who joined the Army Air Corps. (Mary Ruth Clinton.)

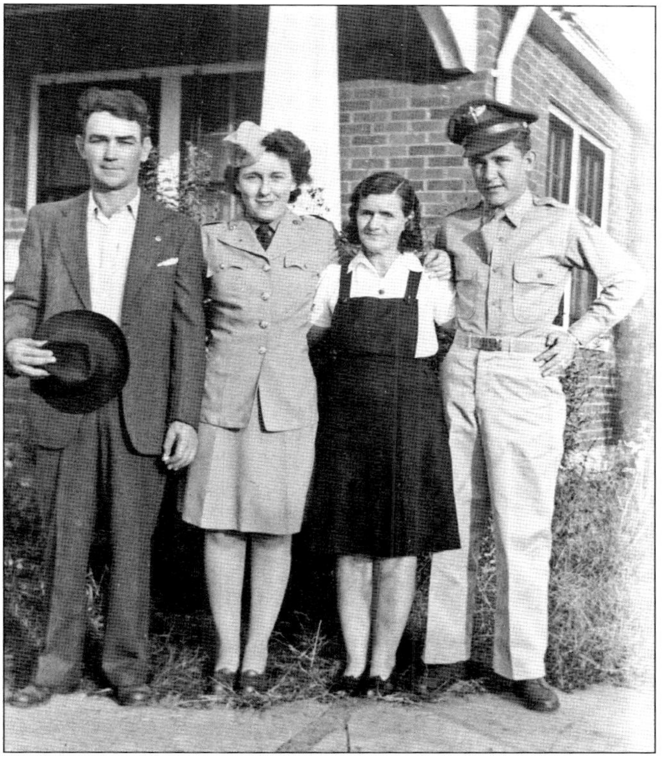

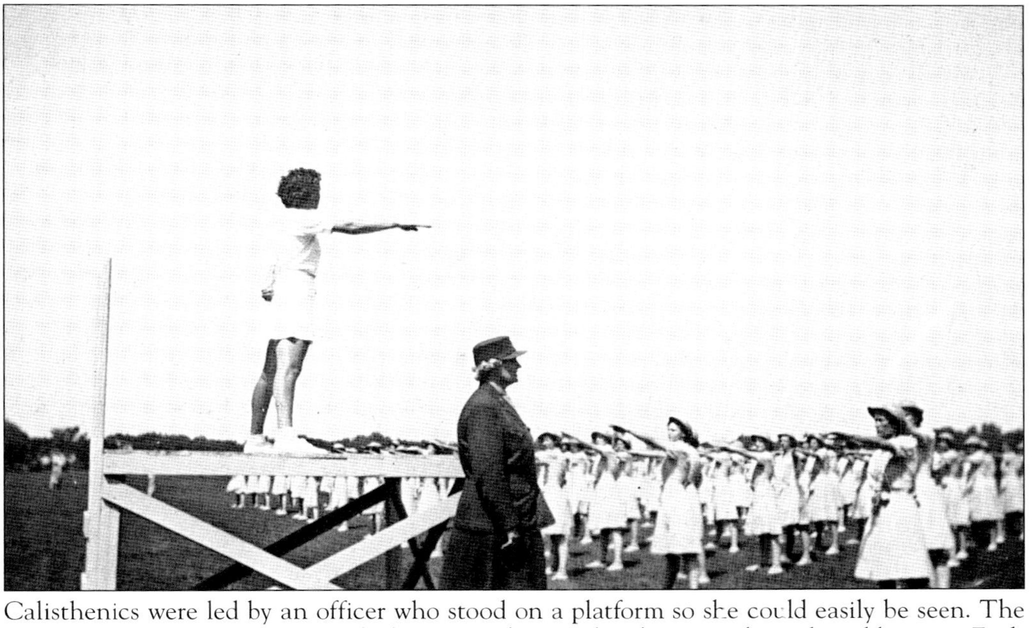

Calisthenics were led by an officer who stood on a platform so she could easily be seen. The women had been issued green-and-white-striped seersucker dresses and matching bloomers. Each woman was a soldier and had to be able to carry equipment and do the manual work a male soldier would have been doing. Physical fitness along with a good diet kept the women in good "fighting" condition. (CCNMP.)

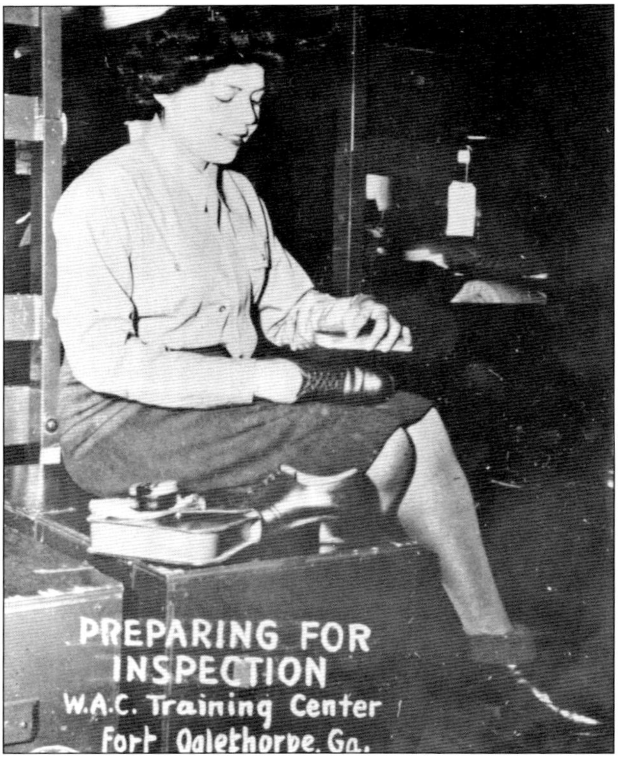

A WAC prepares her property for inspection. After polishing her shoes, she will check her foot locker, her clothes locker, and her bed. Quarters had to bounce off the tight bed coverings. Everything had to be kept according to army regulations. Inspection was Saturday morning. Once that was completed, the women marched to the post parade grounds for a troop review. (CCNMP.)

The army created recruiting posters used to inform women and the public on the daily lives of WACs. "Daily Callisthenics," "Preparing for Inspection," "Bakers' School" and this poster of "Marching to Class" show various parts of a WAC's life at the post. Families understood how their daughters, sisters, mothers, and grandmothers worked to fulfill their oaths to defend their country. (CCNMP.)

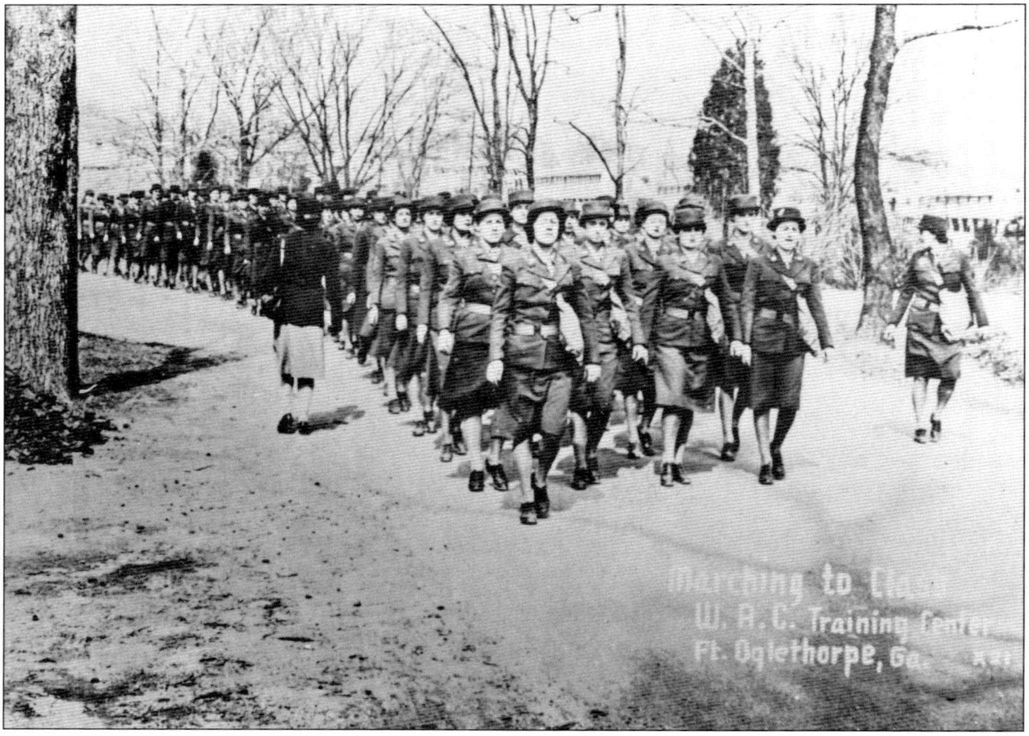

The Bakers' School was one of several specialized schools for WACs after basic training. Their work would probably be stateside to fill the position of men who could then go on to the fighting overseas. Some women would go overseas and find themselves in battle areas and in harm's way. They all served with pride, representing the Women's Army Corps. (CCNMP.)

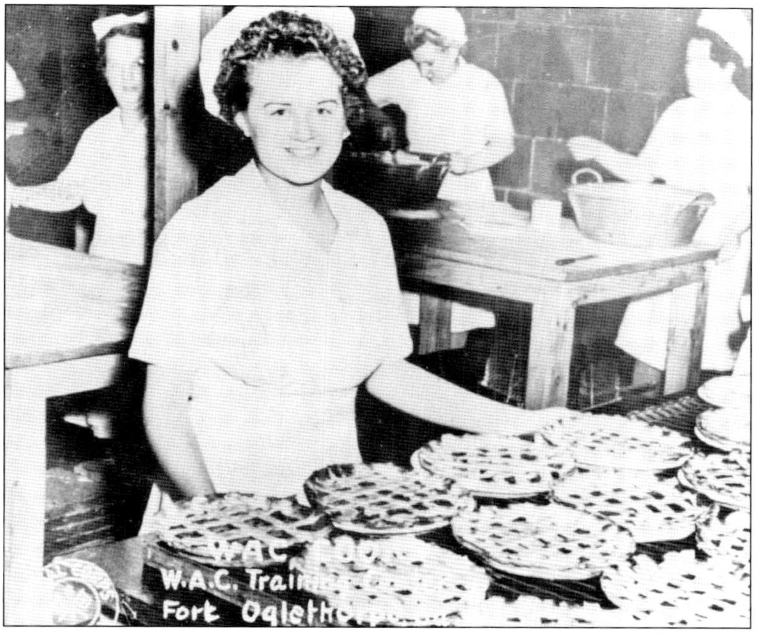

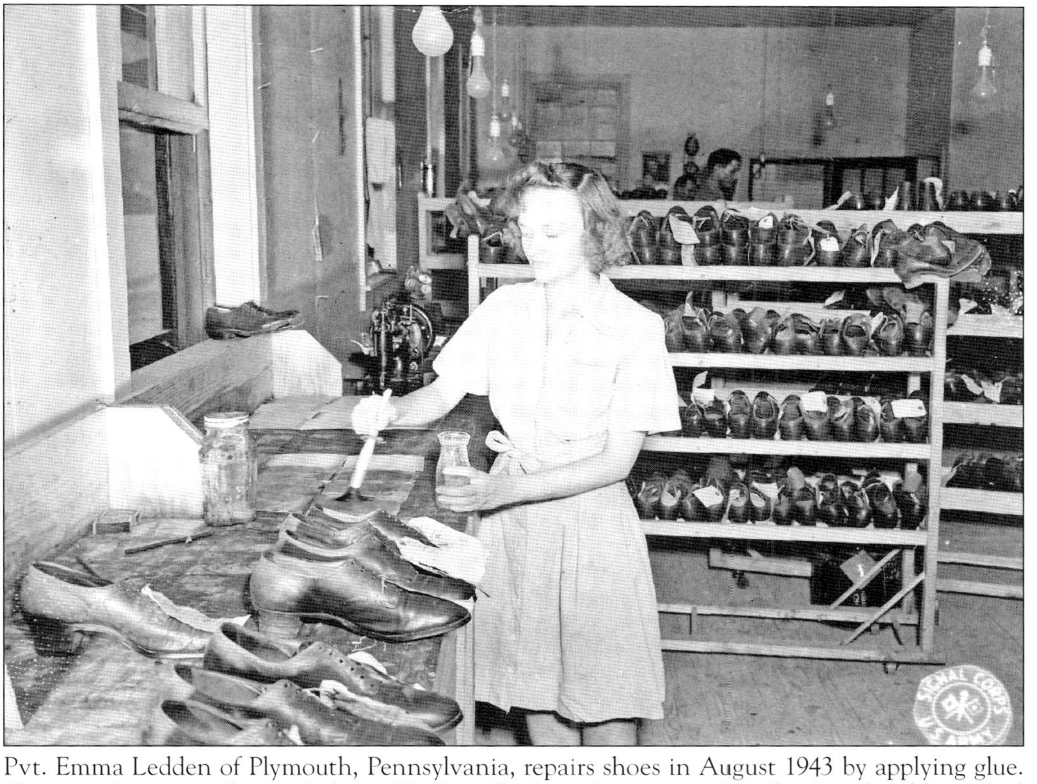

Pvt. Emma Ledden of Plymouth, Pennsylvania, repairs shoes in August 1943 by applying glue. She wears her seersucker work dress. WACs walked, on the average, 44 miles a week. Their oxford shoe sizes ran from 3½ to 12. With war shortages on most materials, leather shoes were repaired again and again. (CCNMP.)

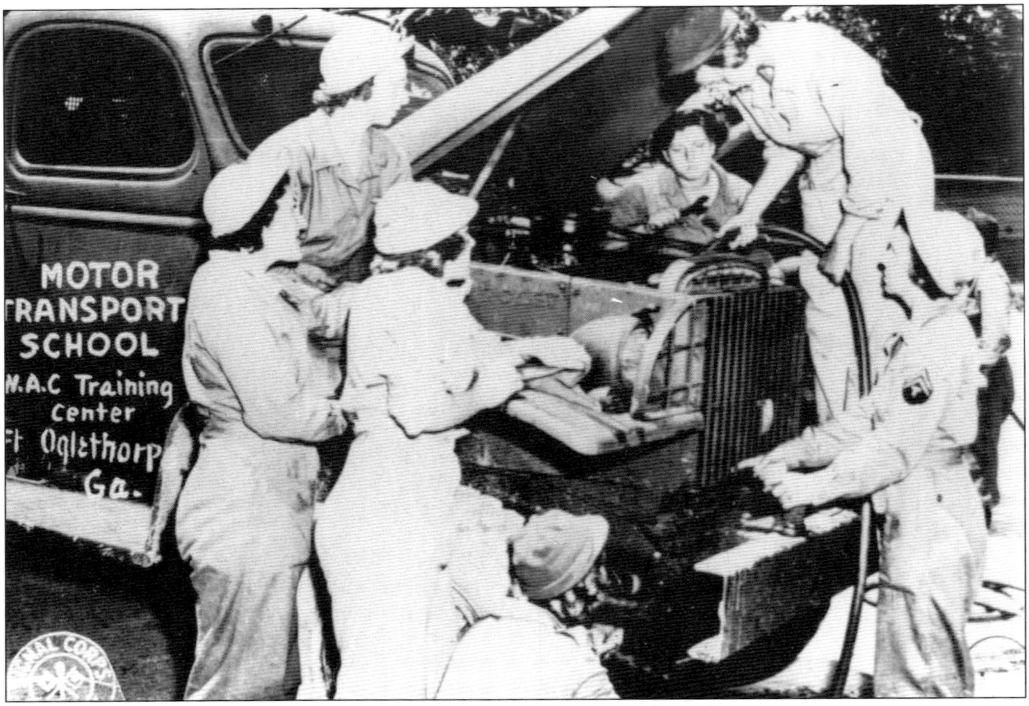

The Motor Transport School trained women for convoy work and moving equipment, supplies, and troops. They drove heavy-duty trucks as well as the smaller vehicles. The Motor Pool School provided mechanics who could repair all vehicles at the post. A third group, civil servant contractors, provided transportation to and from the railroad station as new recruits came and graduating WACs left. (CCNMP.)

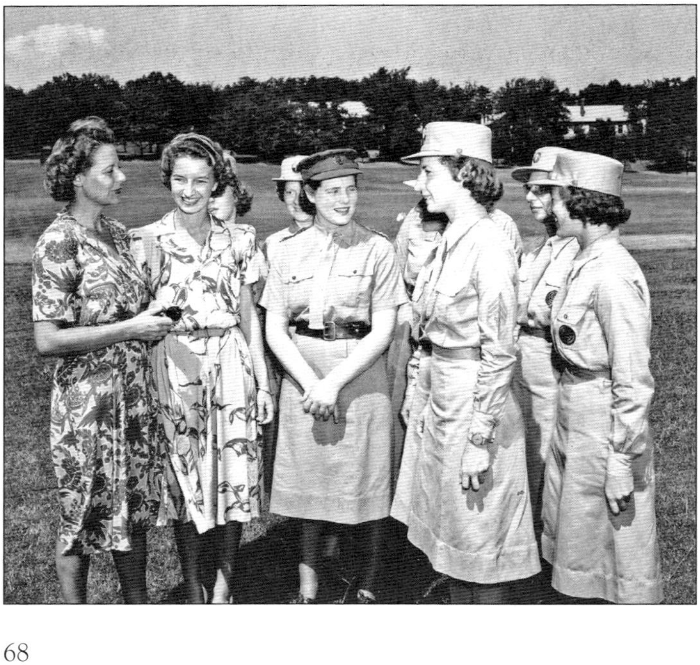

In August 1943, shown from left to right are Alice Marble (American) and Mary Hardwick (British), tennis champions, talking with Subaltern Mary Churchill, daughter of Prime Minister Winston Churchill of England, and WACs at the post. Churchill visited the post to learn about the training. The next day, the two athletes played exhibition matches for the WACs. Stylish dresses and fancy hairdos are sacrificed by the WACs for tan uniforms and "Hobby" hats. (CCNMP.)

After Pearl Harbor, military police (MPs) were stricter in admitting civilians onto the post grounds. Passes were required and checked by the MPs at each gate. License tags and drivers' names were recorded. (NARA.)

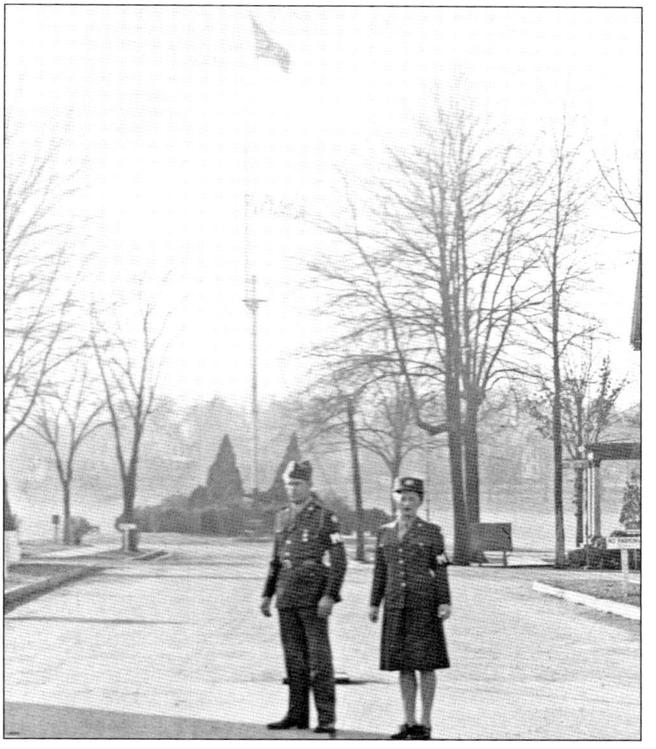

Again POWs were brought to Fort Oglethorpe. The few hundred men worked outside the camp, especially in agricultural positions. Some prisoners cleared wild onion from grazing pastures at Happy Valley Dairy Farms in Rossville before milk was homogenized. Prisoners prepared their own food in their mess hall kitchen. In 1944, Col. Howard Clark, commandant of the post, looks over the shoulder of a pastry cook as he rolls out his dough. (NARA.)

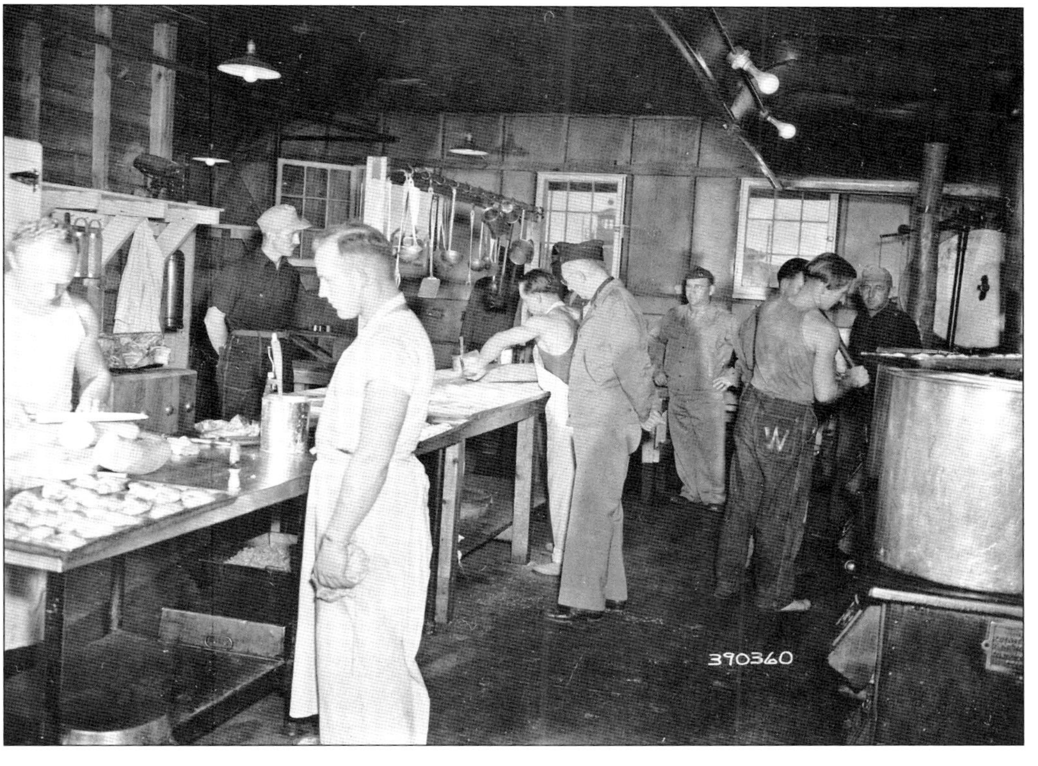

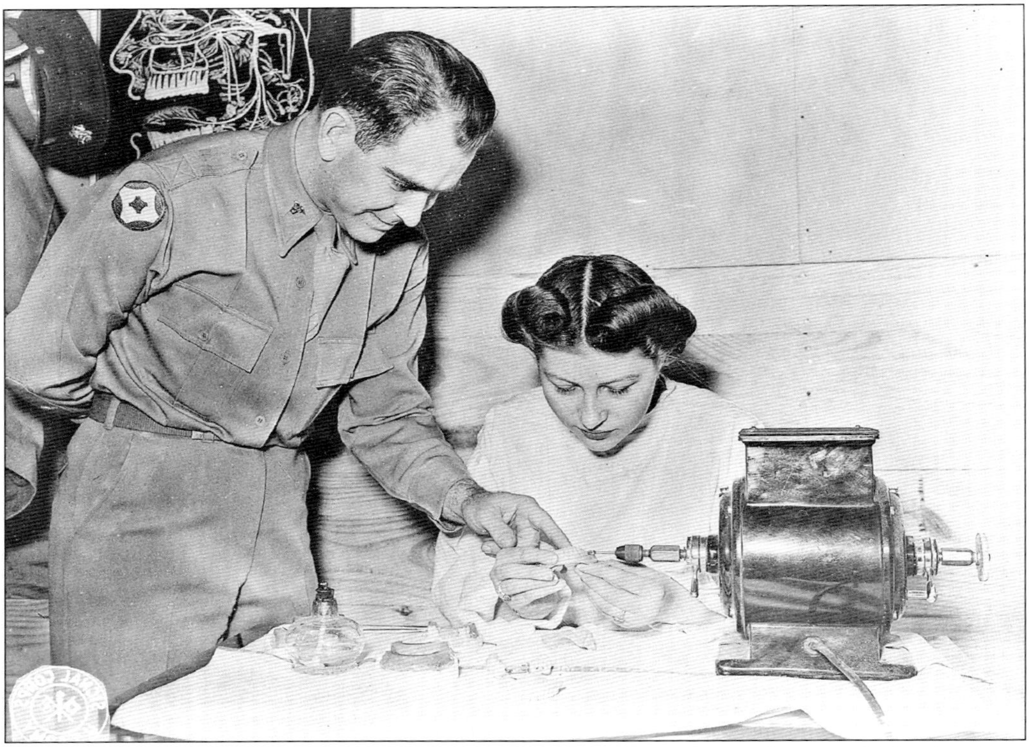

Maj. Eugene Delose Jr. of Louisiana instructs Anna Mae Corcoran in the dental lab. Auxiliary Corcoran is one of three dental technicians in his lab. Specialized schools trained clerks, secretaries, cooks, bakers, military policewomen, medical technicians, chemists, photographers, and film technicians. The government also hired civilian seamstresses to make alterations to the clothing issued the WACs. (CCNMP.)

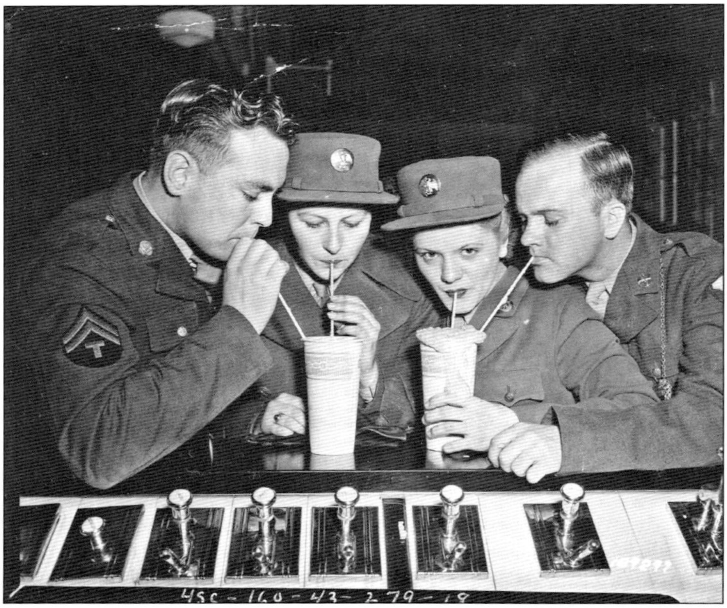

During a break at the WAAC dance in March 1943, these two couples enjoy sodas at the Service Club fountain. T. Sgt. John Luntz, Eau Claire, Wisconsin, and partner Auxiliary Anna Mae Corcoran of Ironwood, Michigan (left), both work in the army hospital's Dental Clinic. Auxiliary Mary Kirasic of McKeesport, Pennsylvania, and Pvt. William Gethy of Youngstown, Ohio, just met at the dance. (CCNMP.)

Pvt. Catherine Miller, Elmira, New York, spends time with a special visitor to the post, actor Walter Pidgeon. Private Miller had been in the WAC eight months and was a graduate of the Motor Pool School. She wears her fatigues as she drives her motorcycle and her side car around the area and shows off her handsome passenger to the other WACs. (NARA.)

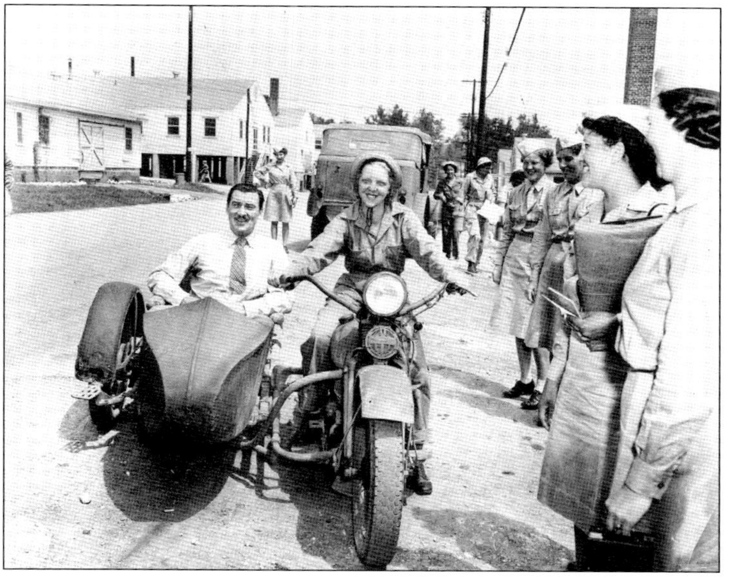

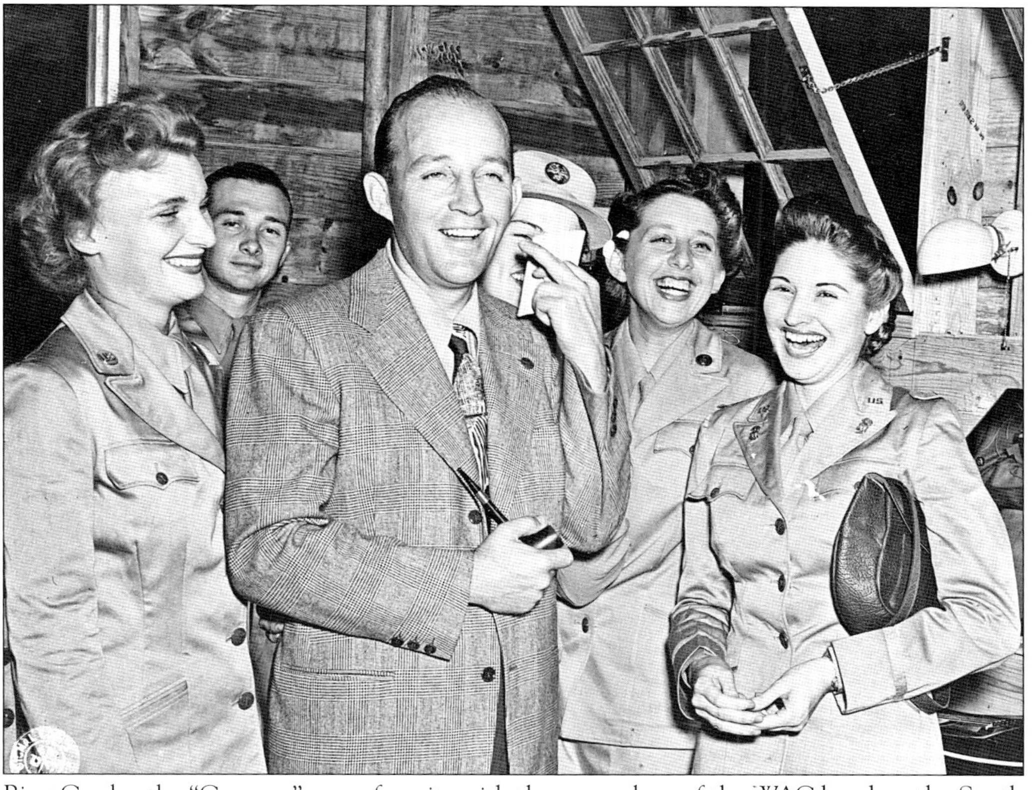

Bing Crosby, the "Crooner," was a favorite with these members of the WAC band on the South Post. Other Hollywood stars who visited the post included Al Jolson and John Payne. Entertainers and special guests performed at the outdoor theater east of the main gate. The amphitheater, completed in May 1945, was built from used materials, financed by profits of the Post Exchanges, and seated 1,500 people. (CCNMP.)

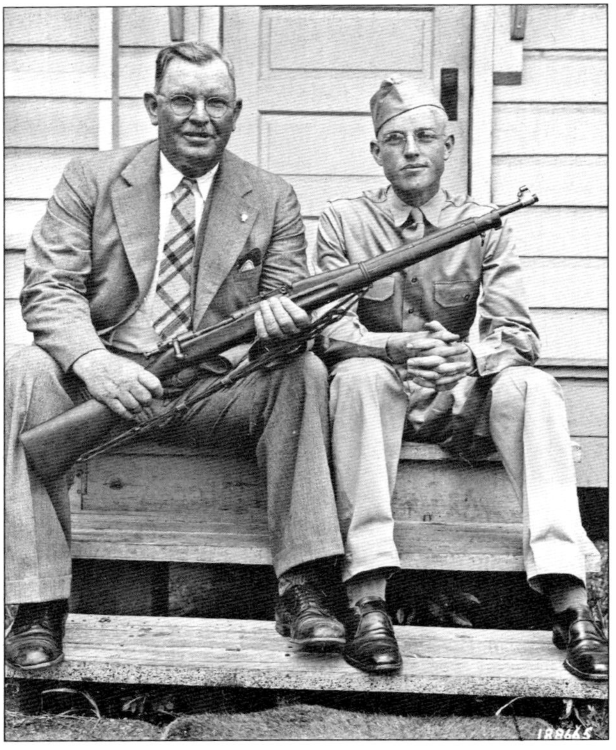

Sgt. Alvin York, a World War I hero, seated next to his son Edward York, visited the post on June 17, 1943, for the celebration of the 200,000th Selective Service inductee into the wartime army at Fort Oglethorpe. His visits were always morale boosters, and he reviewed the WACs as well. (NARA.)

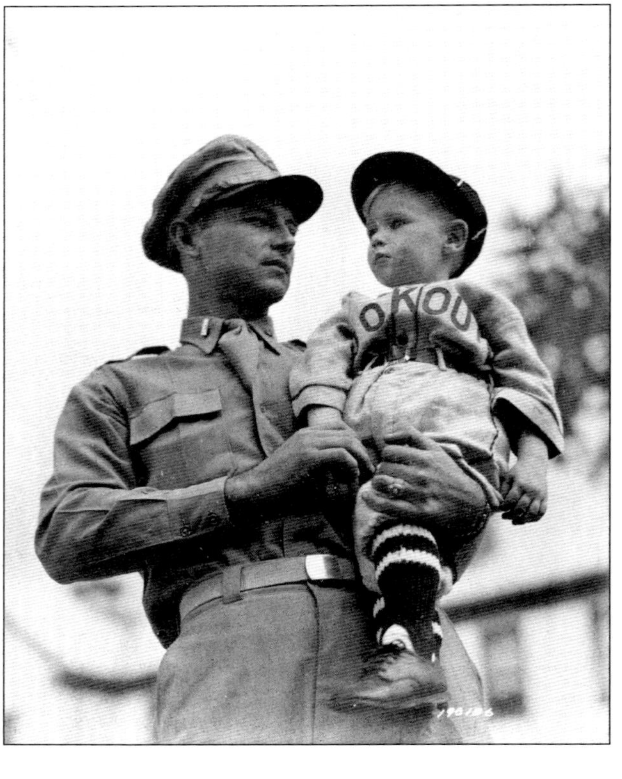

In September 1943, Lt. Johnny Beazley, St. Louis Cardinals pitcher, met David Delano "Superman" St. Clair at Fort Oglethorpe. Six-year-old David had been introduced to the wartime public as a likely candidate for mascot to accompany a major league all-star team on an overseas tour. Beazley, a promising pitcher, permanently damaged his pitching arm on these tours and never reached his potential as a professional ballplayer. (NARA.)

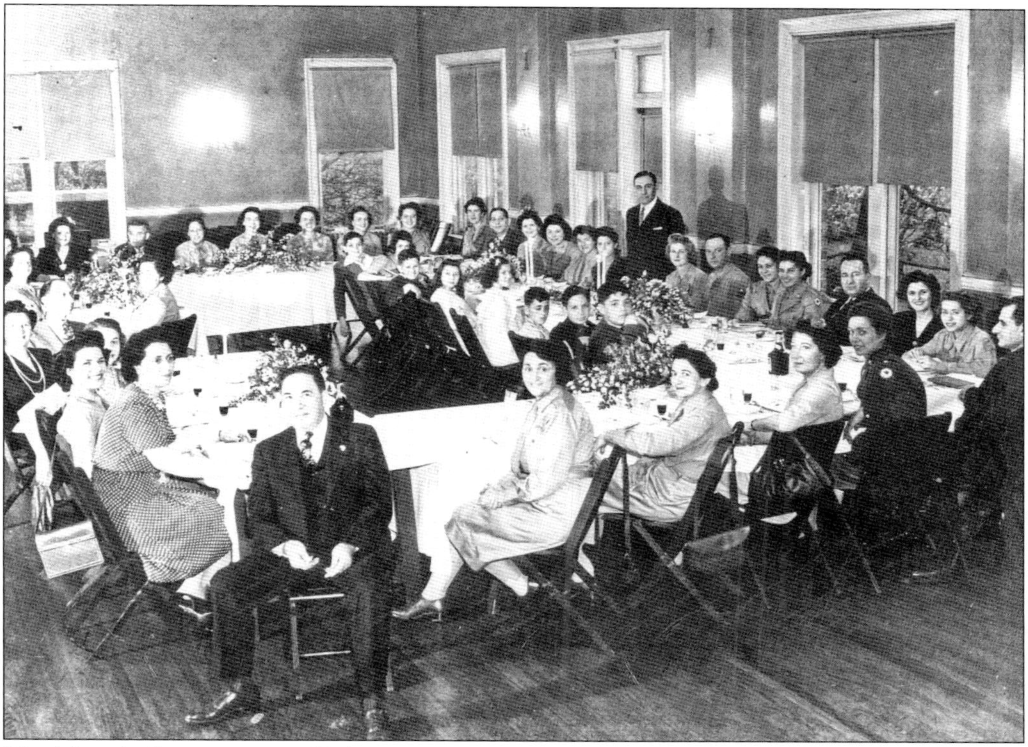

The Mizpah Congregation of Julian and Bertha Ochs Memorial Temple entertained WAC Jewish recruits at a dinner party in 1943 on McCallie Avenue in Chattanooga. Some Jewish people shown here are Rabbi Feinstein, Morris Levine, Norman Moore, Manny Harris, Lester Cohn, Louis Diamond, Ella Gould, and Morris Goldman. Other individuals and church groups also invited WACs to become part of their extended congregation family. (Joy Adams.)

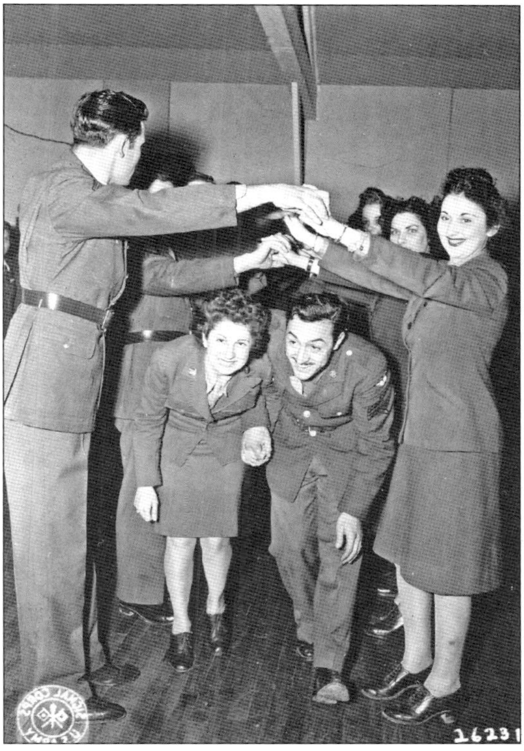

WAACs filled their free time with baseball, swimming, and bowling. They ate dinner at the Patten Hotel, visited USO canteens in Chattanooga, and watched movies at the post theater. Auxiliary Jessie Ann Bucare of Pittsburgh, Pennsylvania, and Sgt. Angelo Bommarito of Detroit, Michigan, come through the line at a dance at one of the social clubs on the South Post. Is that the Chattanooga Choo-Choo they are dancing to? (NARA.)

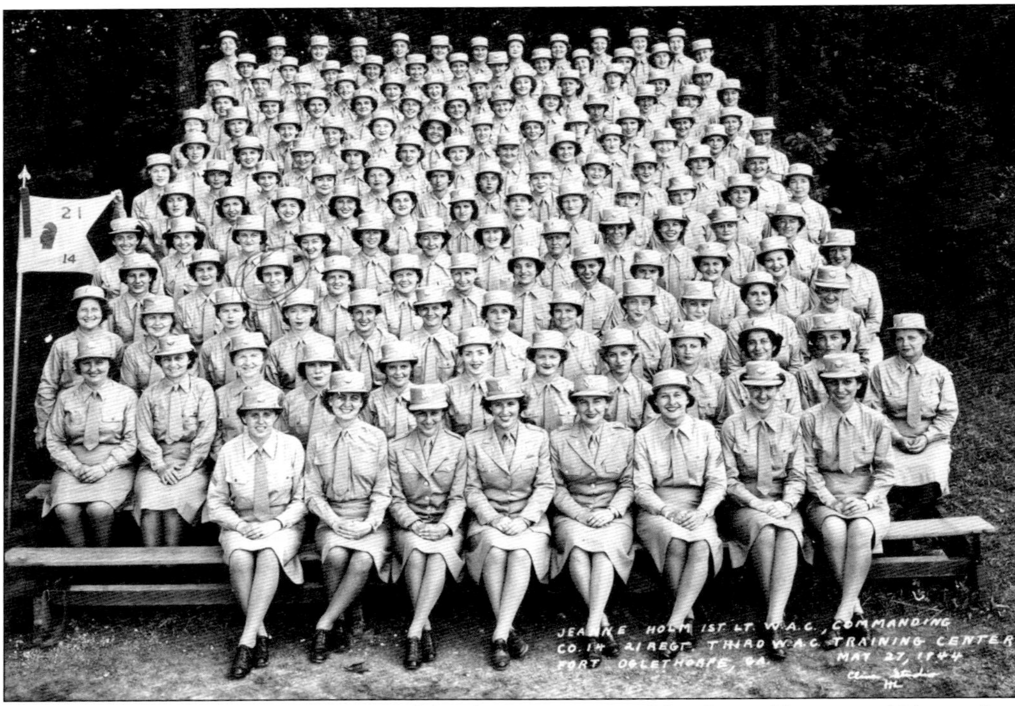

Each company of each regiment posed for their pictures on bleachers. Above are 144 members of Company 14, 21st Regiment, on May 27, 1944. In 1988, some 60 WAACs/WACs, pictured below, returned to the post to dedicate a plaque placed just east of the bandstand. The plaque recognizes the women who passed through Fort Oglethorpe and served their country during World War II. (Both, SCM.)

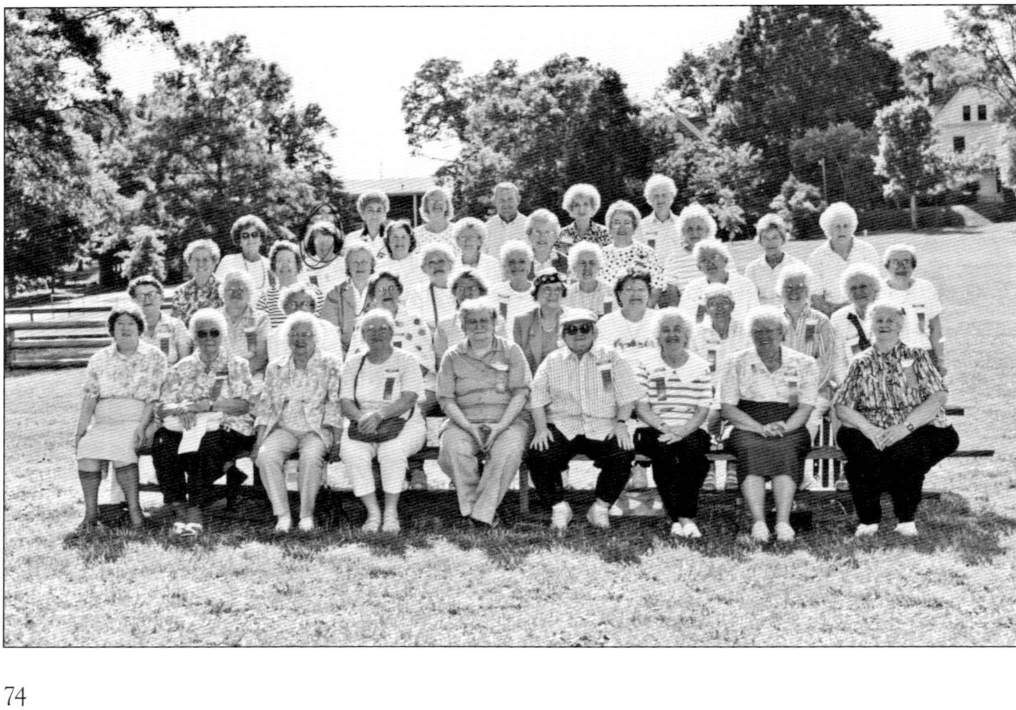

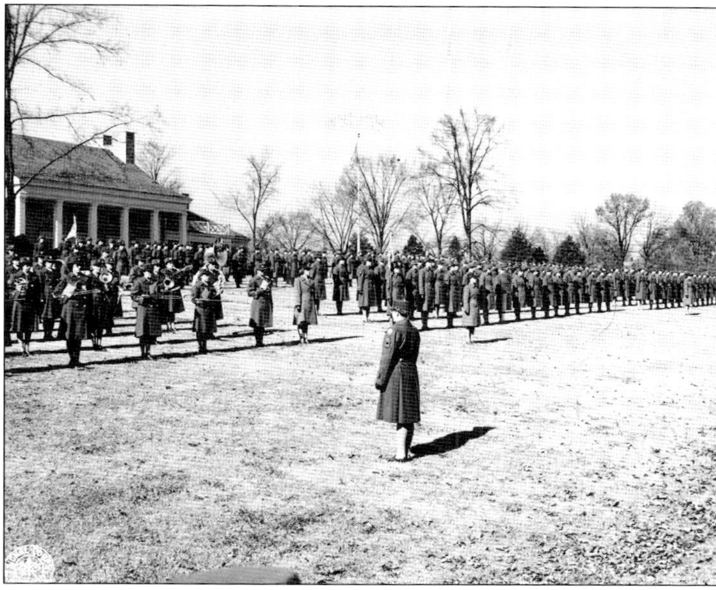

The WAC band and guard of honor assemble in front of the park headquarters building on the battlefield. They await their guests of honor, state governors who are cooperating with the WAC recruiting program, and the ceremonies for "All States' Day," November 17, 1943. The third WAC training center received a special permit from the Department of the Interior to use the Chickamauga Battlefield land. (CCNMP.)

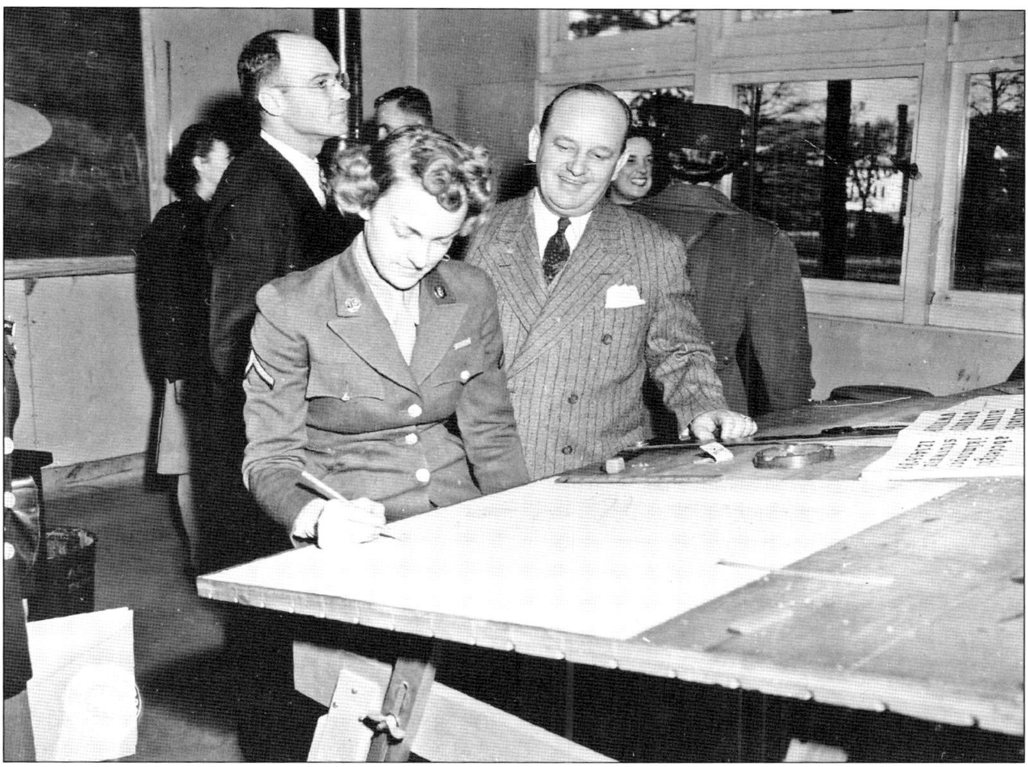

Each governor was escorted by a WAC from his state. Here Georgia governor Ellis Arnall watches Pfc. Alma Swartz of Adrian, Michigan, as she paints a poster in the Publications Arts Department. The WAC needed many more women toward the end of the war to tend to the wounded soldiers returning from the Pacific theater. Among special training in nursing, these women learned Braille to help blind veterans. (NARA.)

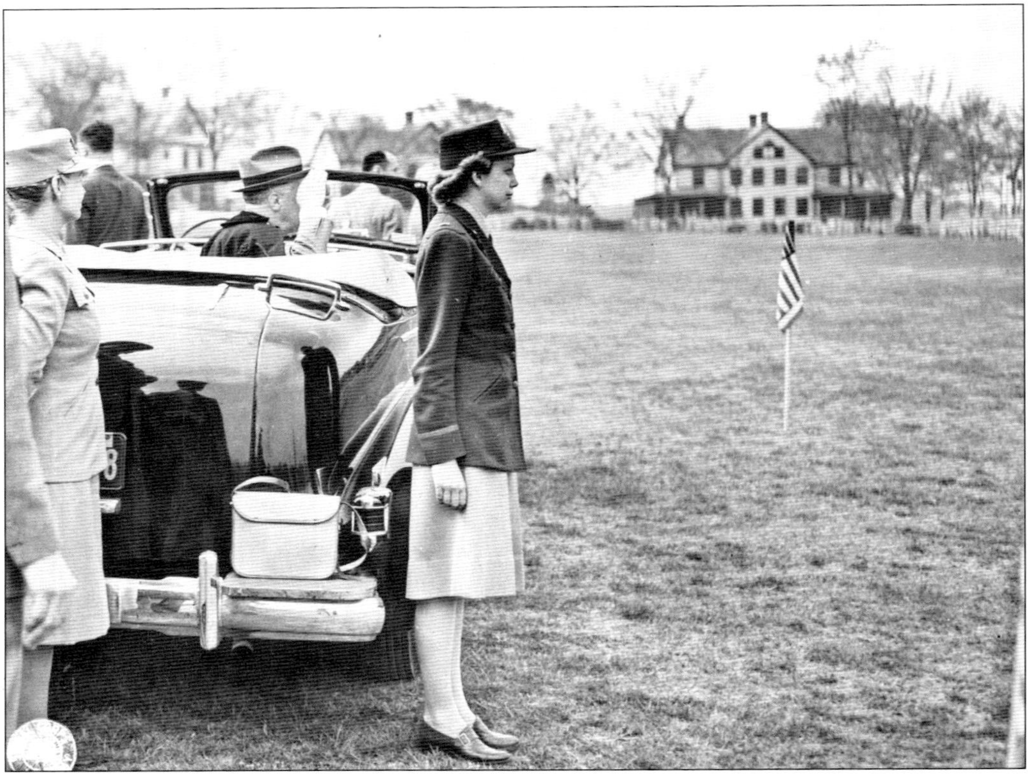

Above, Pres. Franklin Roosevelt made a surprise visit to Fort Oglethorpe to inspect the WAACs on April 7, 1943, on the post parade grounds. As the president salutes, Col. Elizabeth Strayhorn stands at attention. Strayhorn was appointed commandant of Fort Oglethorpe, the first female commandant of any army post. Below, Col. Oveta Hobby, head of the WAAC, and Col. Hobart Brown join President Roosevelt as the WAACs march by. Colonel Hobby takes advantage of the large bumper on the rear of the president's car and places her handbag there until the review is completed. On July 2, 1943, President Roosevelt signed legislation that made the women's unit a part of the U.S. Army with full rank, privilege, and benefits to its members. In August, the WAACs took their oath as members of the Women's Army Corps and became WACs. (CCNMP.)

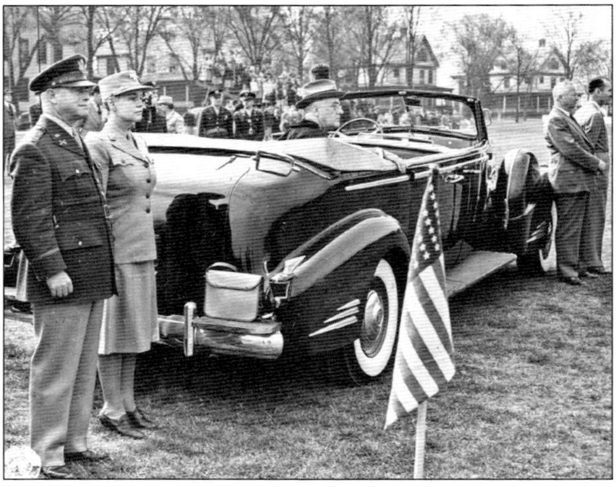

Pres. Franklin Roosevelt died at Warm Springs, Georgia, on April 12, 1945. His body was transported by train to Washington, D.C. As some 7,000 troops, both men and women, pass in review across the parade grounds, the post flag is at half-mast in the president's honor. Many civilians attended to pay their respects. (SCM.)

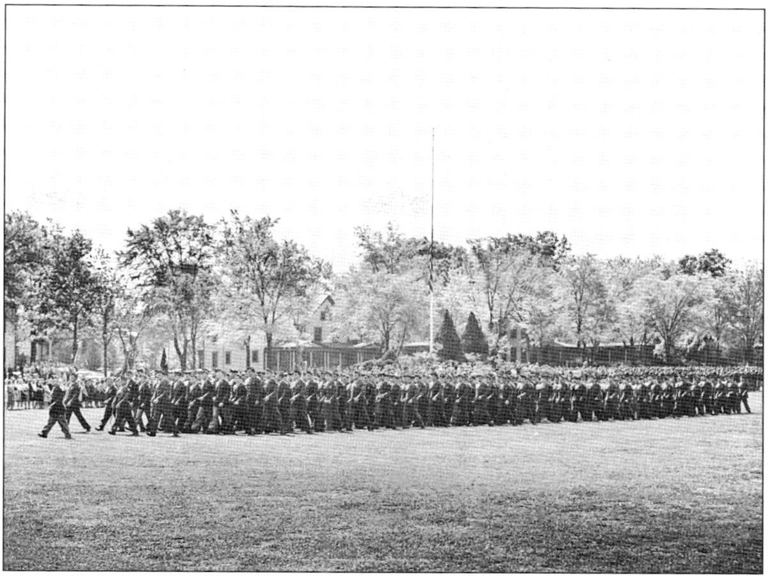

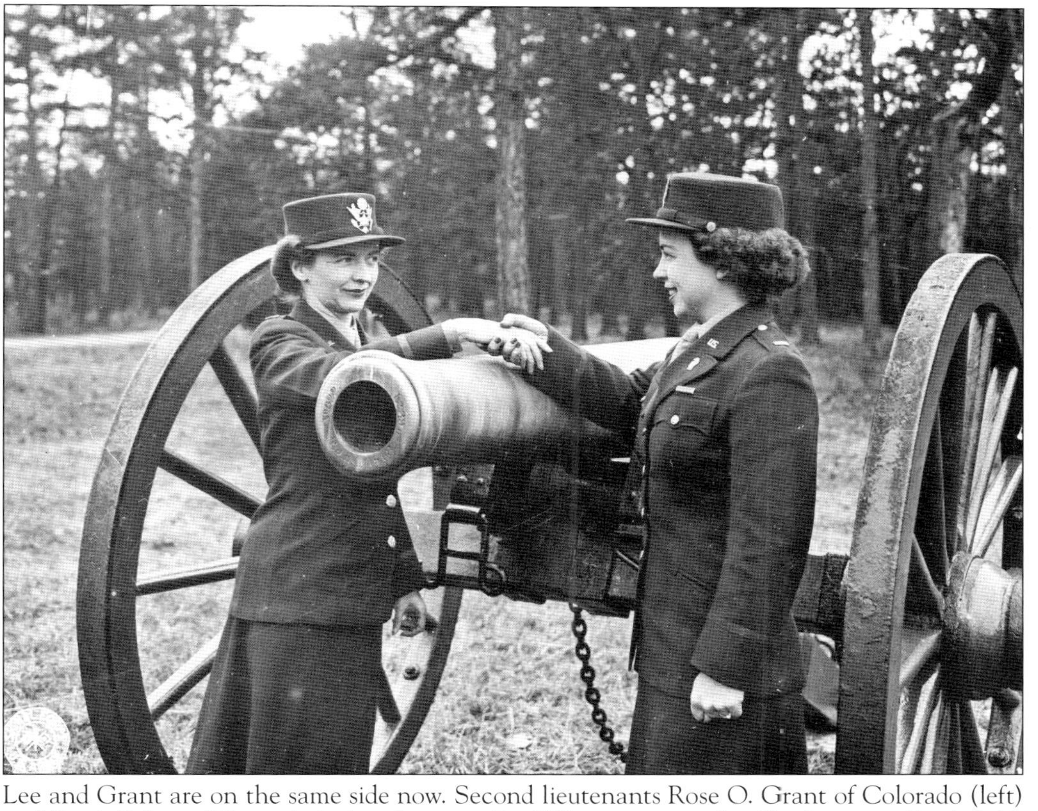

Lee and Grant are on the same side now. Second lieutenants Rose O. Grant of Colorado (left) and Sarah E. Lee of Texas shake hands over a Civil War cannon at the Chickamauga Battlefield. Other famous twosomes serving together were Olsen and Johnson, Dempsey and Carpenter, Barnam and Bailey, Mason and Dixon, Stanley and Livingston, Luckey and Fortune, and North and West. (CCNMP.)

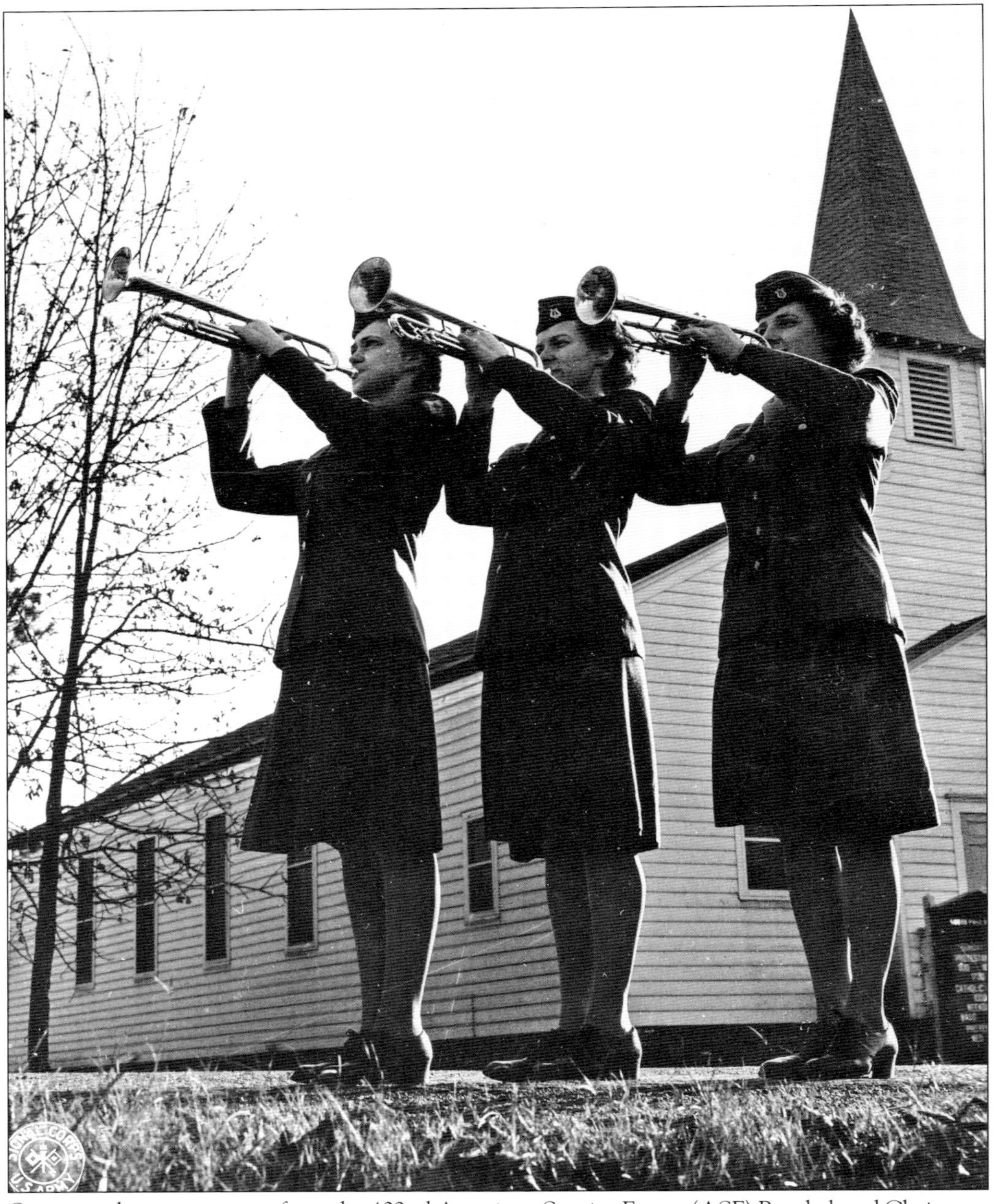

One year, three trumpeters from the 402nd American Service Forces (ASF) Band played Christmas carols each night during the Christmas season before "Taps" was sounded. The tree planted by the local CCC men in the southwest corner of the parade grounds was dark during World War II because the country was at war. In the 1960s, the downtown merchants' Christmas parade ended at the tree and everyone enjoyed the lighting ceremony. (CCNMP.)

Six

Creating a Town

"When I got my report card, I would look at it very carefully to make sure there was at least one 'A' and no failing grade," said a local grammar school graduate of the 1960s. "Then I would run to My Place, to get my free ice cream cone." Jack Ross, owner, generously offered free ice cream to children who brought their report cards in to show him. My Place, first a Mello Kreme ice cream stand and later a family restaurant, is the oldest business in the town of Fort Oglethorpe. It is located on Lafayette Road, near the Harker Road entrance to Barnhardt Circle.

Lafayette Road was moved and widened in 1964, better linking the city of Chattanooga, Tennessee, and the town of Lafayette, Georgia. Later Battlefield Parkway was developed, connecting Fort Oglethorpe to Interstate 75 and to Ringgold, the county seat. This led to more traffic and to the development of downtown Fort Oglethorpe along Lafayette Road. Early businesses included Park Place Restaurant, Piggly Wiggly Grocery (replaced later by Sav-A-Lot), and K-mart. Fort Oglethorpe State Bank, on Thomas Road, was among the first new businesses. The bank was quickly followed by gas stations, a post office, and other ancillary businesses.

The Post Volunteer Fire Department was organized in 1951 with seven volunteers and a 100-gallon booster tank truck donated by the army. Now the department has 70 members, 15 pieces of apparatus, and nine staff/support vehicles valued in excess of $3 million. Today the department, now known as Fort Oglethorpe Fire and Rescue, serves Fort Oglethorpe and western Catoosa County, approximately 25 square miles. The 5,000 acres of the Chickamauga Battlefield are also protected. The department is a charter member of Tri-State Mutual Fire Protection, Inc.

In its early years, the fire department accomplished three goals: the 1954 purchase of a pumper, the purchase of a $3,700 radio system, and the construction of the municipal building, with courtroom, police office, radio room, mayor's office, utilities office, jail, mess hall, bunker, and apparatus room. The funds were raised at the annual Labor Day at the Post celebrations, where the firemen cooked and sold their famous barbecue.

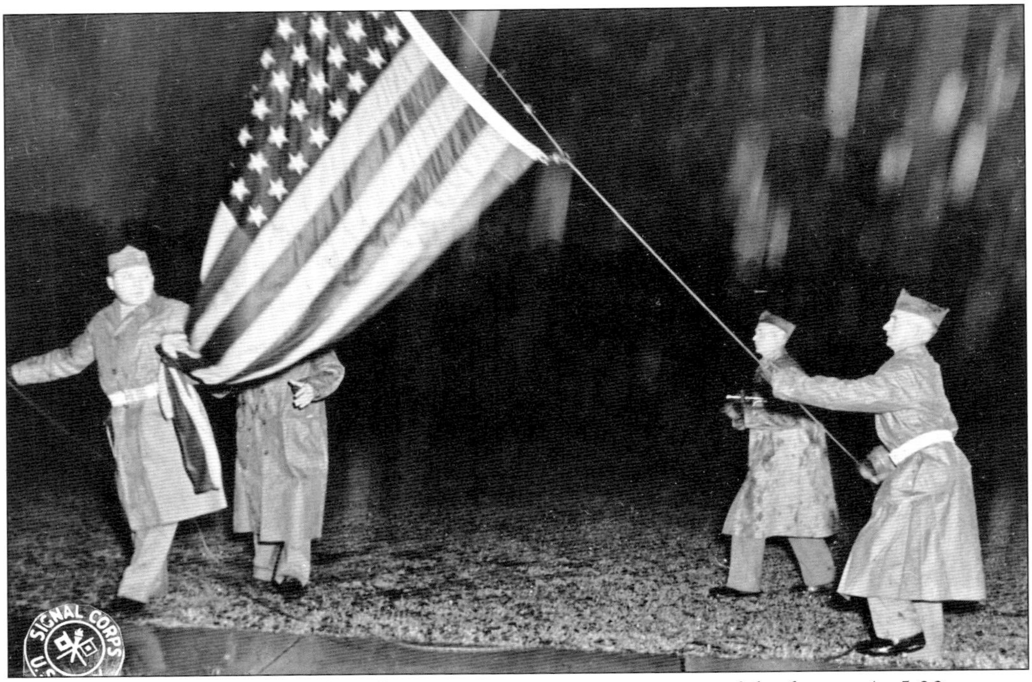

The post could not accommodate the massive training movements of the future. At 5:00 p.m. on December 31, 1946, the flag was lowered officially for the last time by (above) M.Sgt. Orlander C. Churchwell, M.Sgt. Peck J. Porter, 1st Sgt. Willis Albertson, and Sgt. James H. Bryant, bugler. Special guest Angus Clifford (below, far right) of East Ridge, Tennessee, was a member of the 7th Cavalry unit stationed to guard the post when it was opened in 1904. He appeared in civilian clothes because he did not have a uniform left from his retirement in 1924. Col. Malone Rees (second from left), commanding officer, presented the last flag to M.Sgt. Peck J. Porter in recognition of his 33 years of army service. The ceremony at 5:00 p.m. was witnessed by a number of people who loved the post. At midnight, in a light rain, these men returned to take down the flag for the last time. (SCM.)

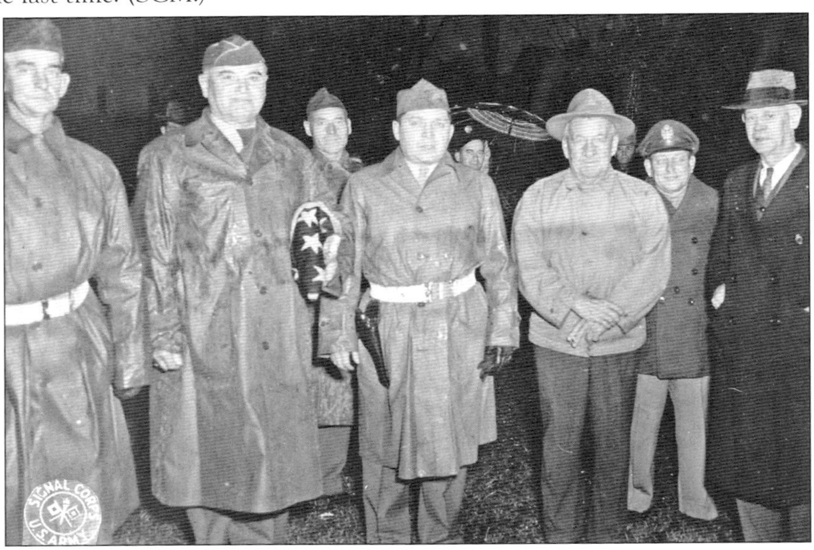

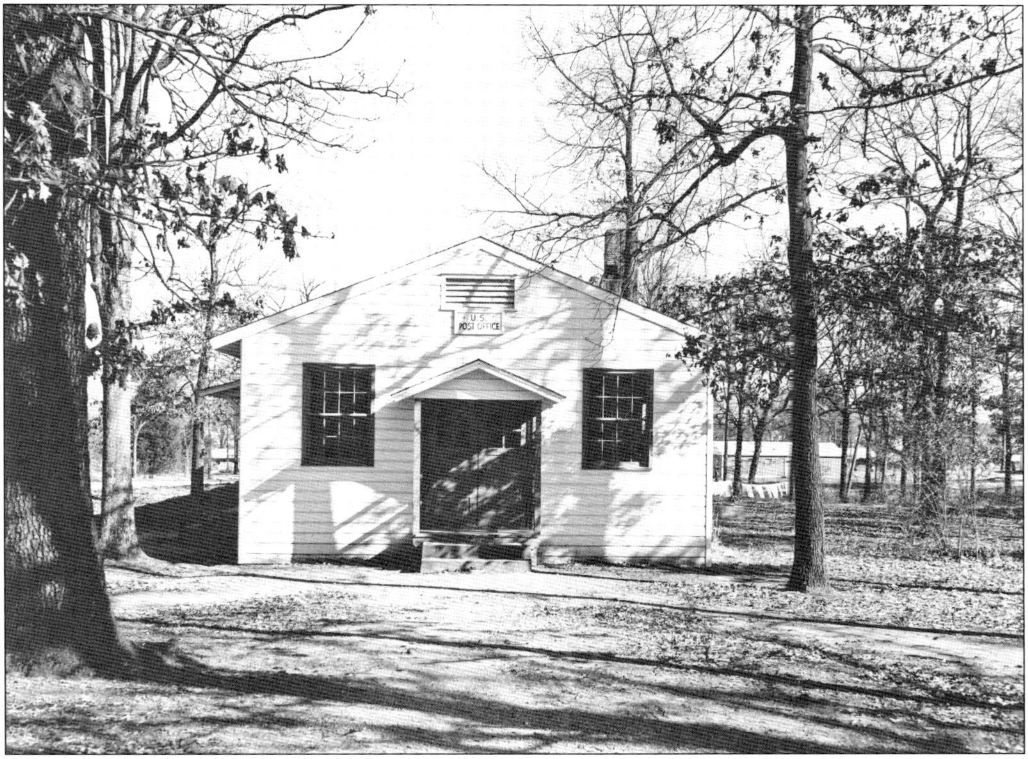

Edna Earle Lockman, first postmistress at the original town post office, announced during her term of service that mail would be delivered directly to homes. Beginning at this small facility east of Lafayette Road in the Cleburne and Martin Streets intersection area, the post office moved across Lafayette Road and then to its present location across Stephenson Road from the then-new municipal building and fire department. (CFO.)

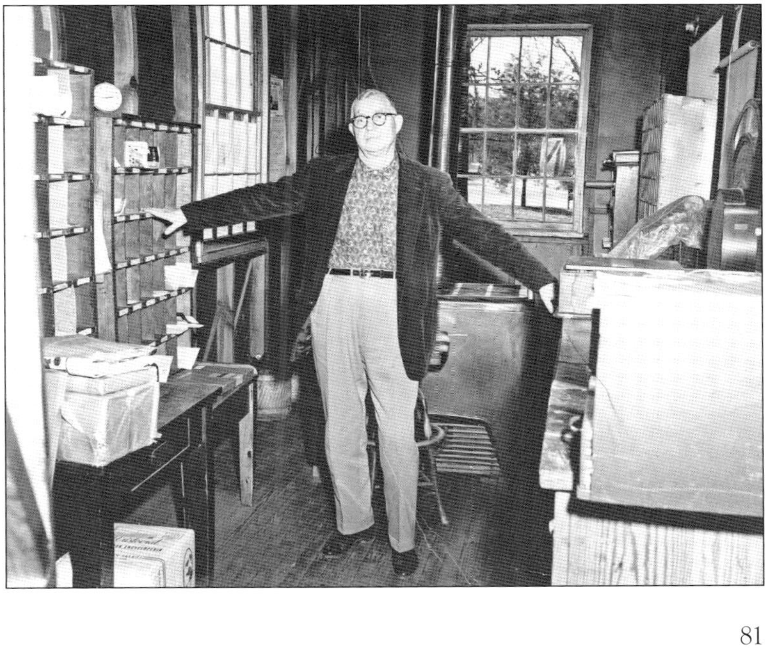

The inside of the post office is not very large. Hershall Powell, who also served as postmaster, reaches out and almost touches the walls of this room. Railway Express delivered parcels to the adjacent room. With post office boxes, a work table, scale, and heater, there was little room for more than one person. (CFO.)

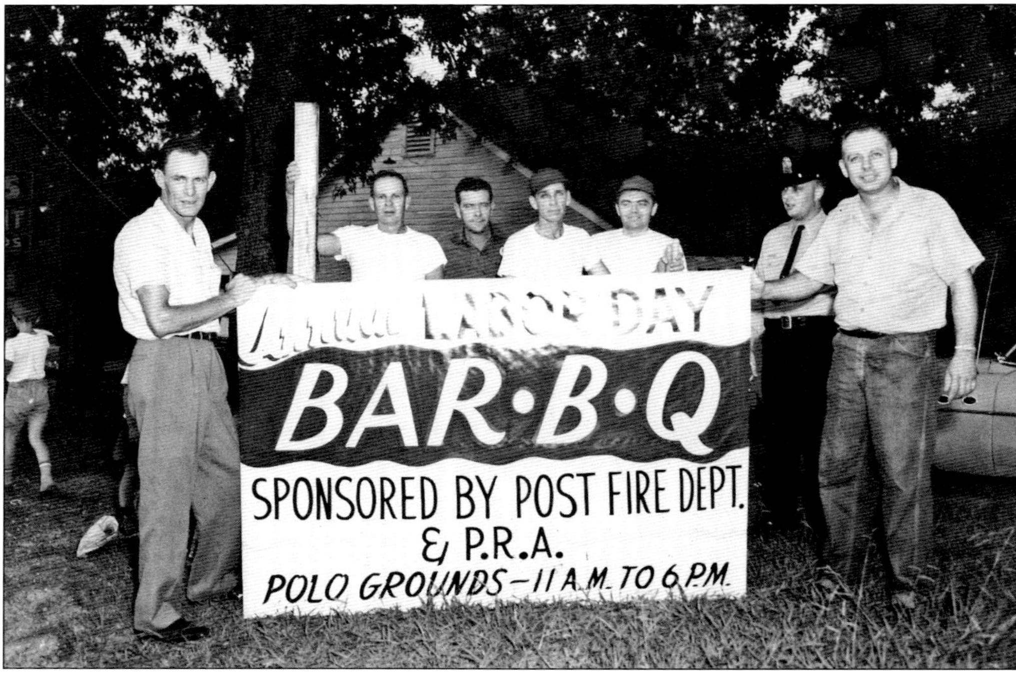

Early volunteers for the Labor Day barbecue cooking marathon are, from left to right, Frank Friel, Junior Lehman, Harold Cook, Jake Norton, Bill Wagner, Marshall Nicols, and Smokey Holder. The barbecue began at 11:00 a.m. on Monday, Labor Day, at the polo field and lasted until 6:00 p.m. Cook and Holder were no longer active volunteers but continued to participate. Volunteers began cooking the barbecue on Friday at the play park on Cleburne Street. Sons of volunteer firemen anticipated the year they could don the big rubber gloves and help in this 24-hour, three-day cook. Blake Strickland, a teenager at the time, said residents could smell the barbecue throughout the city and it was evident by the amount of smoke generated by the cooking pork. (Both, CFO.)

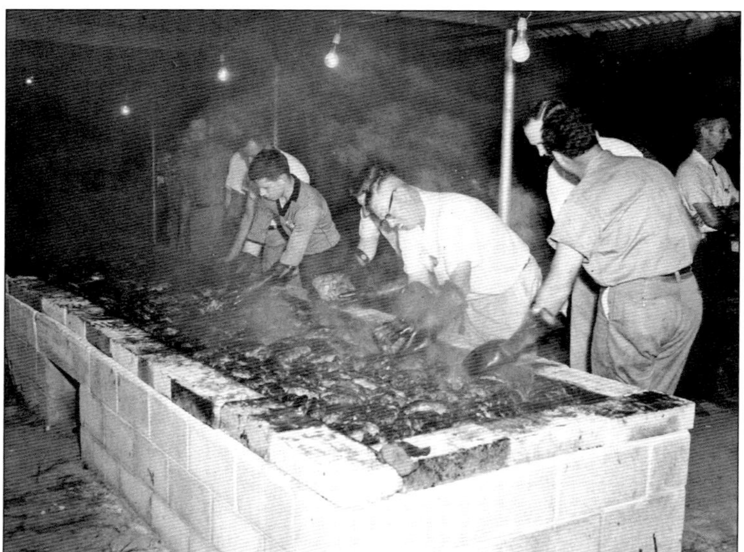

Hanging lights and a corrugated roof were needed for night work and protection from the sun during the day. Men, working in shifts, and boys kept the fires going and the meat turned. Women and girls stand outside the fence. Their husbands, fathers, brothers, and sons were beyond their reach. The women could look, but it was all men's work. (CFO.)

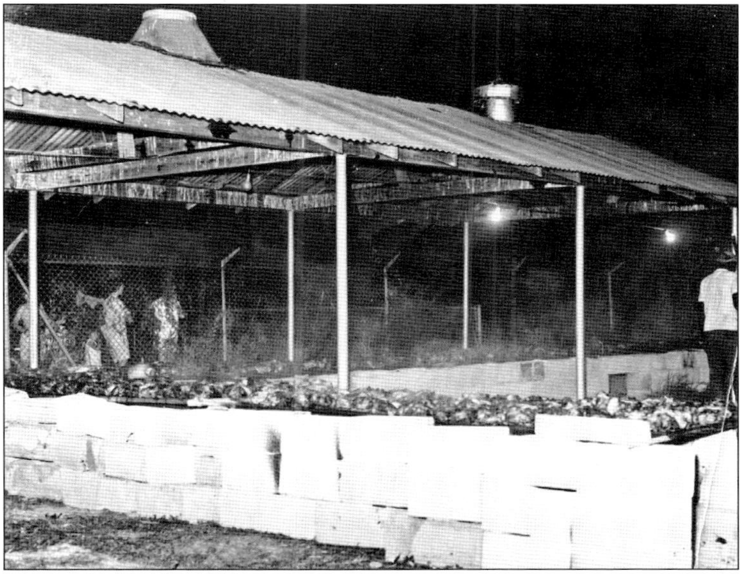

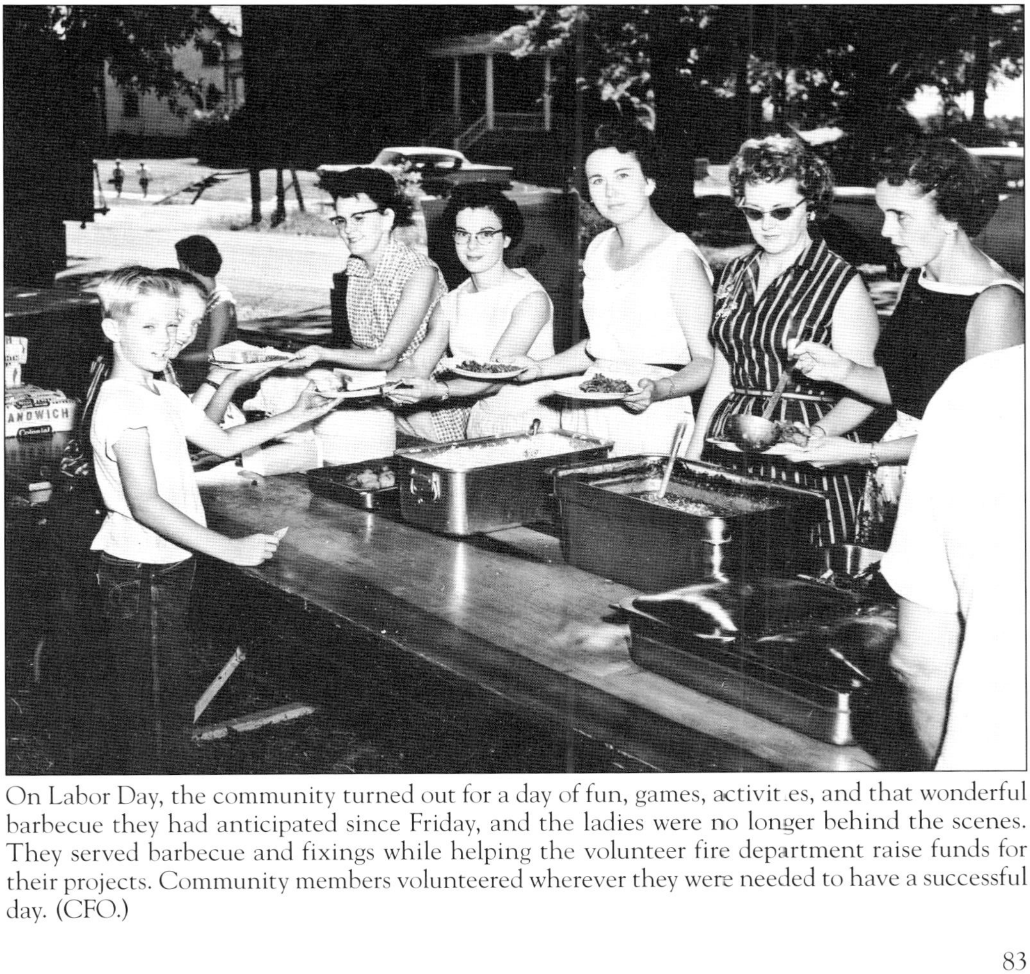

On Labor Day, the community turned out for a day of fun, games, activit.es, and that wonderful barbecue they had anticipated since Friday, and the ladies were no longer behind the scenes. They served barbecue and fixings while helping the volunteer fire department raise funds for their projects. Community members volunteered wherever they were needed to have a successful day. (CFO.)

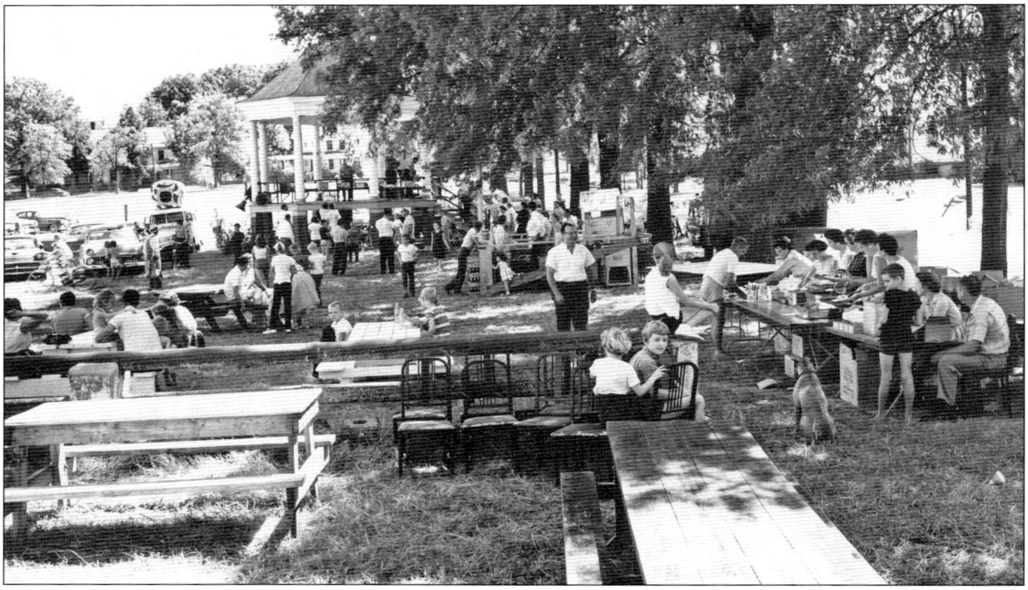

Picnic tables, benches, and chairs are put out around the post bandstand at the south end of the parade grounds. The early crowd arrived by car and one child by bicycle. A four-legged friend is being watched by a boy who stands at the serving table. Trees that have grown to a stately size provide shade for workers and guests alike. (CFO.)

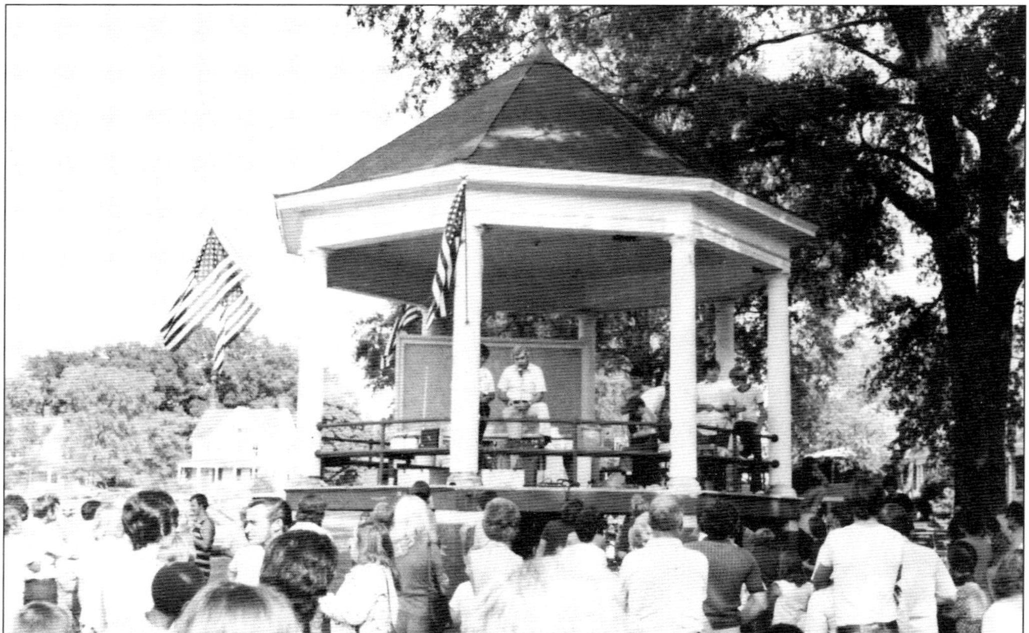

At the bandstand, original to the post in 1904, the mayor prepares to auction off various donations, which can be seen on the seats of the bandstand. A greased pig attracted the adventuresome. The dunking booth challenged the baseball enthusiasts. A pile of sawdust held a cash prize for the observant hunter, and cash atop a greased pole was claimed every year by some persistent climber. (CFO.)

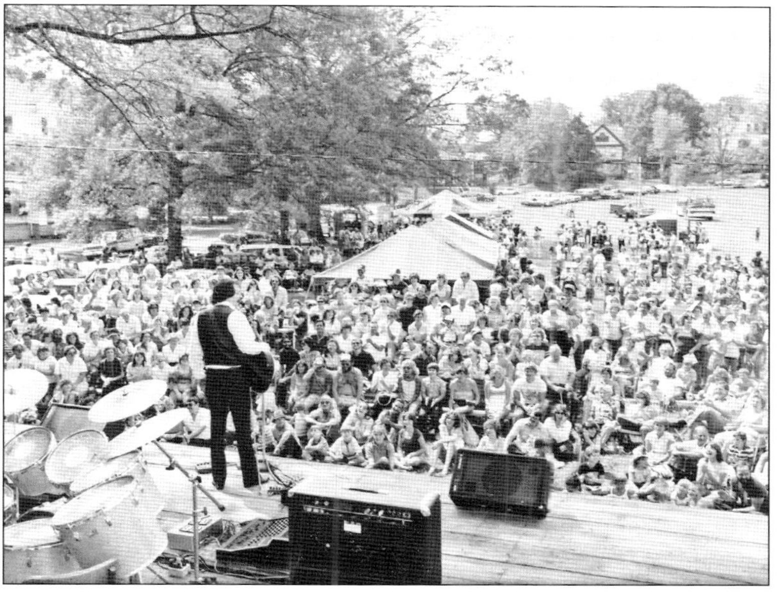

The Labor Day celebration provided an opportunity for local talent to entertain the crowd. Tents identify activity areas, and the stately "Ladies" of Barnhardt Circle with their bevy of windows and welcoming porches witness another community gathering on the parade grounds. Some talent returned often to entertain in their hometown. (CFO.)

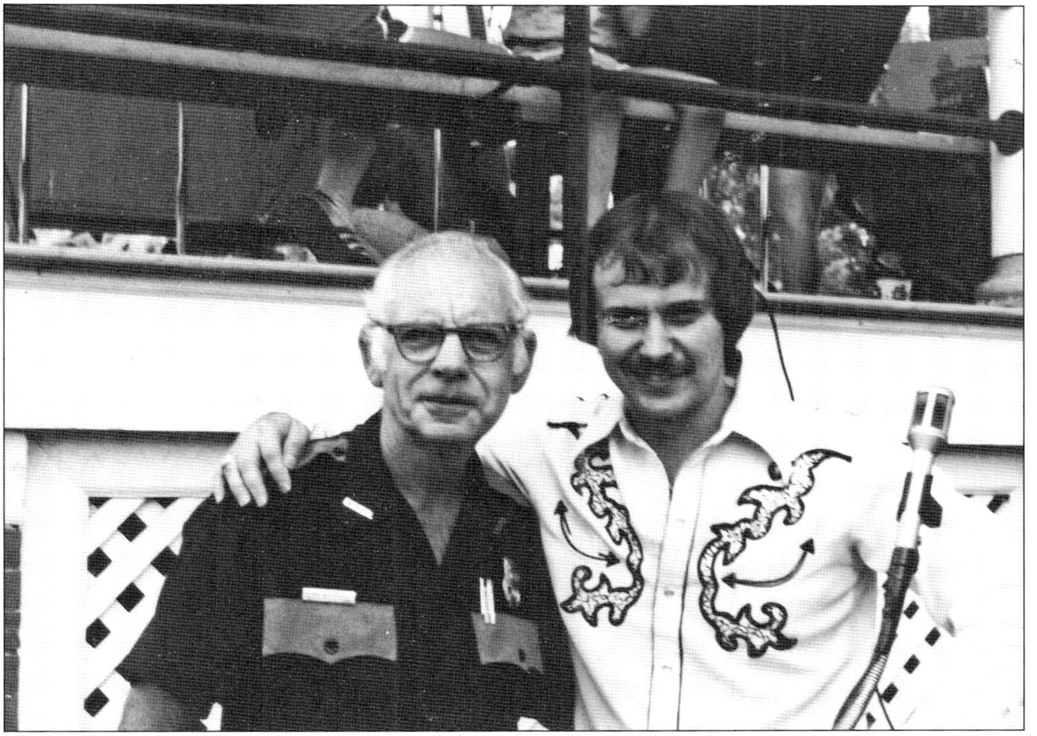

James "Smokey" Holder served the city for 38 years. When he began in 1950, the city dispatcher turned on a red light outside town hall. The patrolman patrolled the town and every few minutes drove by, checking on the light. If it was on, he stopped in and picked up the call. Smokey is shown here with a favorite son of Fort Oglethorpe, James Rogers, singer and entertainer. (JH.)

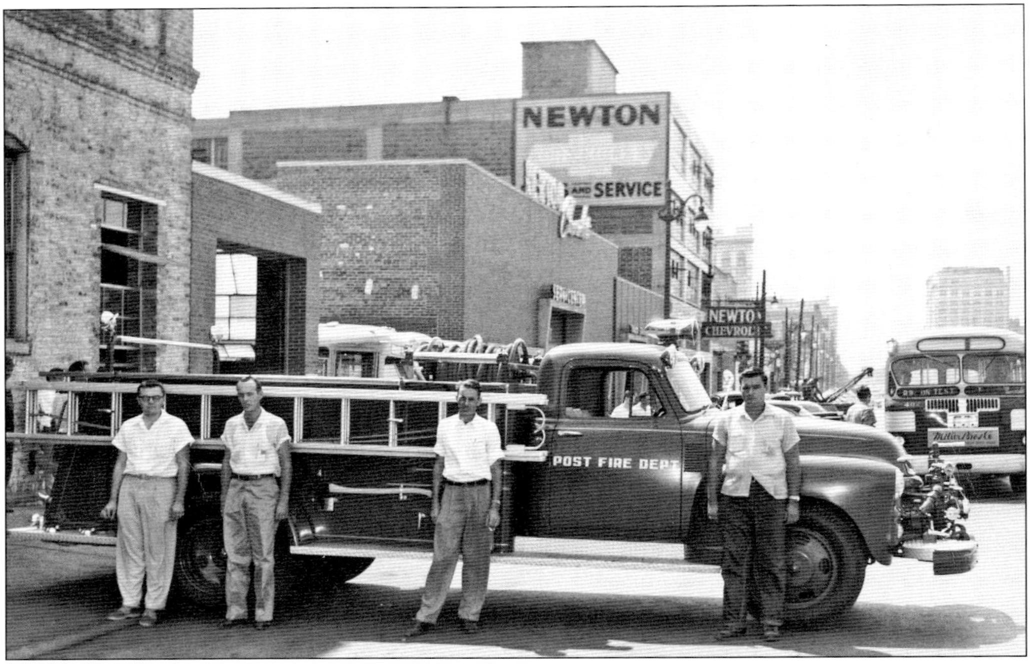

Under Reuben Satterfield, the volunteer fire department's first project was to purchase a new pumper. This 1954 pumper was picked up on Market Street, Chattanooga, near Newton Chevrolet's downtown dealership by, from left to right, unidentified, Darwin Holder, Dennis Stevenson, and Reuben Satterfield. The Fire Police protected firemen from traffic and people and included Lt. Joe Ballew, Nick Matula, Mayor Doyle Phillips, and Z. W. Daugherty. (Courtesy of Marie Holder.)

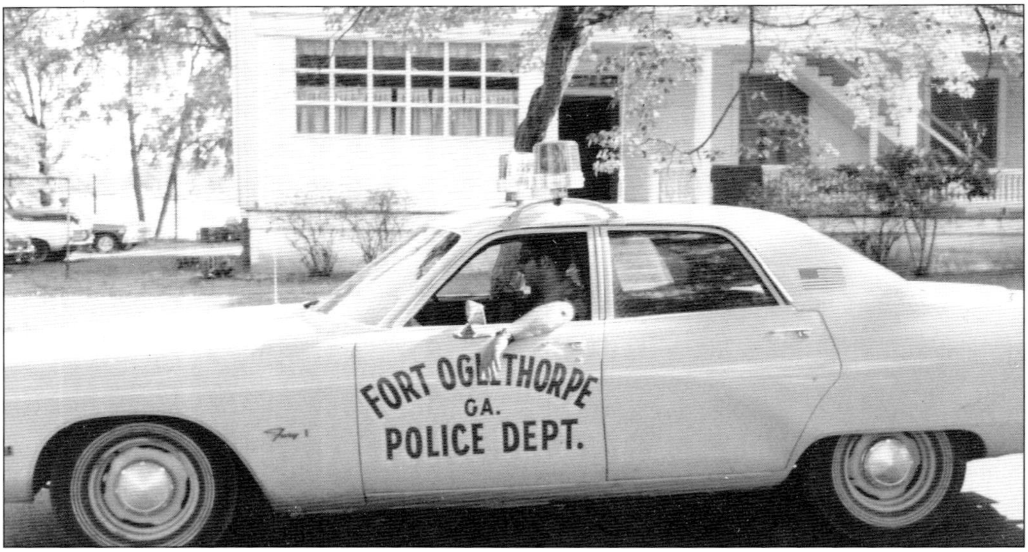

Next the volunteer fire department purchased a two-way radio dispatch unit for $3,700. For many years, the calls for police were made to Chattanooga and then transferred to Fort Oglethorpe. Now Fort Oglethorpe had its own radio dispatcher and radios installed in both fire engines and the police car. A city police car is passing by the Bachelor Officers Quarters on the south end of Barnhardt Circle. (CFO.)

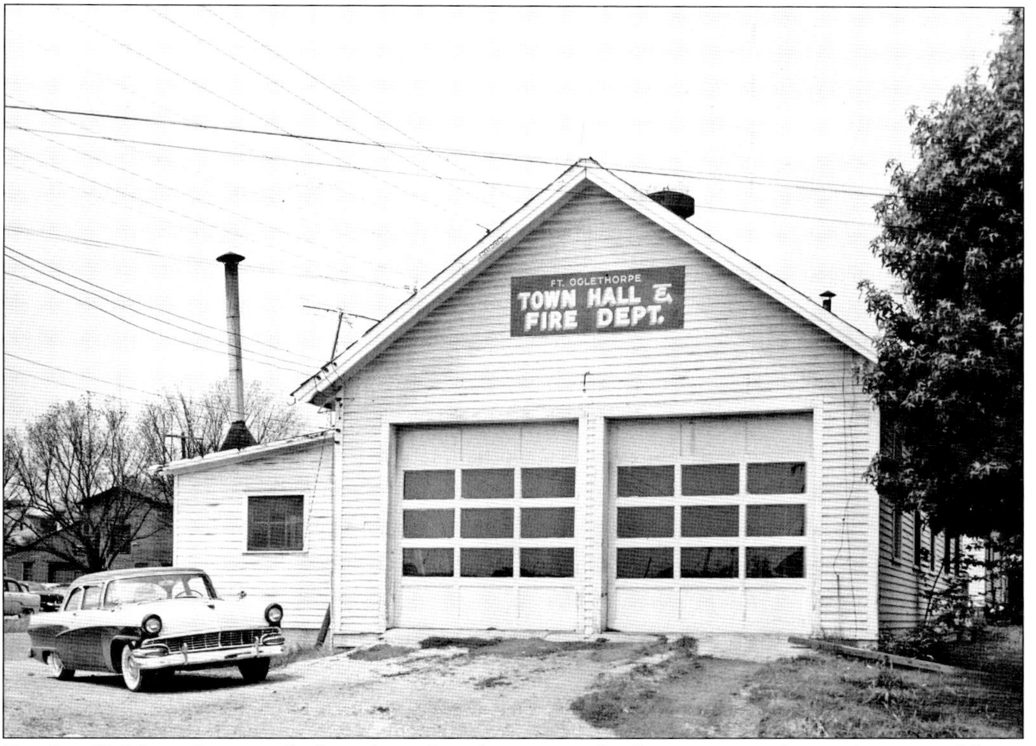

Smokey Holder volunteered when the police department had no car, no radio, and no gun. After a year, Smokey purchased a .38-caliber pistol from a friend for $20. "After I bought the gun," Smokey reported, "I bought a piece of leather and took it to a shoe store and had a holster made." This gun was passed along from officer to officer as the shift changed. (JH.)

Mayor Doyle Phillips points at Forrest Road, indicating where the new municipal building will be constructed. The building committee is, from left to right, T. G. Hixon, Chief Reuben Satterfield (chairman), Mayor Phillips, Dennis Stevenson, and cochairman Nick A. Matula Jr. The fire department charged the city rent for the office space it used and used these funds to retire the bonds sold to citizens. (CFO.)

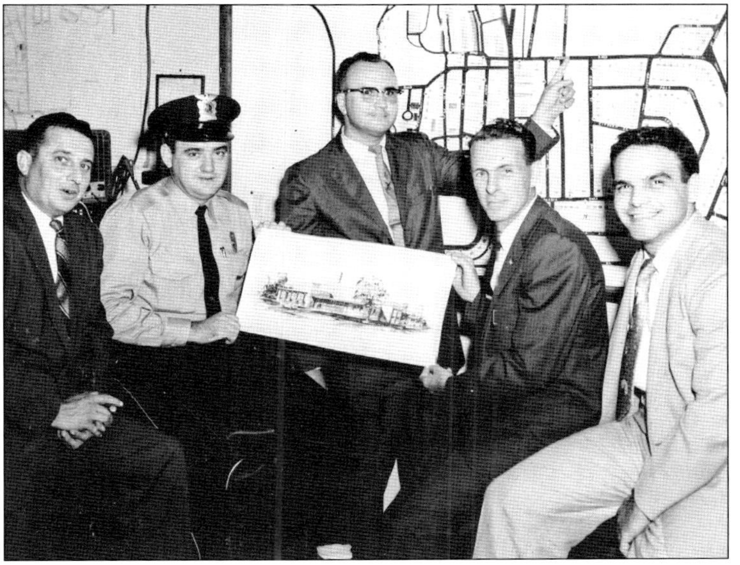

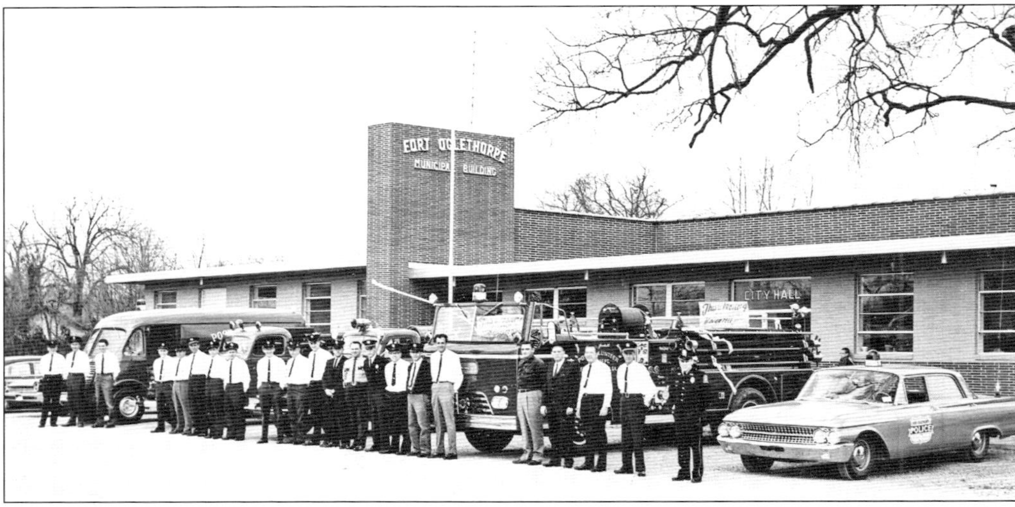

The local residents believed the army had left behind enough resources to begin a city, and on February 17, 1949, the city was incorporated. The city proudly documents its progress in its fire department, police department, and municipal building. Soon the school, library, health building, and ball fields added to the quality of life here. (CFO.)

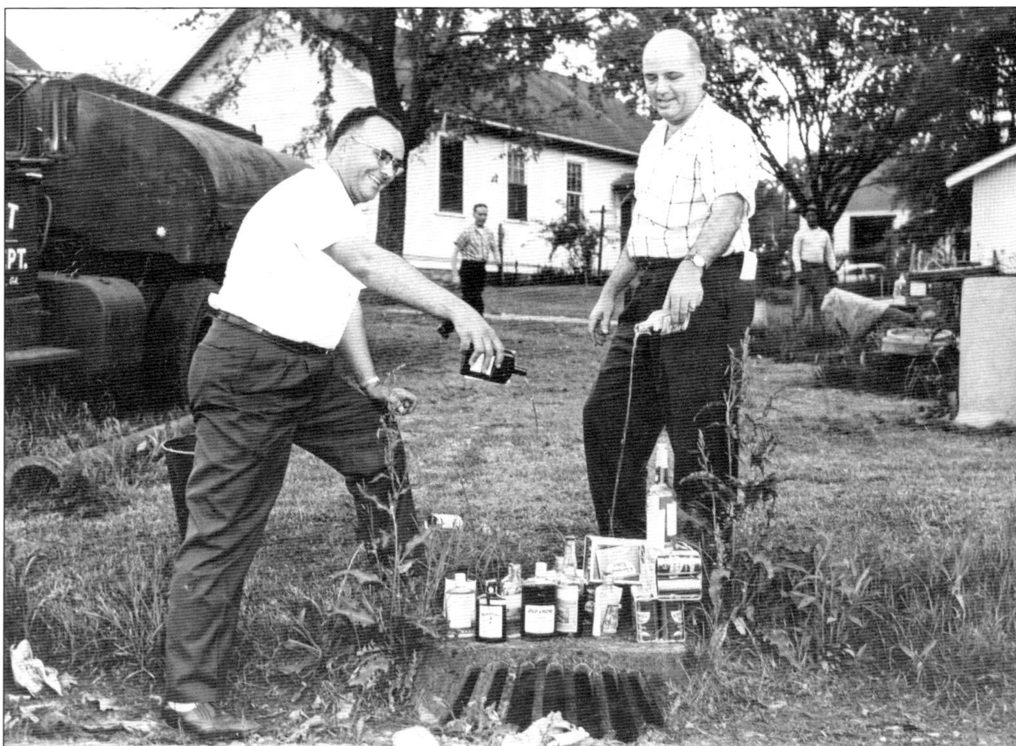

More population and more roads brought more traffic to the city. Mayor Doyle Phillips and an assistant participate in the "Pour-Out" in the early 1960s. Liquor and beer confiscated by police when issuing tickets for driving under the influence are poured down a city drain. The wastepaper basket behind the mayor will make quick work of the cans and bottle. (DP.)

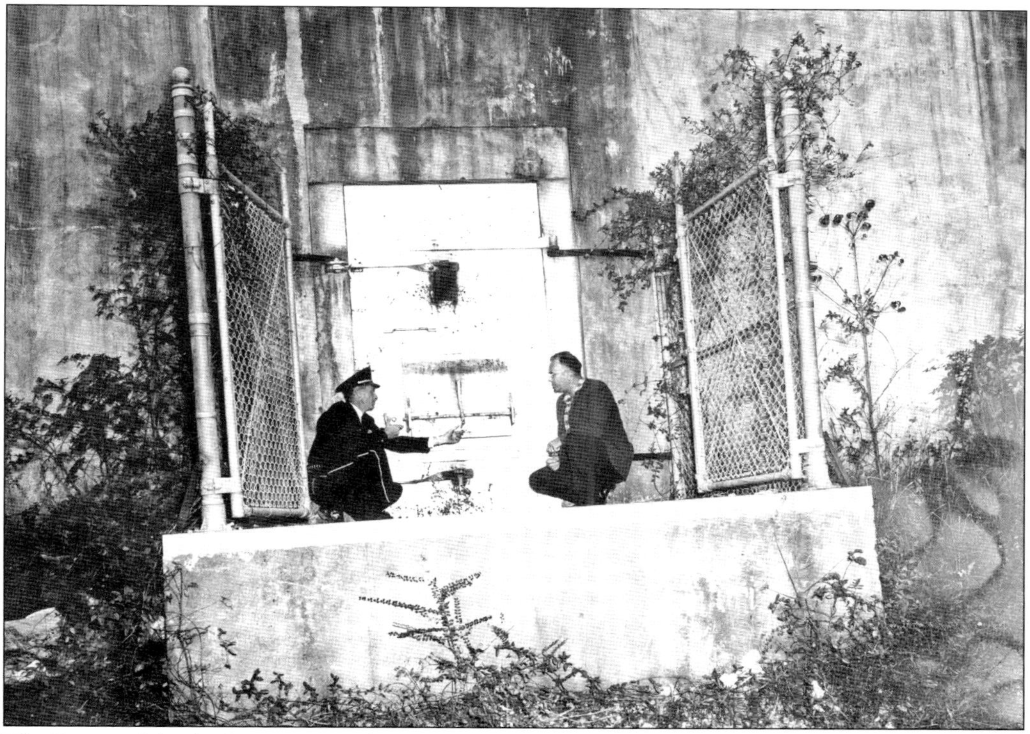

The Russian Missile Crisis occurred in 1962. Americans watched Russian ships on their televisions and listened closely to President Kennedy's remarks. Russian missiles in Communist Cuba, 90 miles off the U.S. coast, made all Americans uneasy. Mayor Doyle Phillips checked out an abandoned army bunker at the old post for possible use for civil defense purposes. Below, the men also looked over supplies that had been put aside to furnish the shelters at the Hutcheson Memorial Tri-County Hospital basement and other buildings around town. Fort Oglethorpe's system was considered to be one of the best in the Southeast. The crisis passed. The Russians turned the ships around, and the missiles were returned to Russia. America relaxed, and the city turned toward new projects. (Both, DP.)

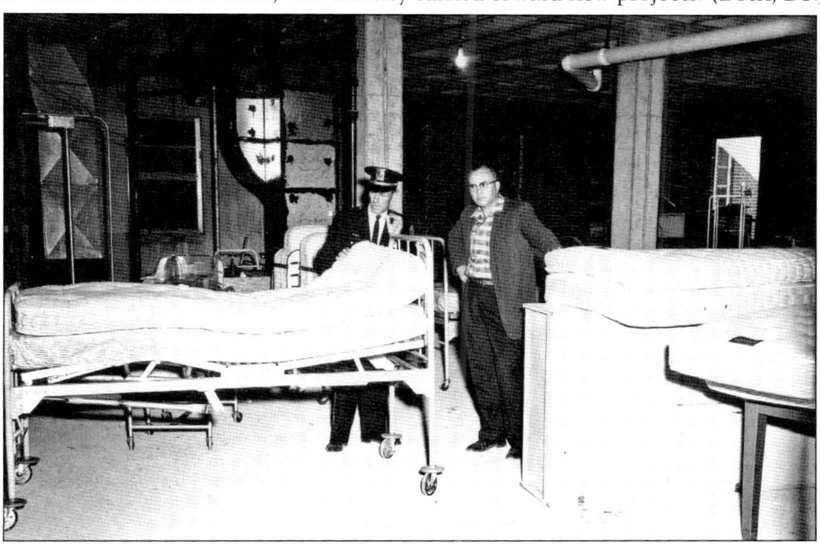

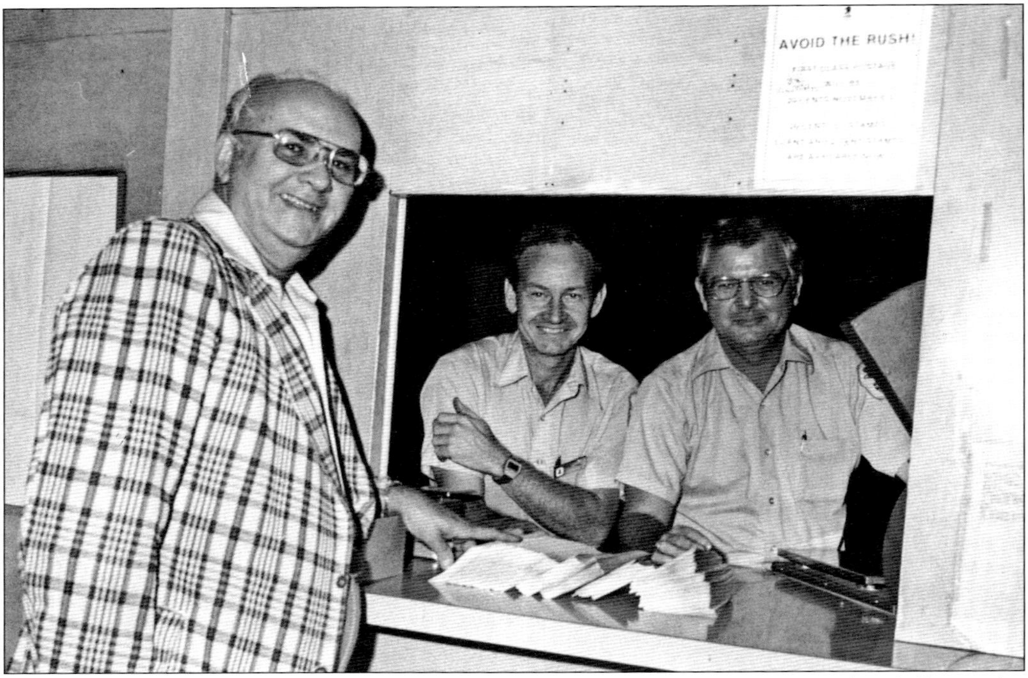

Doyle Phillips enjoys a visit with postal employees Richard Lyons and Carl Little. Phillips is the last customer at the city post office on Lafayette Road. The population of the city had grown, and a larger facility was needed. Margie L. Williams became the postmistress of the new facility on Forrest Road. (DP.)

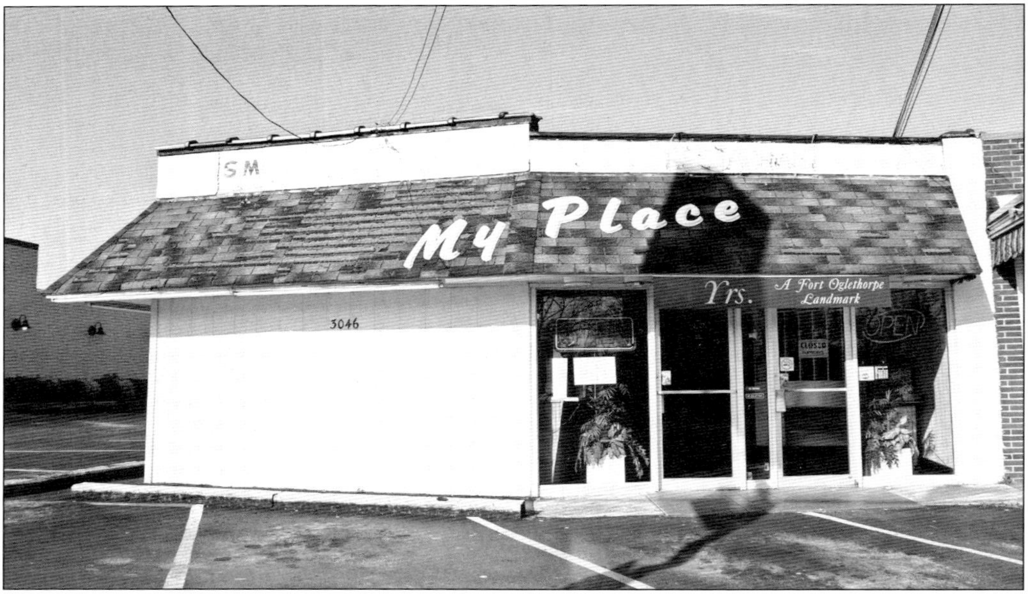

My Place, the oldest business in the city, began as Mello Kreme. Owner Jack Ross was quoted one time in a *Busy Shopper* interview that he would give a free ice cream to any local student with at least one A and no Fs on his report card. Although the offer was never repeated publicly and was never advertised, in print Jack continued to honor the offer decades later. (LP.)

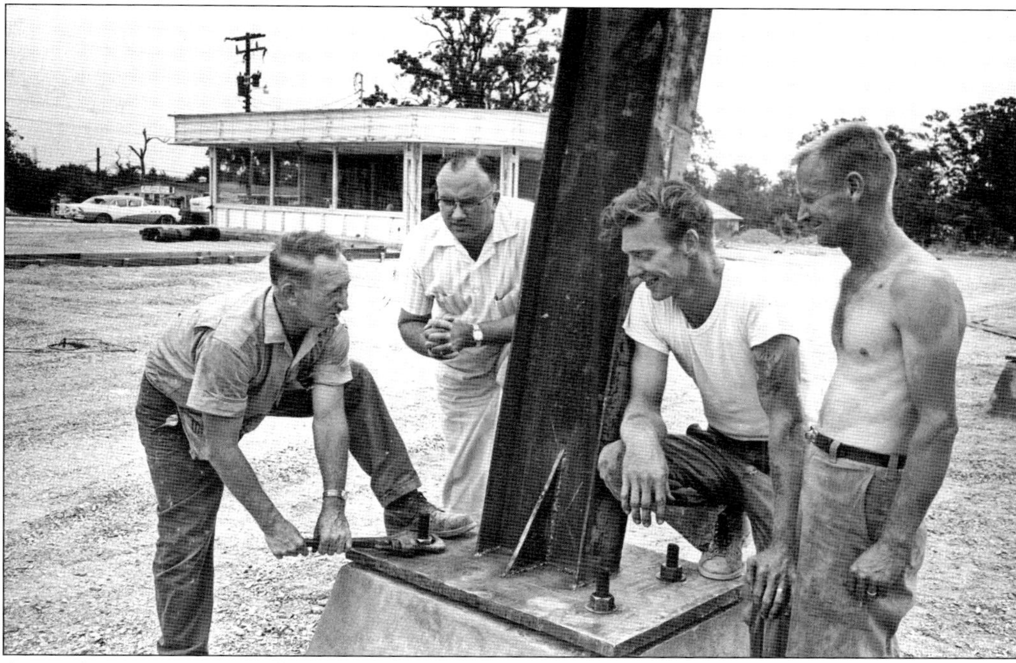

Around 1960, Roy Lewis (left), president of the Rossville Merchants Association and operator of Roy's Grill there, tightens a bolt on a standard for the new 32-foot, $10,000 sign that will mark his new restaurant (background) in the heart of downtown Fort Oglethorpe, just north of the Park Place shopping center. Mayor Doyle Phillips, second from left, looks on. (DP.)

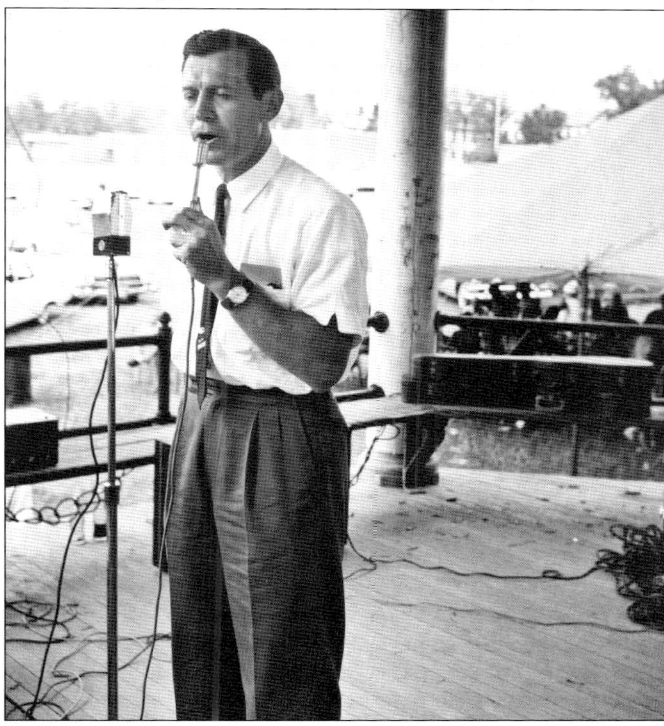

Politicians stumped for local votes throughout Georgia. The popularity of Labor Day at the post drew statewide candidates as well as local candidates. In 1962, popular Carl Sanders was candidate for governor of Georgia. After enjoying barbecue and shaking hands with old friends, Sanders walked to the microphone on the bandstand and "stumped" for votes. (CFO.)

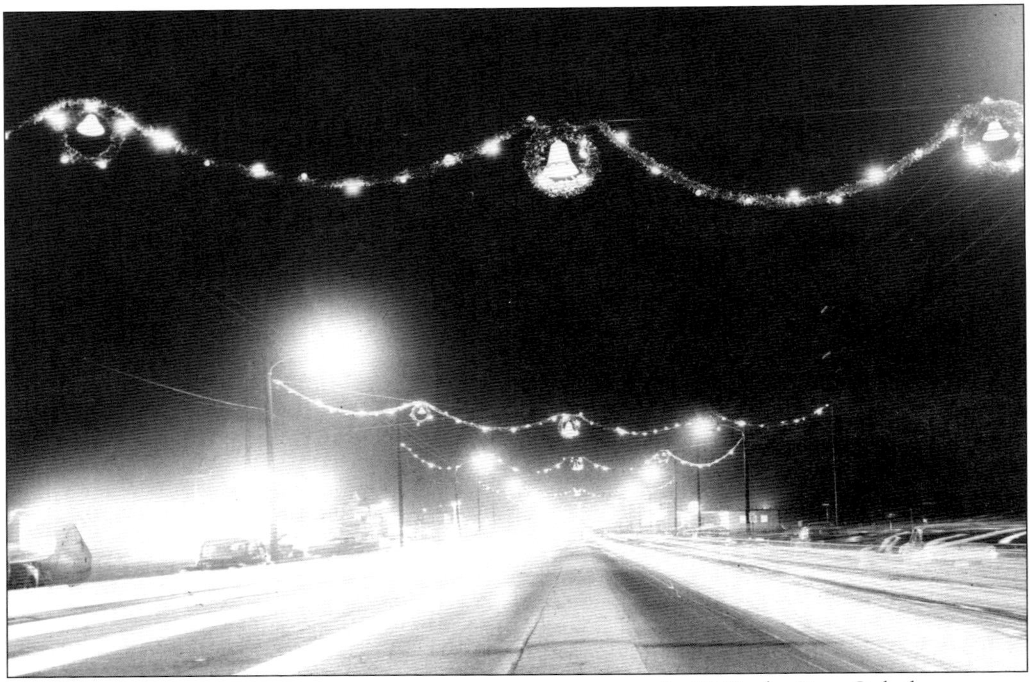

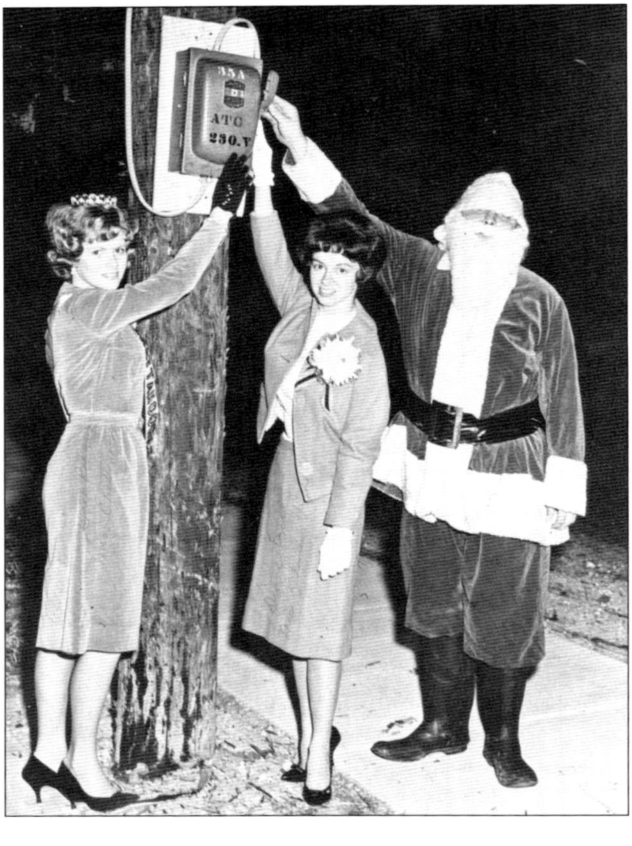

In 1962, the Fort Oglethorpe Merchants' Association, headed by James O'Neal, determined to attract more citizens downtown for their shopping needs. The association provided the business district with Christmas lights for the first time. The lights spanned Lafayette Road and provided a cheerful holiday glow to the shopping season. (DP.)

The city's Christmas parade ended with the lighting of the post Christmas tree, planted by the local CCC camp. This night, in 1962, three dignitaries prepare to light the tree. From left to right are Gail Robinson, Miss Chattanooga; Dianne Ezell, 1963 Lakeview High School queen; and Frank McDowell, Santa Claus. Generations turn out for the parades, and today they are filmed by UCTV-3 for those who missed the parade and for shut-ins. (DP.)

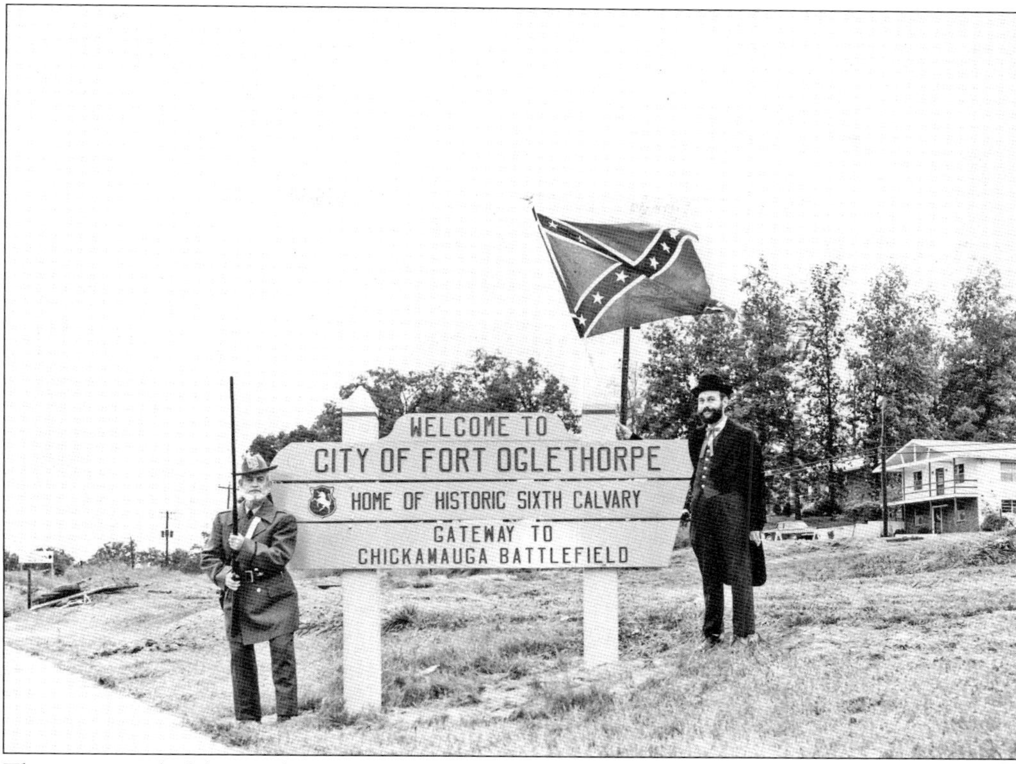

The centennial of the Battle of Chickamauga was an active period for the city. The battle occurred September 19–20, 1863. The reenactment activities included a barbecue, formal ball, military demonstrations, and general fun for local citizens. O. C. Churchwell (left) and John Holland (right) stand guard at the city's gateway leading to the battlefield. The Confederate flag leaves no doubt into whose territory the visitors enter. (DP.)

"Smoothies Arrested!" No beard? Go to jail! Mayor Doyle Phillips is jailed because he had no beard for the Battle of Chickamauga commemorative programs. City rules were strictly enforced. Standing guard are John Holland (left) and Johnny Woods (right). The mayor attempted escape, but watchful citizens defied his attempt. (DP.)

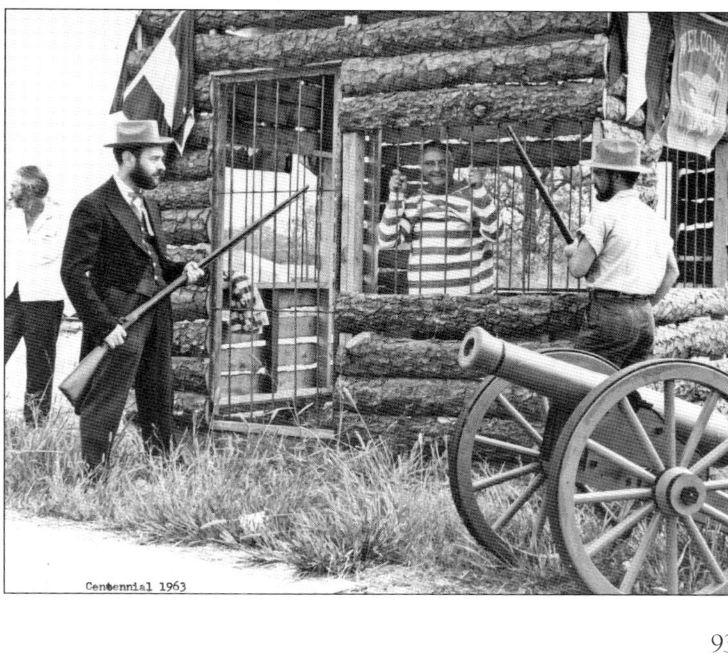

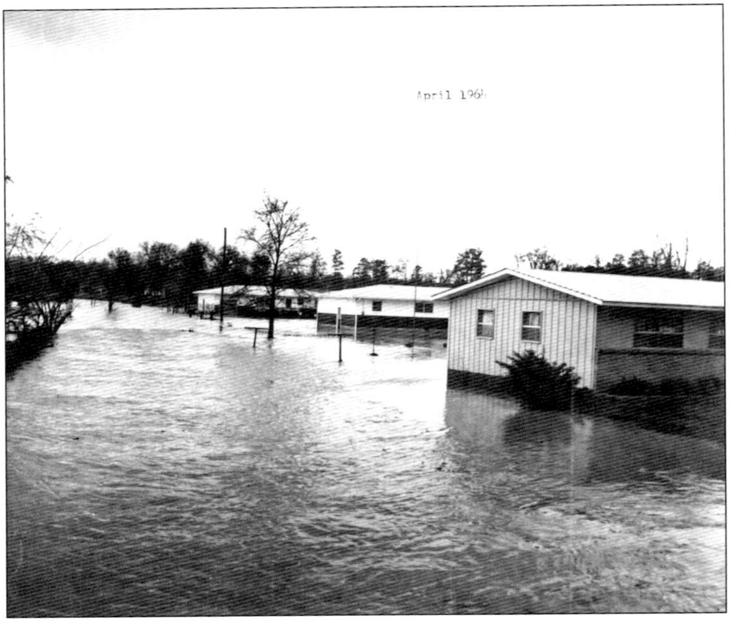

This 1964 flood shows the effect of severe rain on local drains and culverts that tried to empty into Black Branch, which roams throughout the city. This creek, Chickamauga Creek, and, ultimately, Spring Creek in neighboring East Ridge backed up and flooded their respective neighborhoods. The construction of the Brained Levee in Chattanooga now relieves the town, and severe flooding has decreased in frequency. (DP.)

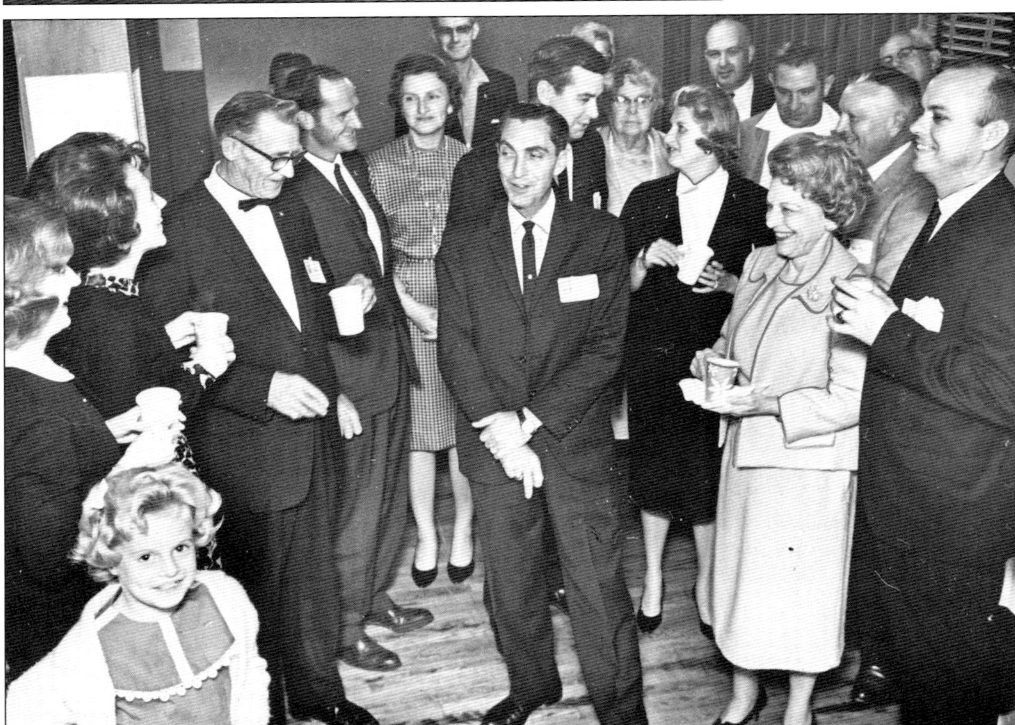

The campaign kicks off. Leonard Fant (front, right) and his "Clean the Town Up" ticket open their campaign headquarters in October 1964. The Fant slate for mayor and five council seats swept the opposing ticket in the November election. Among those in the picture are members of his slate: George Hackler, Jack Chandler, Glenn Parker, John Norris, Jim O'Neal, and Leonard Fant. (Leonard Fant.)

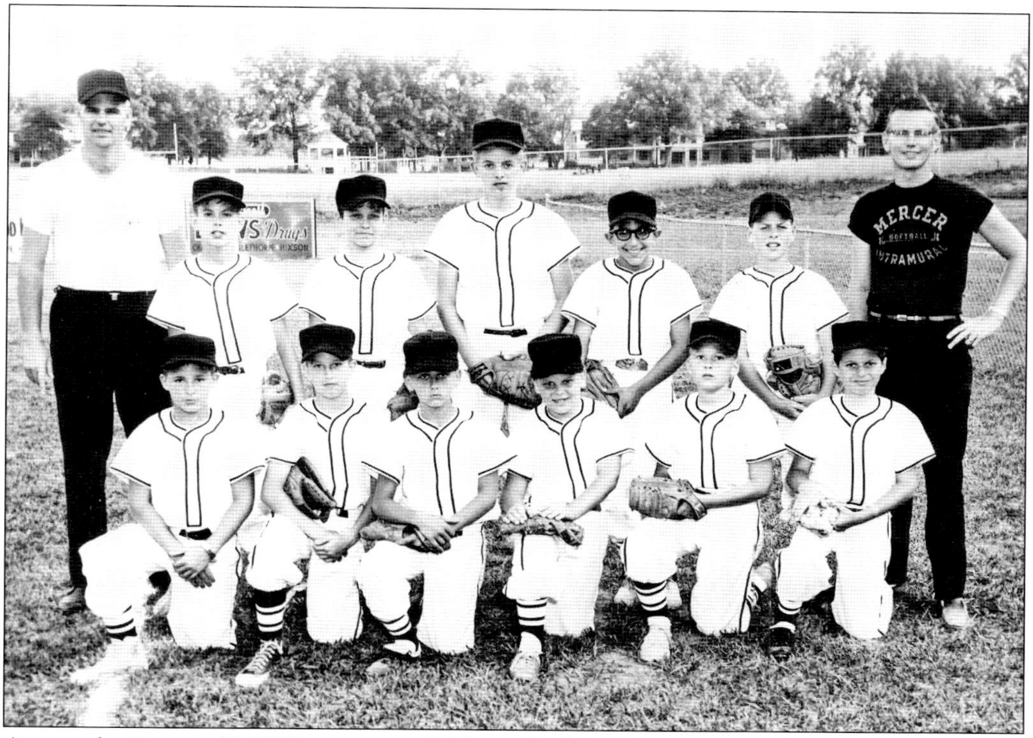

Among the 11-year-old All-Star team in 1965 were Rick Honeycutt (second row, second from right) and Steve Brown (second row, center). Coach Wayne Honeycutt (far left) managed Little League teams for years and served on the town recreation association for 17 years. The Rick Honeycutt Golf Tournament and Youth Foundation donates all proceeds to youth and recreational projects in and around the Fort Oglethorpe area. (WRH.)

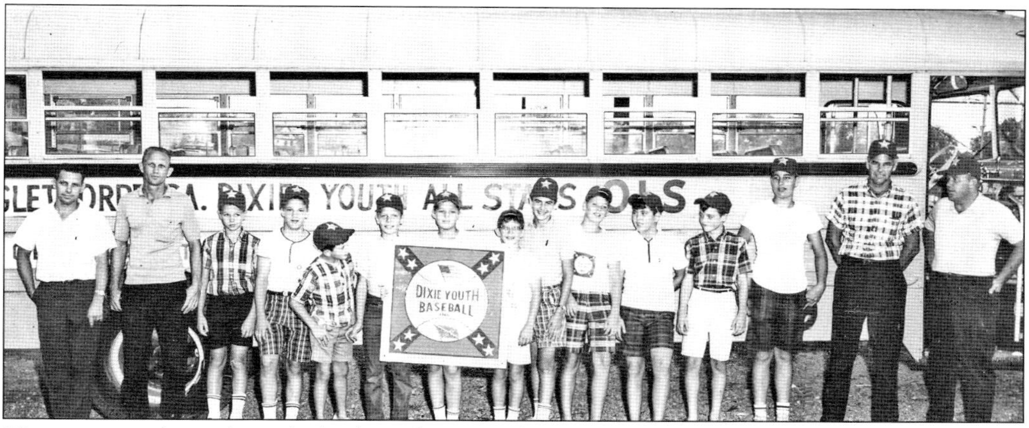

These young players brought back to the town the 1966 Georgia State Championship in Dixie Youth Baseball. The town has been known to meet the returning team at the interstate exit and provide a police escort into and through town and the neighborhoods. Citizens joined in and blew their horns to announce the return of the local heroes. (WRH.)

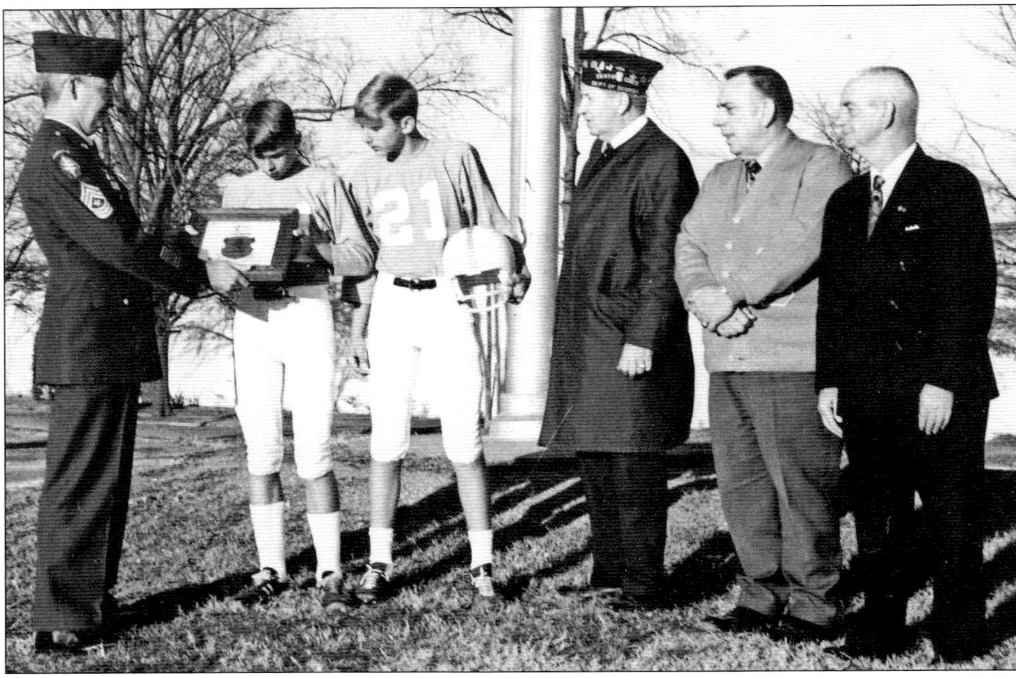

The Fort Oglethorpe Elementary School adopted the regimental insignia of the 6th U.S. Cavalry as its official emblem and are now called the "Warriors." Pictured from left to right are Sgt. Maj. Loner Westmoreland; Kenneth Sholl and Danny Painter, captains of the school football team; Sgt. Hubert Mazerole, commander of the Fort Oglethorpe VFW and American Legion; Alvin B. Perry, principal; and M.Sgt. O. C. Churchwell (retired). (SCM.)

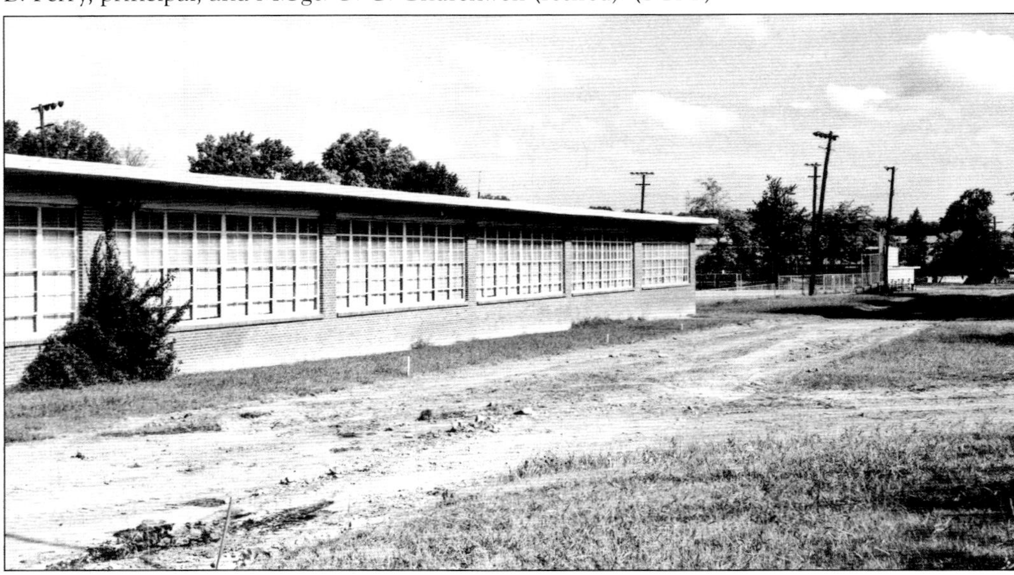

Fort Oglethorpe needed a local school for its children, and parents remembered their children riding a bus into Chattanooga for an hour before their classmates woke up. The elementary school was built on the parade grounds across from the headquarters building. A baseball diamond can be seen north of the school. Landscaping has not been completed at this time. (CFO.)

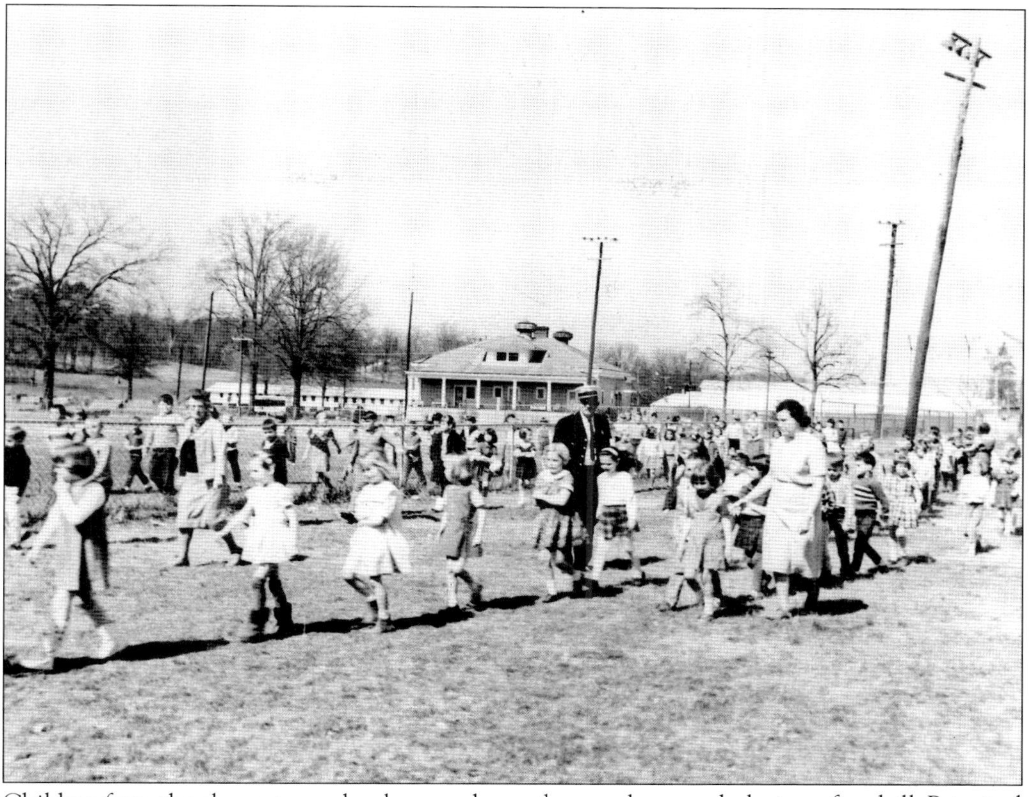

Children from the elementary school proceed over the parade grounds during a fire drill. Principal Eva Henry Skeen and fire chief Frank Friel assist the children. Chief Friel began the Post Volunteer Fire Department's fire prevention program in the 1960s. To the north, the post guardhouse and horse stables can be seen. The troop barracks, which had been on each side of the guardhouse, are gone. (CFO.)

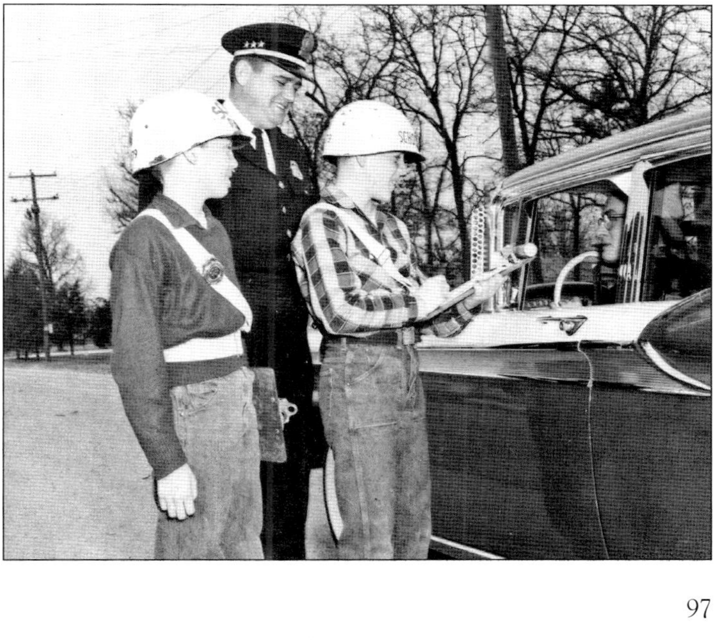

Two safety patrol members get "on the job training" under the watchful eye of Chief Reuben Satterfield. The unlucky recipient of the boys' attention is Mayor Doyle Phillips. Mayor Phillips was always available for news photographers. He believed in advertising the city and its quality of life. His successors continued to advertise in this way. (DP.)

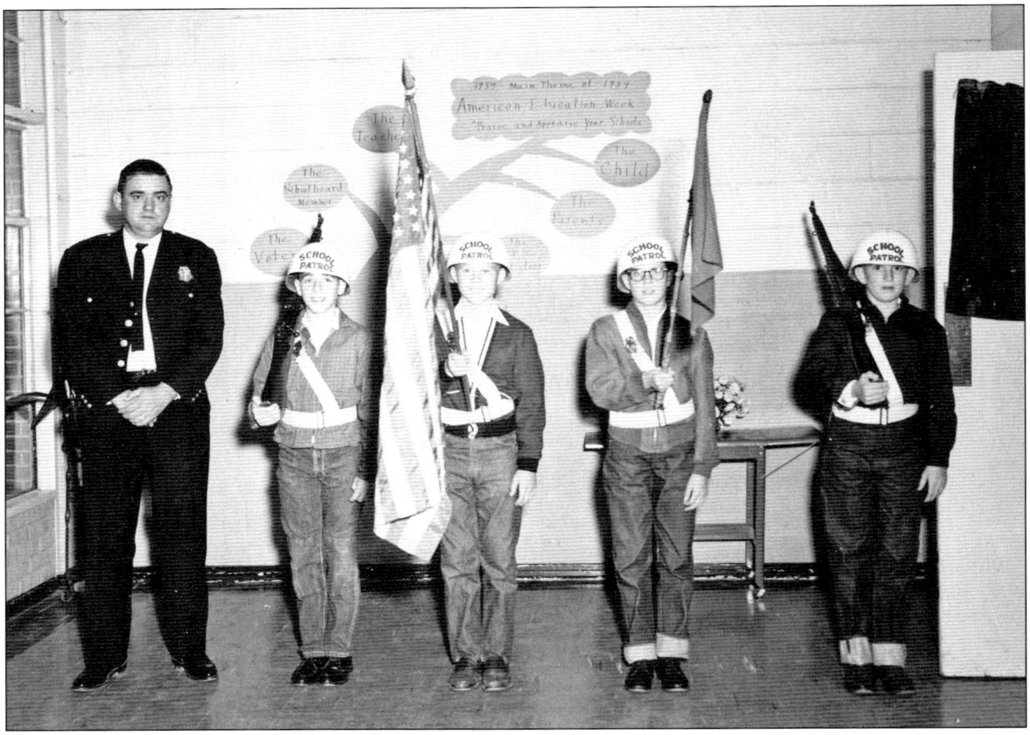

Chief Reuben Satterfield is shown with four members of the school safety patrol serving as a color guard. These boys are shown in 1959 with their hats, belts, and badges. The color guard served at club meetings, and their presence reminded everyone that school and traffic safety was everyone's responsibility. Both the police and fire departments involved the youth of the city in their outreach. (DP.)

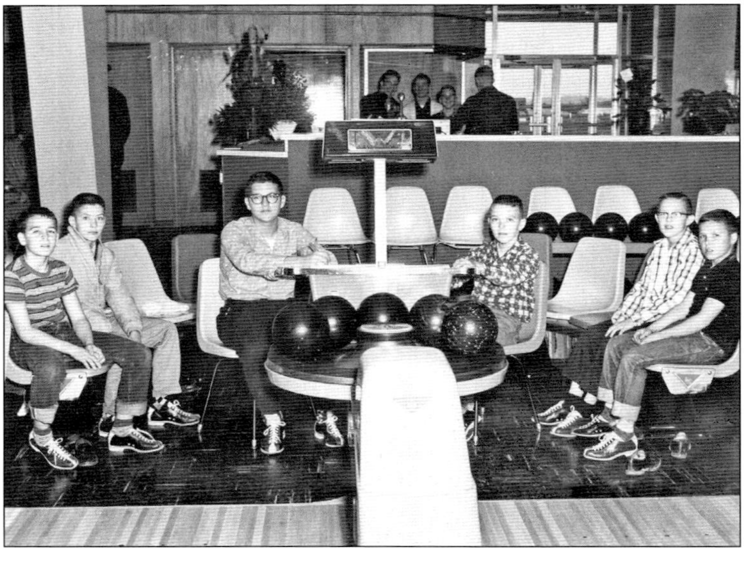

The bowling alley on Lafayette Road was a popular hangout for all age groups in the city. Church groups had leagues, and teenagers congregated there to shoot pool and down Cokes. And young kids bowled. The three boys on the right are, from left to right, Tommy Bridges, David Gibson, and Jim Alexander. The bowling alley closed in May 2008 and is missed by several generations. (DP.)

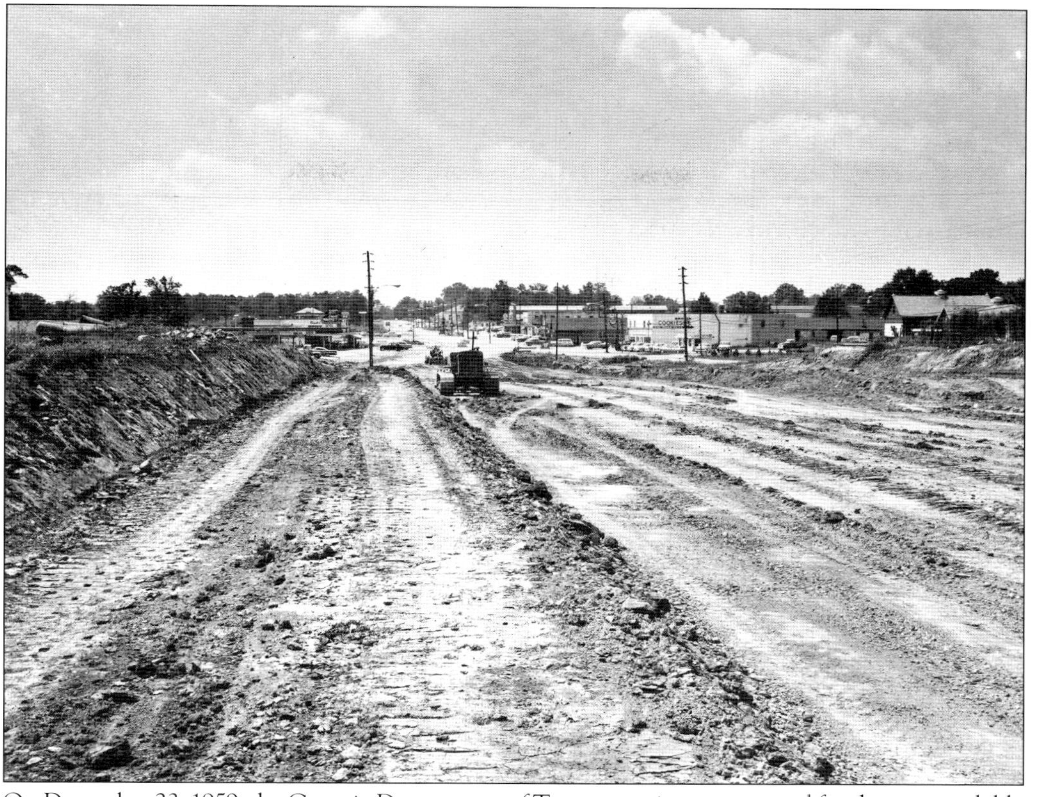

On December 23, 1959, the Georgia Department of Transportation announced funds were available and the project to move and widen U.S. Highway 27 between Rossville and Fort Oglethorpe from two lanes to five lanes would proceed. Both cities anticipated great economic growth from the new artery. Shortly after the road opened, a new shopping center opened, bringing a Piggly Wiggly grocery store and a drugstore to town. (DP.)

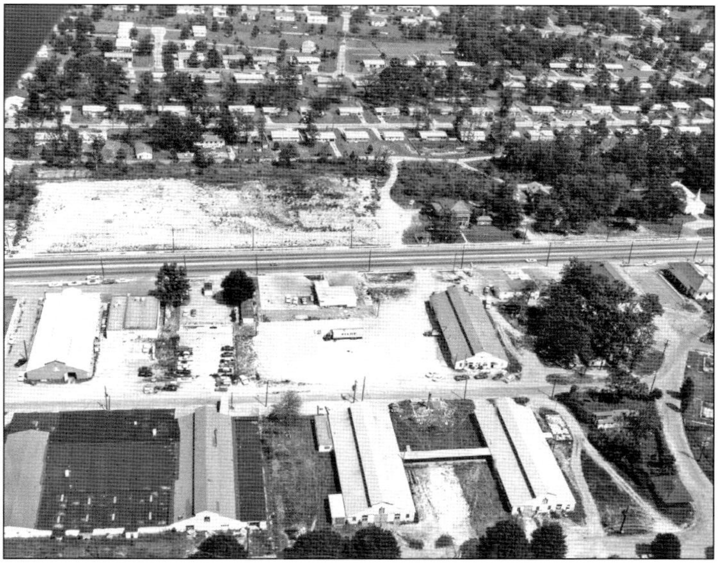

Doyle Phillips kept wonderful scrapbooks of projects and activities during his years as mayor. This aerial photograph of downtown Fort Oglethorpe in the mid-1960s shows growth. For many years, the town grew to the east of Lafayette Road, filling in areas of the CCC, CMTC, and prison camps. Today annexation has moved the city limits in all directions to include the battlefield to the south. (DP.)

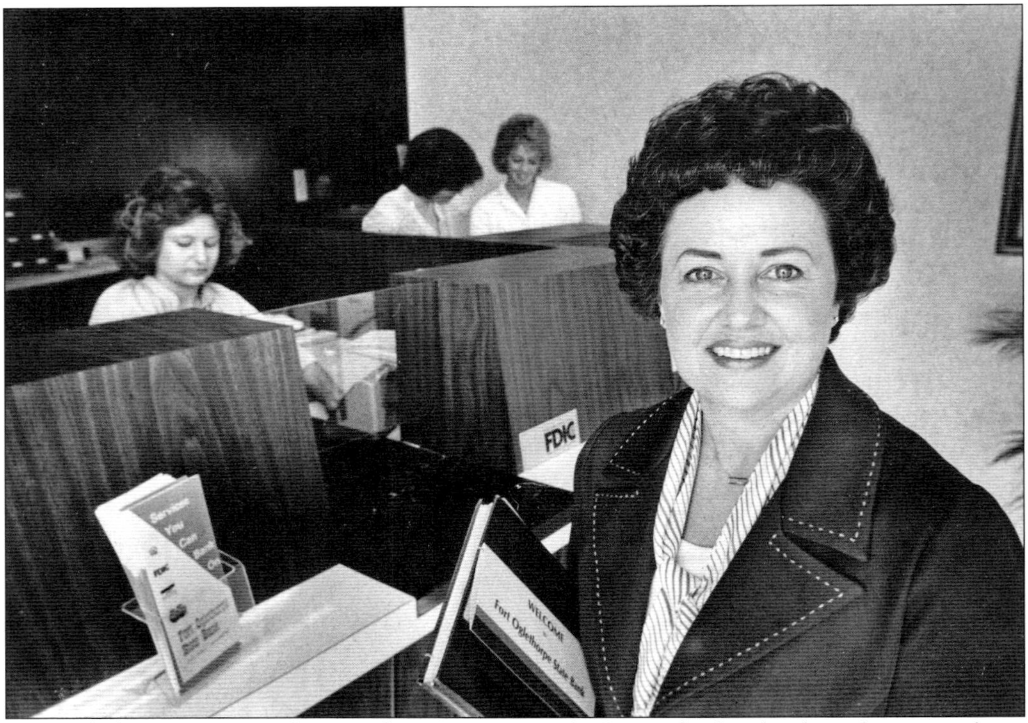

Fort Oglethorpe State Bank opened on August 7, 1964. It was the first bank in the city and was located on Thomas Road, just down from the hospital. One of the first people hired was Rena Honeycutt (above), who later became assistant vice president and manager of the Fort Lake branch opened in 1970. That branch received much of the new business along the new Lafayette Road. Later Fort Oglethorpe State Bank was taken over by Capital Bank. Rena was selected 1985 Citizen of the Year by the Catoosa Chamber of Commerce and, below, rides in the local parade. A career mother, after work Rena became a baseball mom, supporting her husband's coaching and her son's playing. (Both, WRH.)

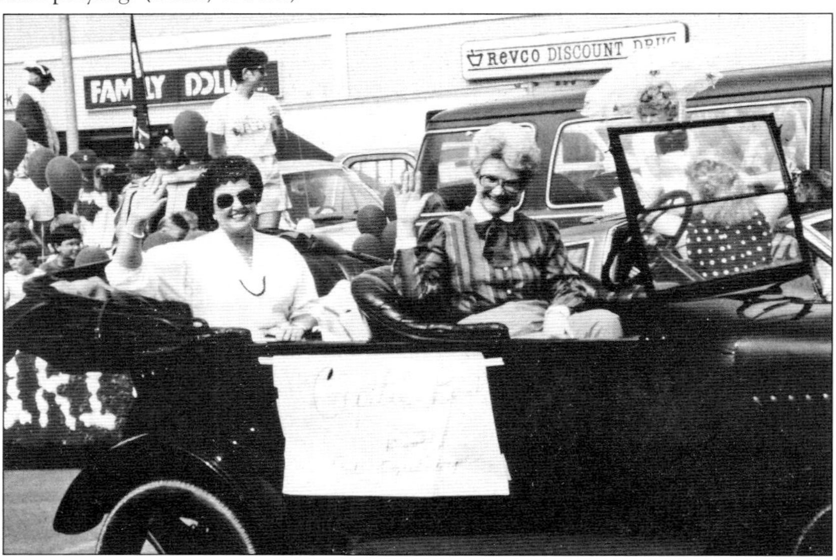

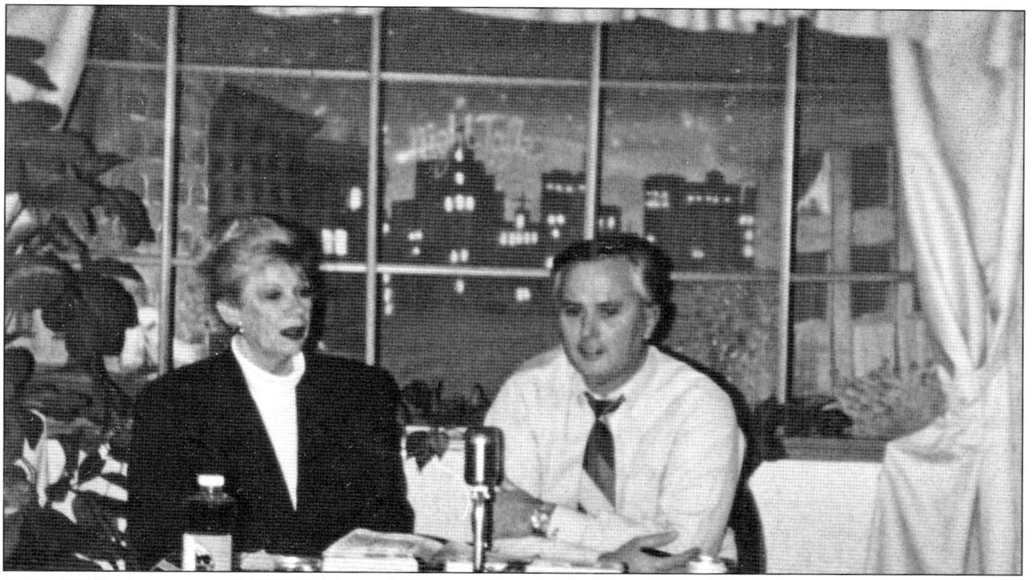

Judy O'Neal, owner of UCTV-3, and Ronnie Bowman, then the sheriff of Catoosa County, are shown on the set of Judy's evening show in 1986. These two created the "Stockings Full of Love" campaign to raise funds for Christmas presents for needy children in Catoosa County. The program has been copied in neighboring Dade and Walker Counties. (Judy O'Neal.)

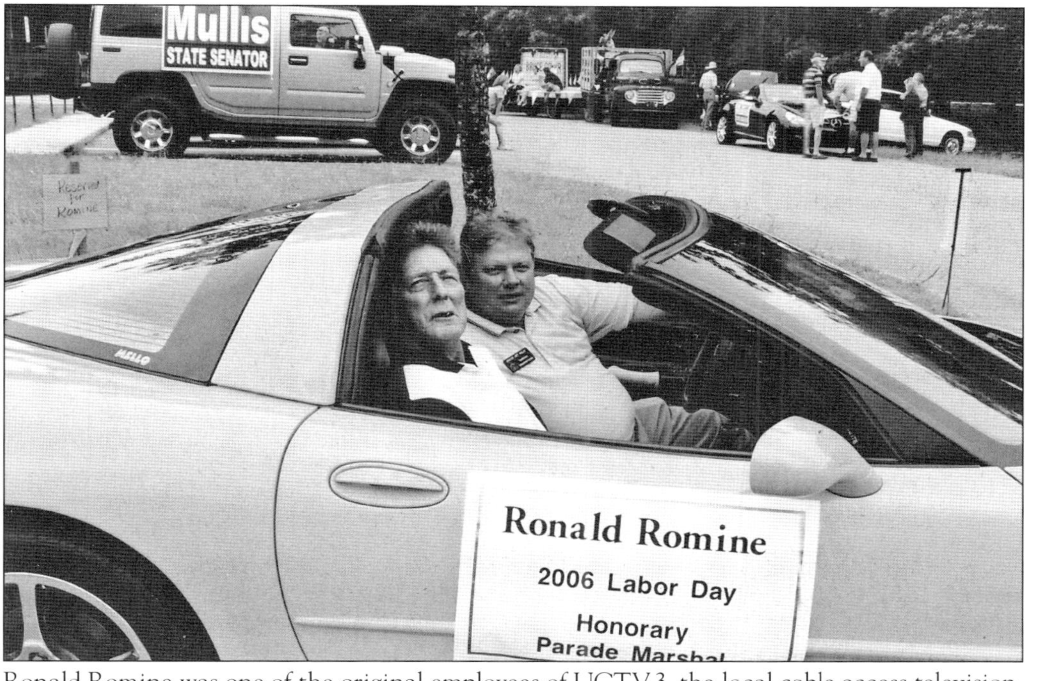

Ronald Romine was one of the original employees of UCTV-3, the local cable access television. Romine taped the area city council meetings, the county commissioners meeting, and Christmas parades. He was honorary parade marshal for the 2006 Labor Day parade and was driven by Jeff Mullis, present state senator from this area. Romine will be remembered for his tall, slender stature, and his ever-present smile. (Kathy Romine.)

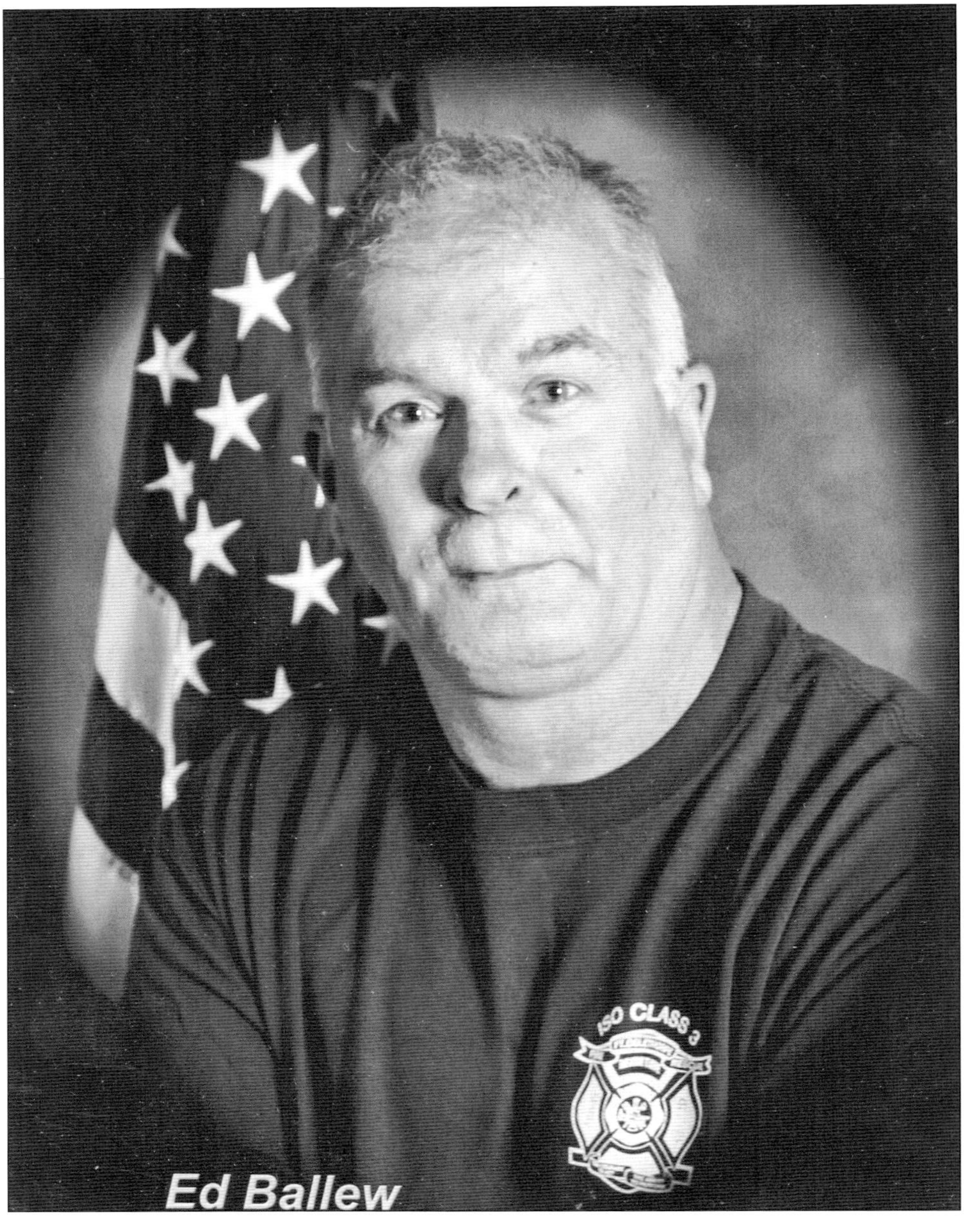

Fire prevention education was important. In June 1997, eight officers and firefighters, including Ed Ballew, learned alternative ways to teach fire safety. The department then created the Clown Battalion. Members adopted costumes and names, and puppets delivered their messages. A special clown character named "Turnout" appeared. The department extended the programs offered to school-age children to include senior citizens. At that time, over 60 percent of the population of the city were senior citizens, many of whom were widows and widowers living alone. Ed Ballew was a gentleman who was lost to our city in a traffic accident in 2008. Ed and Carol Ballew are in the following photograph. (Clown etiquette requires clowns to be addressed by their clown names only; therefore, their actual names do not appear with pictures of them in clown dress.) (Carol Ballew.)

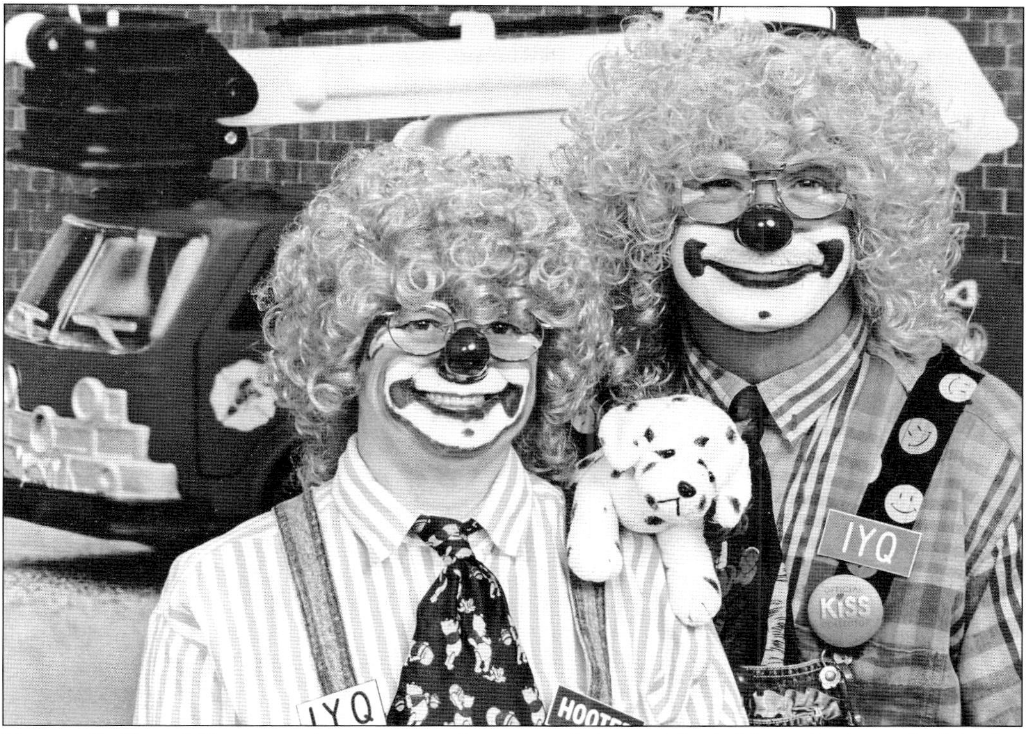

Hooter (left) and Turnout, above, are ready to spend time with children. Both worked in fire education and treasured these opportunities. Below, Turnout, whose name refers to the clothing firefighters don when responding to a fire, took on a special ministry with a friend. They visited T. C. Thompson Children's Hospital in Chattanooga every Tuesday. A social worker said she had never had such faithful and reliable volunteers in her 16 years of coordinating special visitors to her children. When queried as to why he worked with children, Turnout said, "The bottom line on this clowning thing is putting smiles on the kids' faces." (Both, Carol Ballew.)

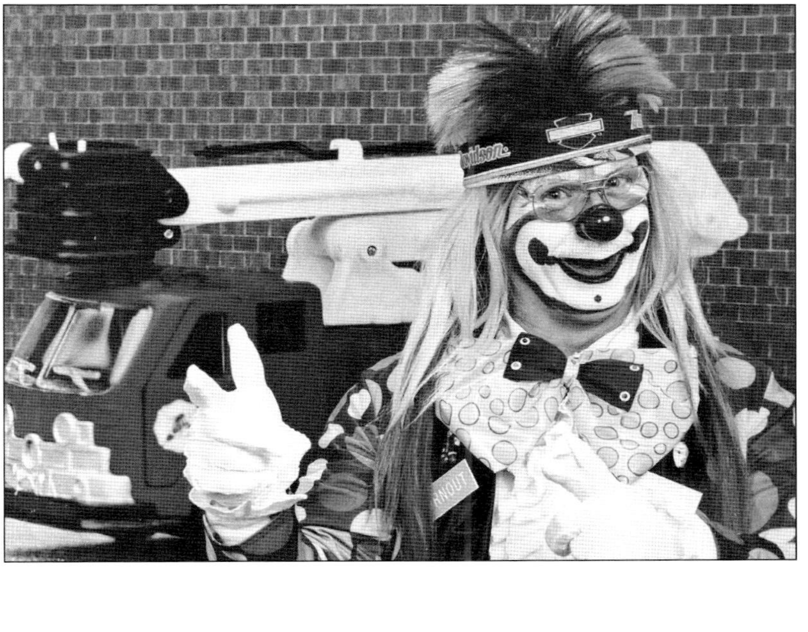

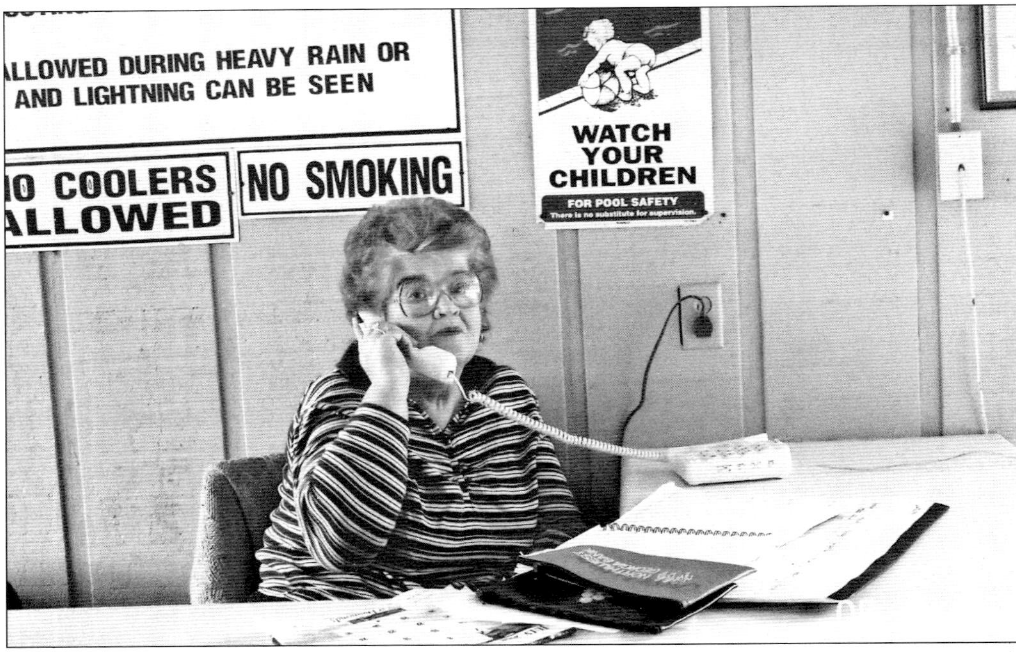

Gilbert-Stephenson City Park is one of the jewels of the city. The land was the site of the World War I POW camp. Now a playground, walking trail, tennis courts, picnic pavilions, and swimming pool draw residents from surrounding towns and counties. The pool is opened to the public for a daily fee and can be reserved for group use. Arlene Crye has answered the phone and booked groups for over 15 years. To thank her, the city honored Arlene by naming the new pool the Arlene Crye Municipal Pool. The new pool was opened for the 2008 swim season and continues to be a popular family recreation spot. (Both, CFO.)

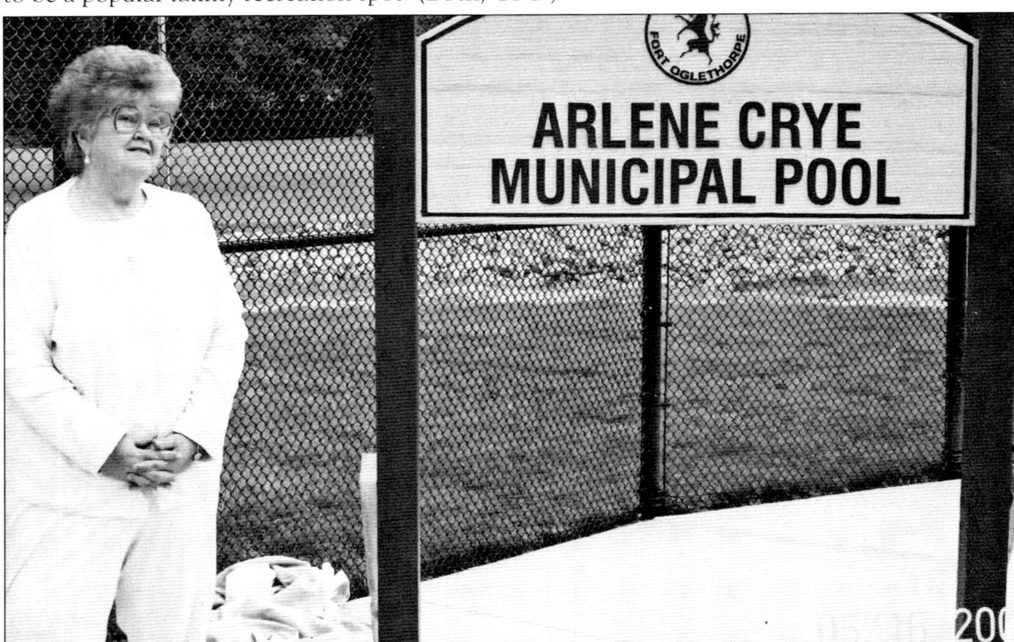

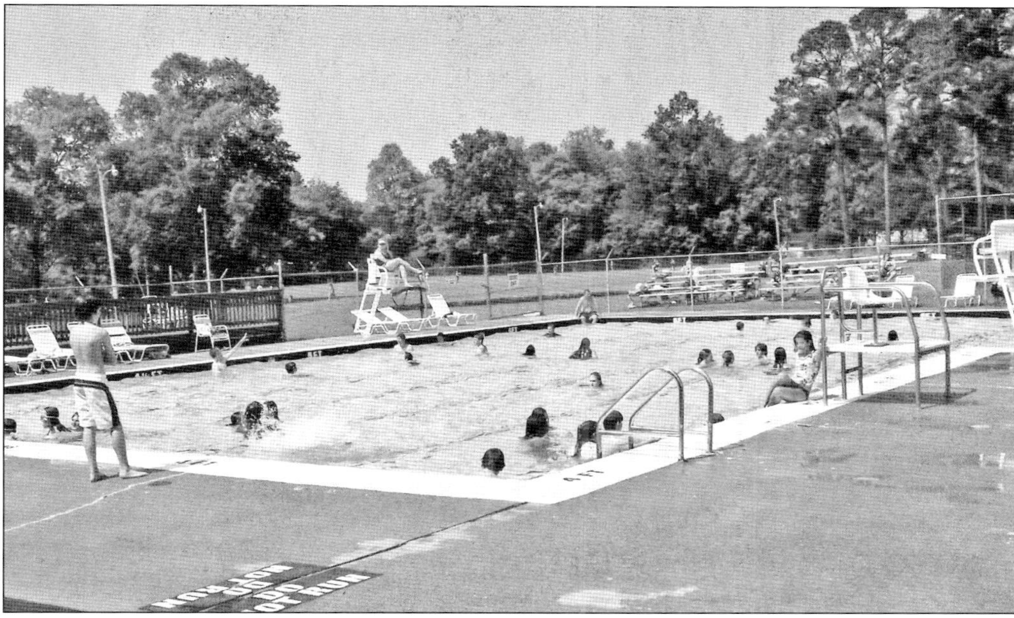

The previous city pool was the home of the Fort Oglethorpe Marlins, the swim league directed by the Lakeview Fort Oglethorpe Recreation Association. Many ribbons have been awarded to Marlin teams and individual standouts. This program exemplifies the dedication, commitment, and talent of the volunteers who make up the recreation association. (CFO.)

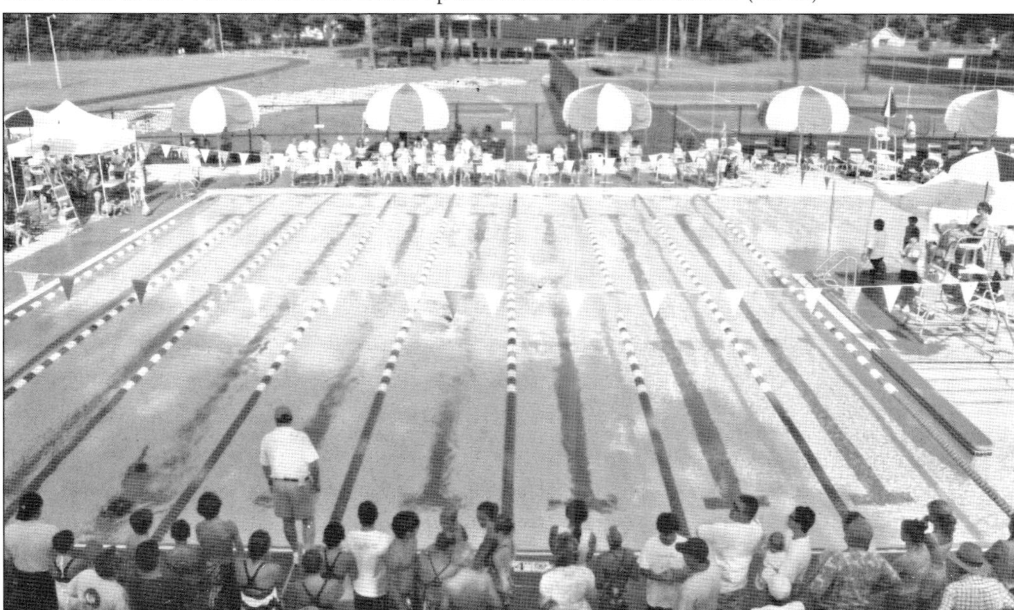

The new pool, umbrellas, and lounges invite swimmers and visitors alike to the competition. Fort Oglethorpe hosted the 2008 district swim meet, which included Chattanooga area teams as well as teams from neighboring Georgia counties. This pool is one of two pools in the state of Georgia that qualify to host the state swim meet. Recreation and economic development come together to benefit youth and taxpayers. (CFO.)

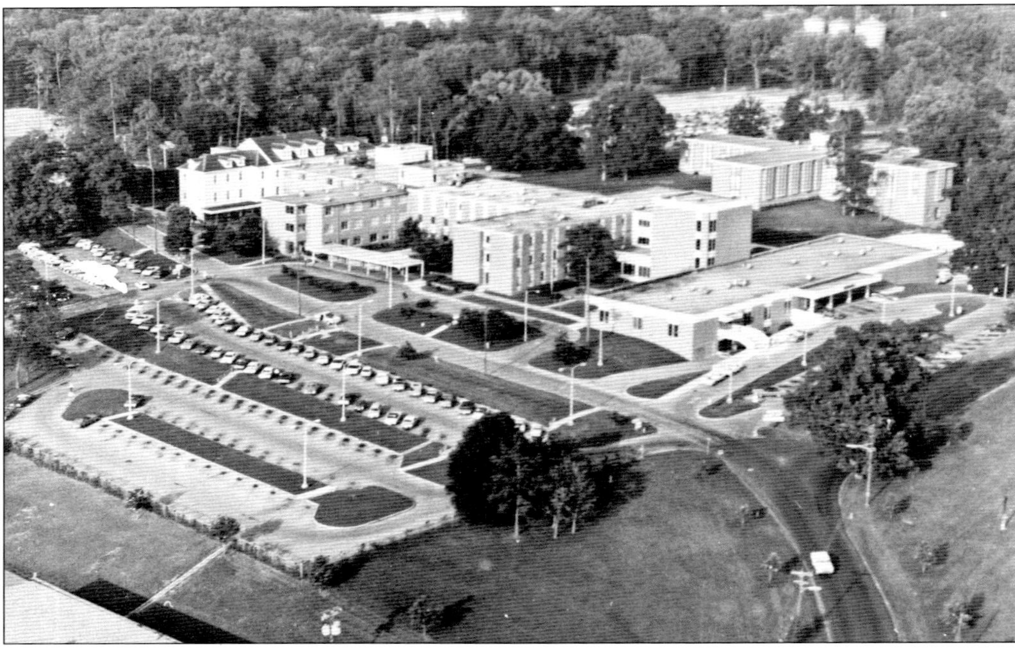

The Hutcheson Regional Medical Center encompasses the original hospital and various expansions developed under Tri-County Hospital. The post hospital is located left of center and is a white three-story building with three sections with dormers. The original post hospital was used as a test area to determine whether a new service was necessary and viable. The medical center continues to serve citizens of Catoosa, Dade, and Walker Counties of northwest Georgia. (HRMC.)

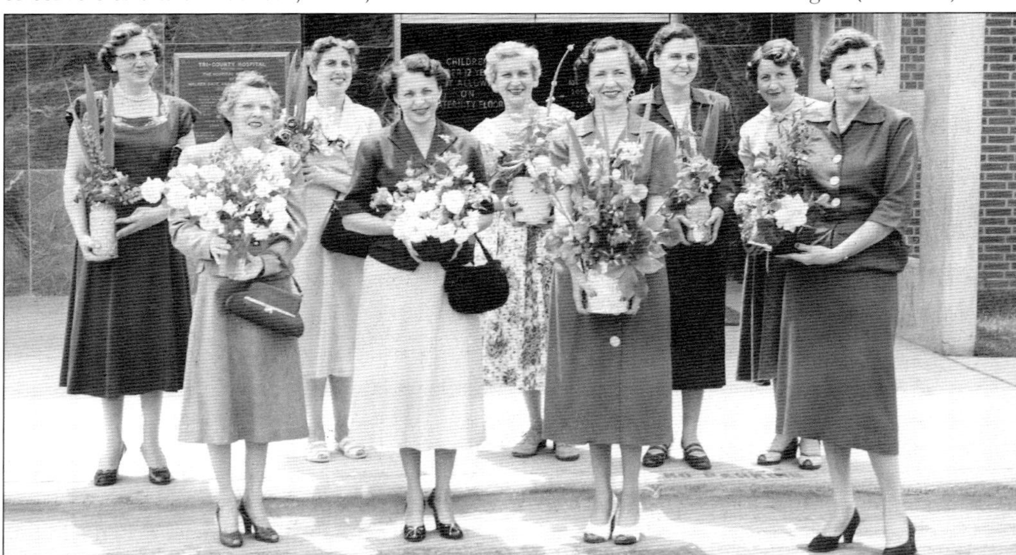

Volunteers are a major resource at every hospital. Tri-County has seen many groups work there. Gray Ladies gave way to Pink Ladies. The Pink Ladies welcomed their male counterparts as the Red Men. And today the coed group wears blue. These Gray Ladies, from 1957, were honored for their service and represent the continuing support of Catoosa, Dade, and Walker Counties for the medical center. (HA.)

On April 2, 1973, Lt. Gov. Lester Maddox used a giant scalpel to break ground for a $6.5-million expansion at the Hutcheson Regional Medical Center. Shown here with the governor are, from left to right, Congressman John Davis, Col. Frank Gleason (hospital board chairman), Governor Maddox, Catherine Morrison, Oscar Hilliard (hospital administrator), and unidentified. (HRMC.)

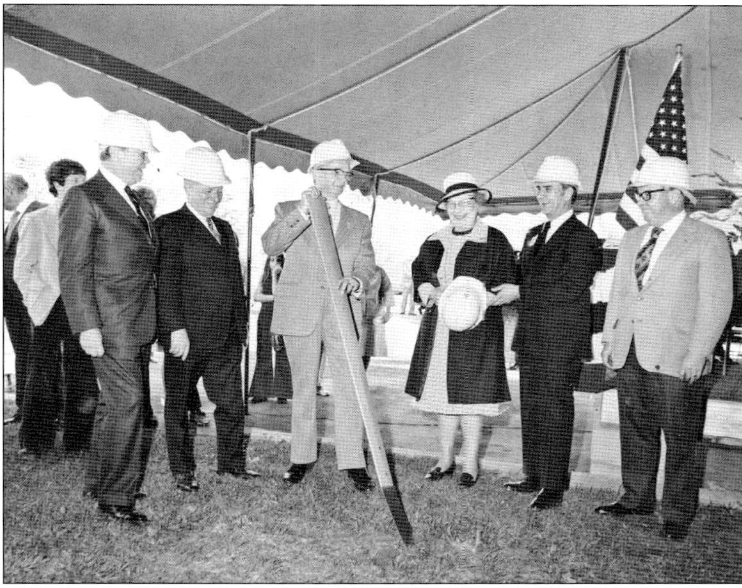

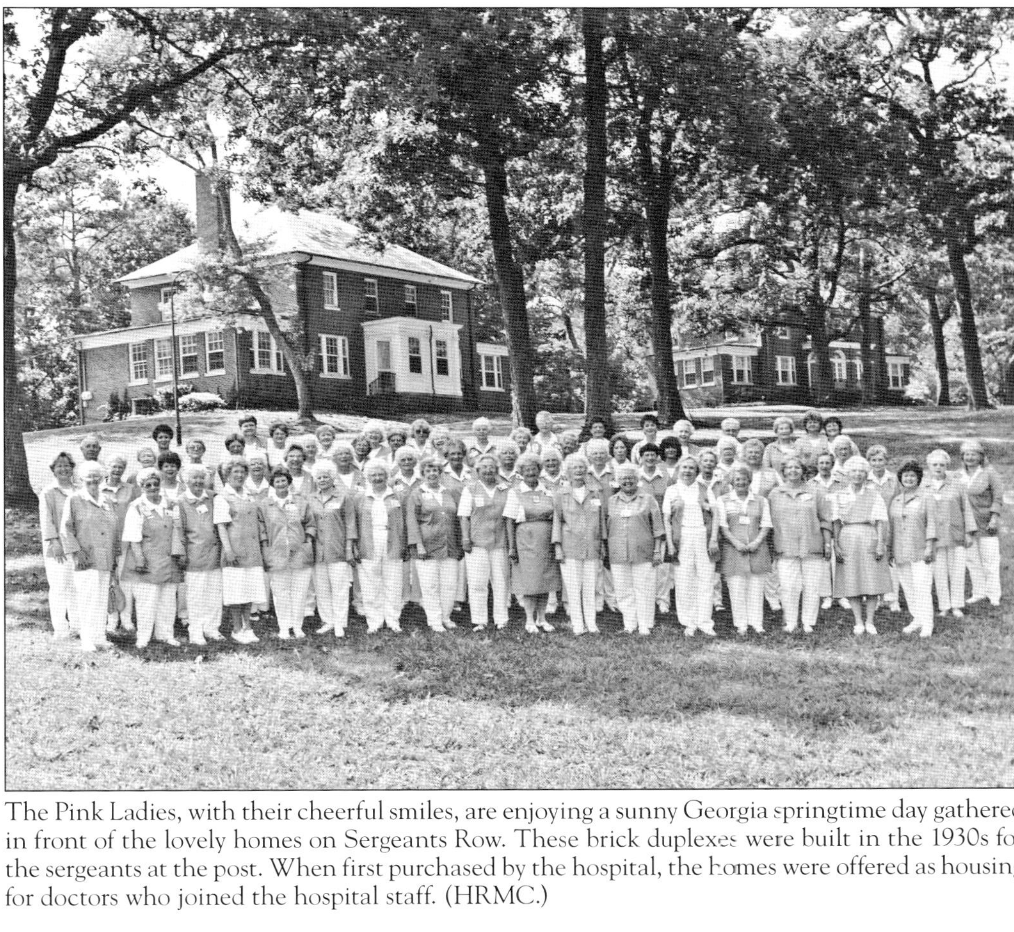

The Pink Ladies, with their cheerful smiles, are enjoying a sunny Georgia springtime day gathered in front of the lovely homes on Sergeants Row. These brick duplexes were built in the 1930s for the sergeants at the post. When first purchased by the hospital, the homes were offered as housing for doctors who joined the hospital staff. (HRMC.)

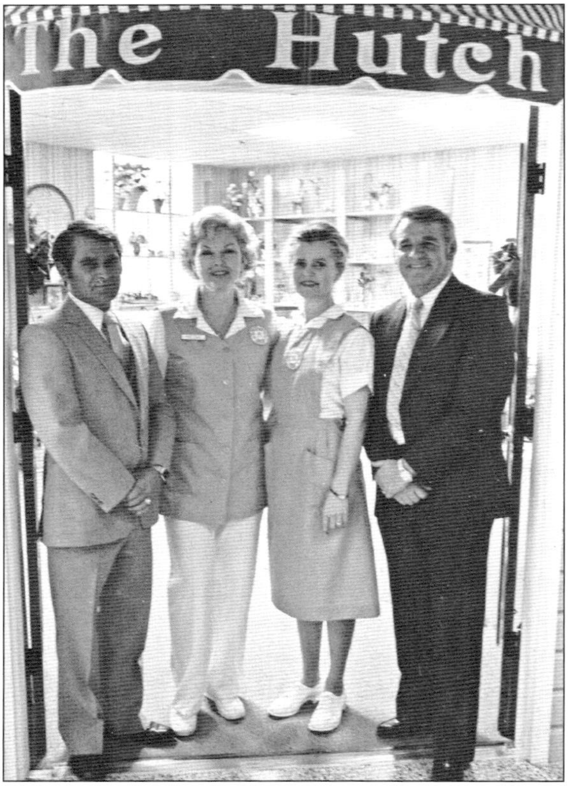

The hospital volunteer corps determined to assist in raising funds for new services at the hospital. The Hutch at Hutcheson Regional Medical Center serves visitors and the community by providing delightful gifts for newborns, children, and patients of all ages. Shown in the doorway of the Hutch are, from left to right, Walker County commissioner Roy Parrish, president-elect Peggy Jorges, Pres. Joan Atkins, and Catoosa County commissioner James Moreland. (HA.)

In the 1960s and 1970s, the *Chattanooga Times* newspaper featured Times Flower Day. Area garden clubs were invited to participate in bringing flowers from home, making arrangements, and giving them to hospital patients and nursing homes. Each club was assigned a specific day. Here are the members of the Fort Oglethorpe Garden Club, from left to right, Bobbie Fant, Roseann Hackler, Gerri Spears, ? Deck, and Wynall Purcell. (Leonard Fant.)

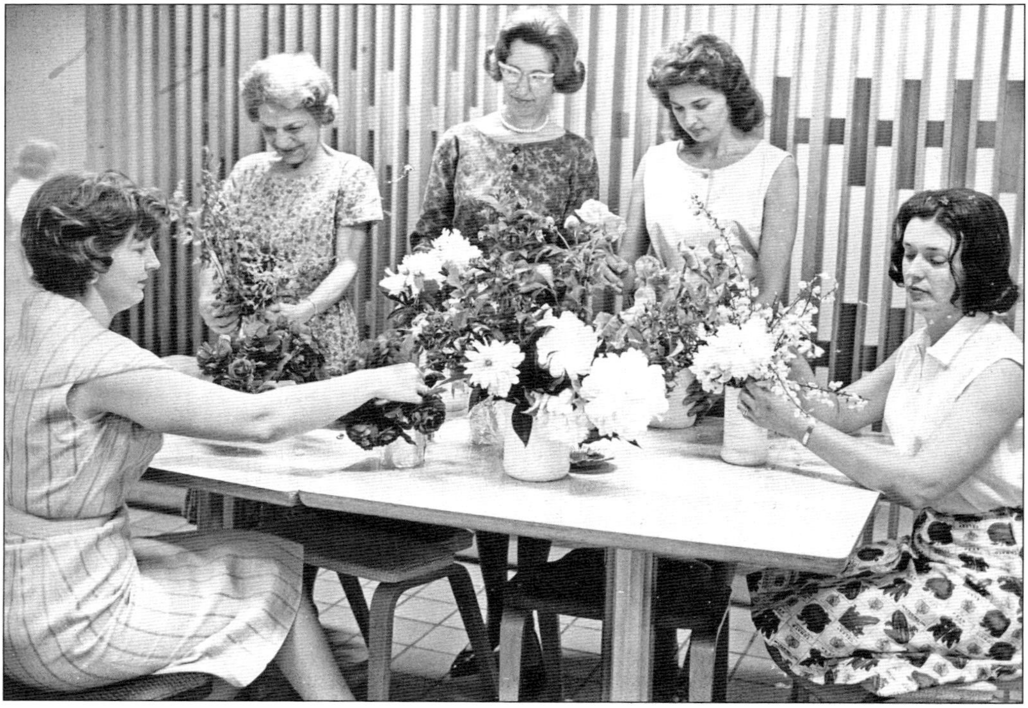

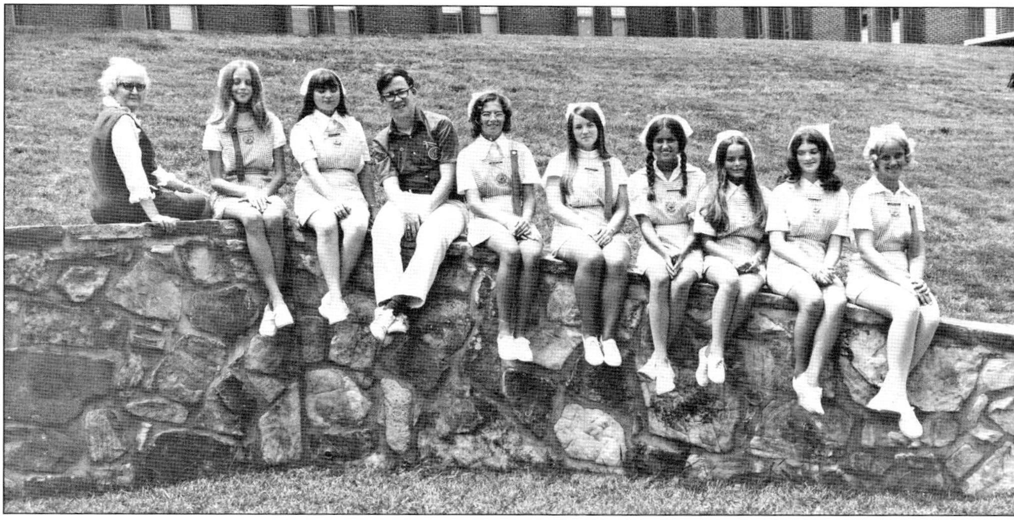

These young people were officers of the Candy Stripers and Teenage Volunteers at Tri-County Hospital for 1972–1973 and represented a large number of young ladies and gentlemen who volunteered their time at the hospital. Membership was drawn from the tri-county area of northwest Georgia served by the hospital—Catoosa, Dade, and Walker Counties. Hazel Brock was the supervisor for this well-organized group. (HRMC.)

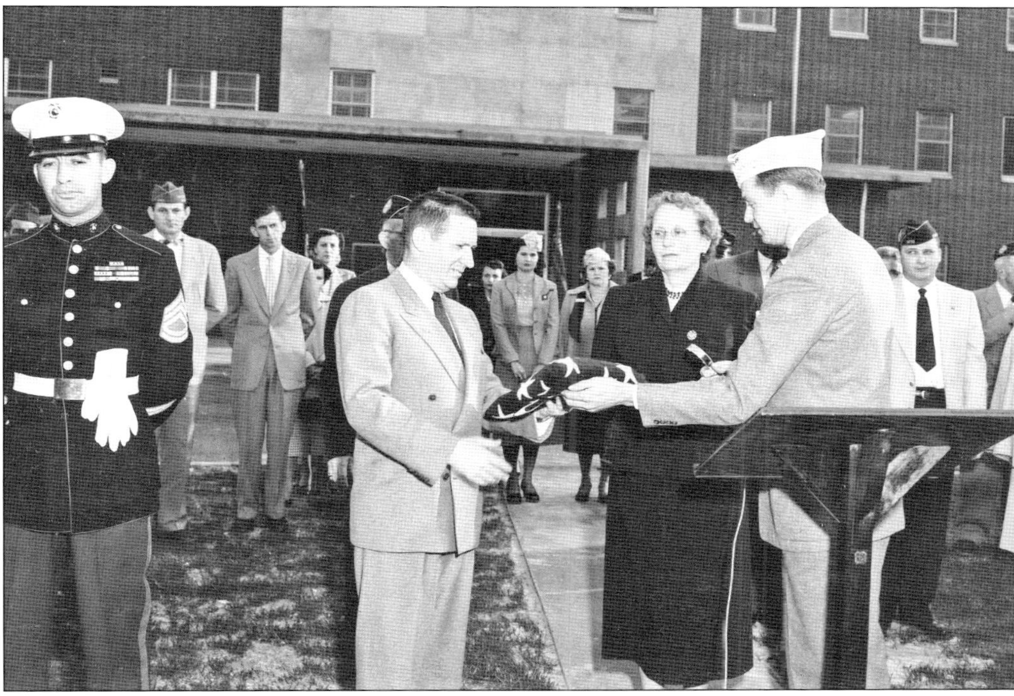

Mrs. Henry Paquette (center) donates the flag that covered her husband's coffin to Frank Gleason (left), chairman of the hospital authority of the Hutcheson Regional Medical Center. Her husband, M.Sgt. Henry "Parky" Paquette, served in the 6th Cavalry for 30 years. Mrs. Paquette said it made her "happy to present the flag because it will fly over the land Parky loved so well." The flag was unfurled at 5:00 p.m., army "retreat" time. (HRMC.)

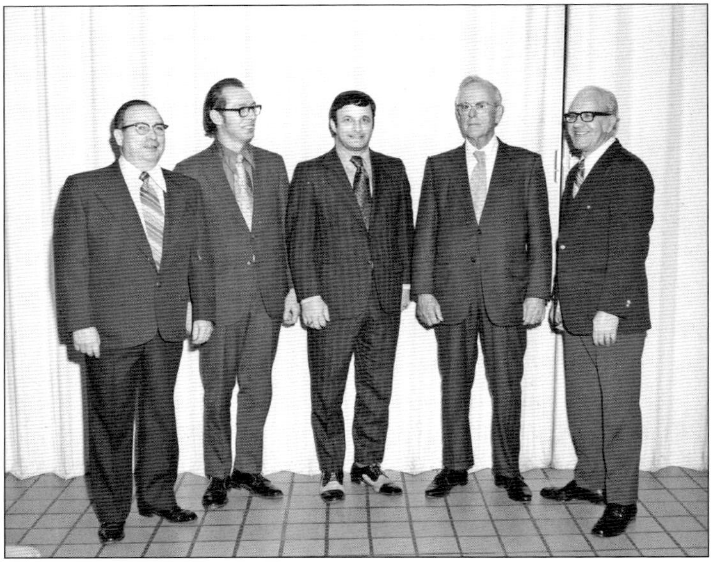

Spiritual assistance is provided by the Chaplain Association of the hospital. The chaplains from various denominations formed a group and met regularly to discuss their ministries. In February 1973, the officers were, from left to right, Rev. Wallace Green, Rev. Ted Youngblood, Rev. Eugene Lewis, Dr. J. Fred Johnson (guest speaker), and Frank Huey, hospital staff. (HRMC.)

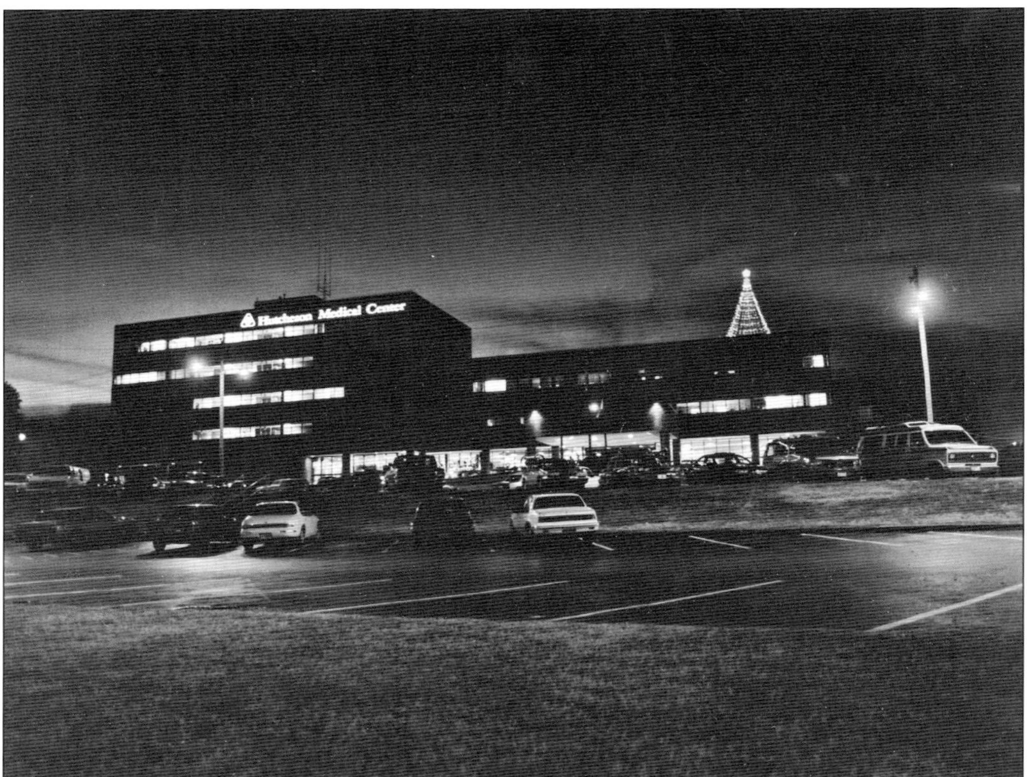

The Auxiliary Love Lights, begun in 1980, added a "Love" light on the Christmas tree for every donation. The tree initially was placed in front of the main entrance to the hospital and now adorns the roof of a hospital wing. "This is only our third tree and yet people have told me the lighting ceremony has already become a Christmas tradition for their family," offered an auxiliary member. (HRMC.)

Seven

Celebrating Our Heritage

During its 50th anniversary, Fort Oglethorpe celebrated growth from a new town founded in 1949 into a thriving economic center in northwest Georgia. The month-long celebration brought together past mayors, councilmen, principals, teachers, students, old-timers, and favorite hangouts during the scavenger hunt.

After the governor and state officials returned to Atlanta and the bunting was removed from the post bandstand, the citizens of Fort Oglethorpe stepped forward into the 21st century. New elementary and high schools, a new community swimming pool at Gilbert-Stephenson City Park, and increased enrollment in the recreation association all attest to the continued population growth of the city.

The annual reunion of the 6th U.S. Cavalry Association still brings back horse soldiers from the 1930s and 1940s. At their 100th reunion in 2000, the city unveiled new patrol cars that had the 6th Cavalry crest on the hoods. The soldiers' affection for this army post continues to thrive, and they share it with their children and grandchildren. The city is honored to receive them each June.

Standing as faithful witnesses to the military past, the remaining post structures are experiencing historic reuse. The PX, gymnasium, and the last free-standing horse stable all contain modern businesses. Around Barnhardt Circle, the Captain's Quarters Bed and Breakfast and Barnhardt Hall (the original Band Barracks) welcome overnight visitors. The remaining officers' quarters are privately owned residences. The post theater is now Calvary Memorial Baptist Church and joins First Presbyterian Church (the post chapel) and St. Gerard's Roman Catholic Church at the east gate site of the original post.

The parade grounds are now used for recreational community events. Regional high school ROTC drill meets, July Patriotism at the Post, Labor Day at the Post, military reenactments, and marathons draw visitors and residents alike to a quieter time in the city's history.

The city's evolving trail system welcomes those who stroll and bike through these historic areas, enjoying the brook, park, greenways, and Barnhardt Circle. The architecture of the postwar homes and shade of the old trees invite reflection and relaxation in Fort Oglethorpe, home of the "Fighting 6th."

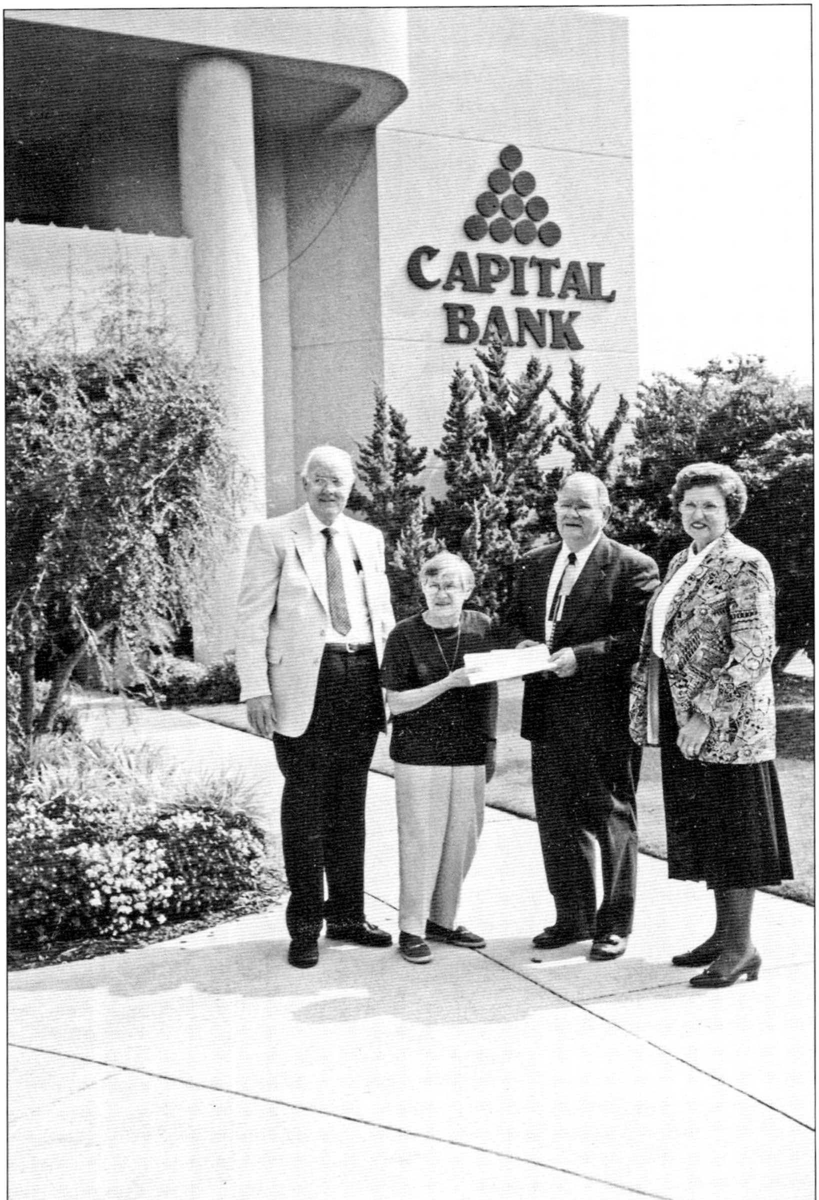

After celebrating the bicentennial of the country and the centennial of the Civil War and the Battle of Chickamauga, the town that was the first town incorporated in Georgia after the end of World War II found that it too had a celebration to plan. This one recognized that the city of Fort Oglethorpe had come of age. The next party was going to involve the entire city. In honor of its relationship to the city and its citizens, Capital Bank announced it would sponsor the month-long series of events in October, celebrating the 50th anniversary of Fort Oglethorpe. Activities began with a Thanksgiving prayer service at the parade grounds and included a scavenger hunt for old-timers, a dinner to recognize past mayors and councilmen, and special programs at the parade grounds. Pictured here are, from left to right, Mayor Doyle Camp; Peggy Stanfield, chairman; L. T. Coe, Capital Bank president; and Virginia Smith, Fort Oglethorpe city manager. (CFO.)

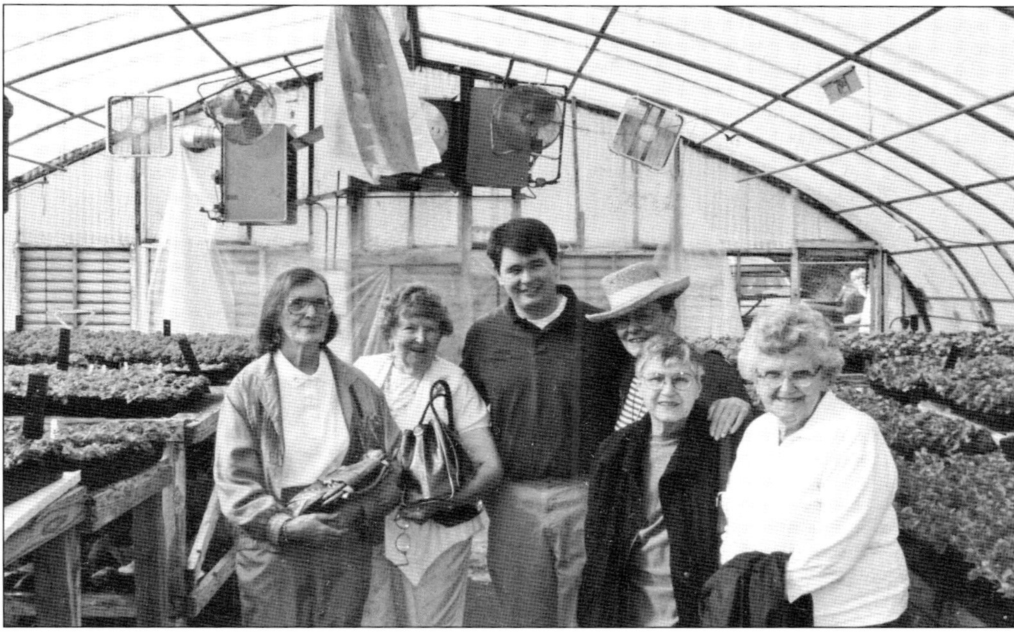

Marigolds cheerfully greeted everyone in town. As part of the golden anniversary of the city, the Marigold Project was developed. Flowers were sold to residents and became a sign of unity throughout the city. Peggy Stanfield, chairman of the festivities, is an active member of this community. She keeps the town's scrapbooks, coordinates the Senior Friends program that meets every Wednesday, and hosts the *Senior Moments* program on UCTV-3. (CFO.)

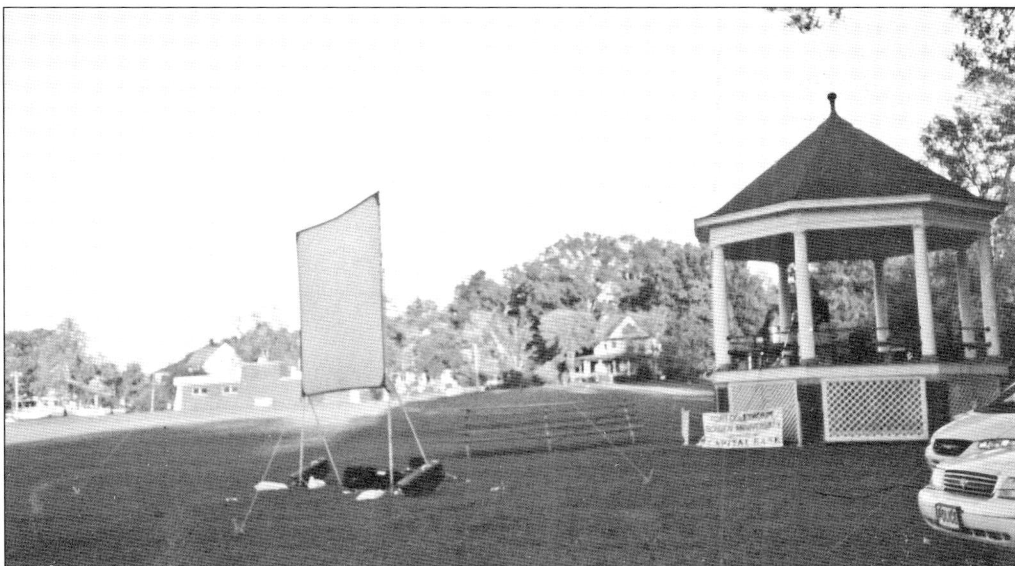

Keep Your Powder Dry was a war movie. Part of the story actually occurred at Fort Oglethorpe. An outdoor movie screen was used for this 1999 evening event. Except for the materials used, it bears a remarkable similarity to the "open air" screen (page 43) used by the World War I German POWs. Fort Oglethorpe's heritage appears often and needs only to be recognized and celebrated—if only with a knowing smile. (CFO.)

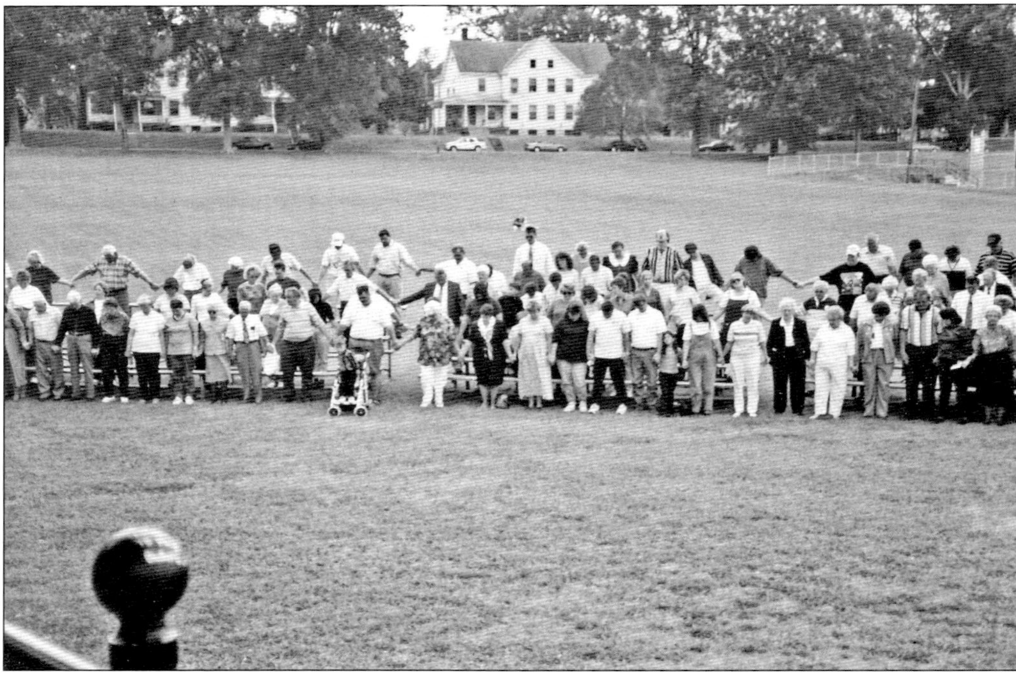

The 50th anniversary of the city was a month-long celebration in October 1999. The Community Thanksgiving Service was held on the parade grounds on October 3. Area ministers lead the group in prayer and music was provided by a community-wide choir. This picture, taken from the post bandstand, shows participants joining hands in a final prayer. (CFO.)

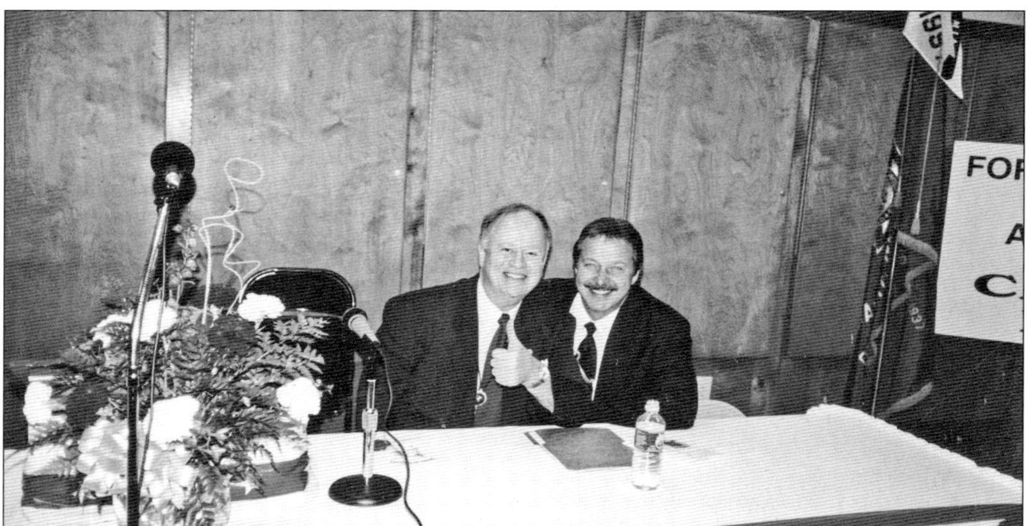

Former mayors and councilmen attended a special dinner in their honor. A special friend of our military heritage and a favorite son share some time together. Max Cleland, a Vietnam veteran and former U.S. senator from Georgia, and James Rogers, a hometown son, together remind us of how common threads in our lives bring us back to our heritage, whether it is our hometown or not. (CFO.)

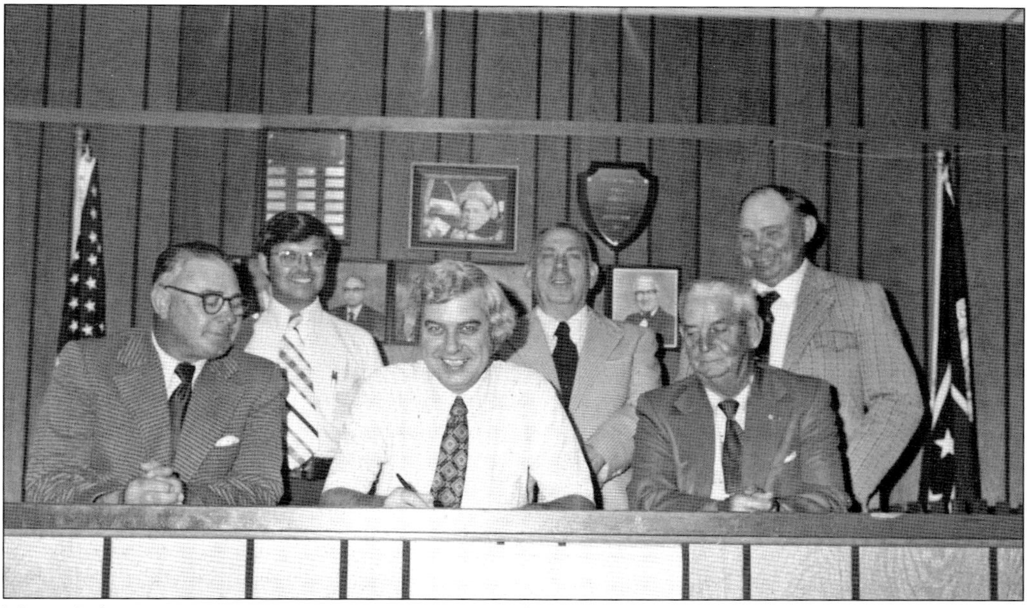

Mayor John Norris signs a petition June 2, 1975, declaring June 15–21 to be "6th Cavalry Week." Present at the signing are, from left to right, John Osborne, city manager James Harris, Mayor Norris, Alvin Perry, O. C. Churchwell, and Joe Hurt. Both the City of Fort Oglethorpe and the City of Chattanooga declared such special weeks over the years. (CFO.)

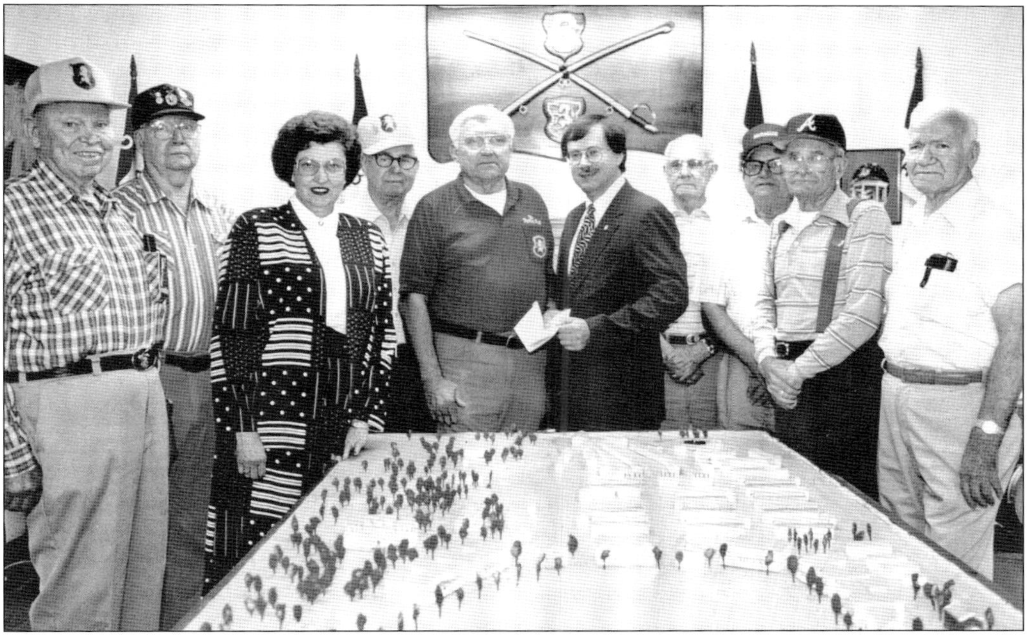

Bill Taylor (center) used his artistic talent to create the layout of the 1940 post shown here. Barracks, stables, officers' homes, landscaping, and roads are detailed and help visitors to orient themselves. State representative Mike Snow presents a check for $10,000 to Taylor to assist the 6th Cavalry Association in completing the upstairs renovation of the museum. City manager Virginia Smith watches on with members of the association and trustees of the museum. (SCM.)

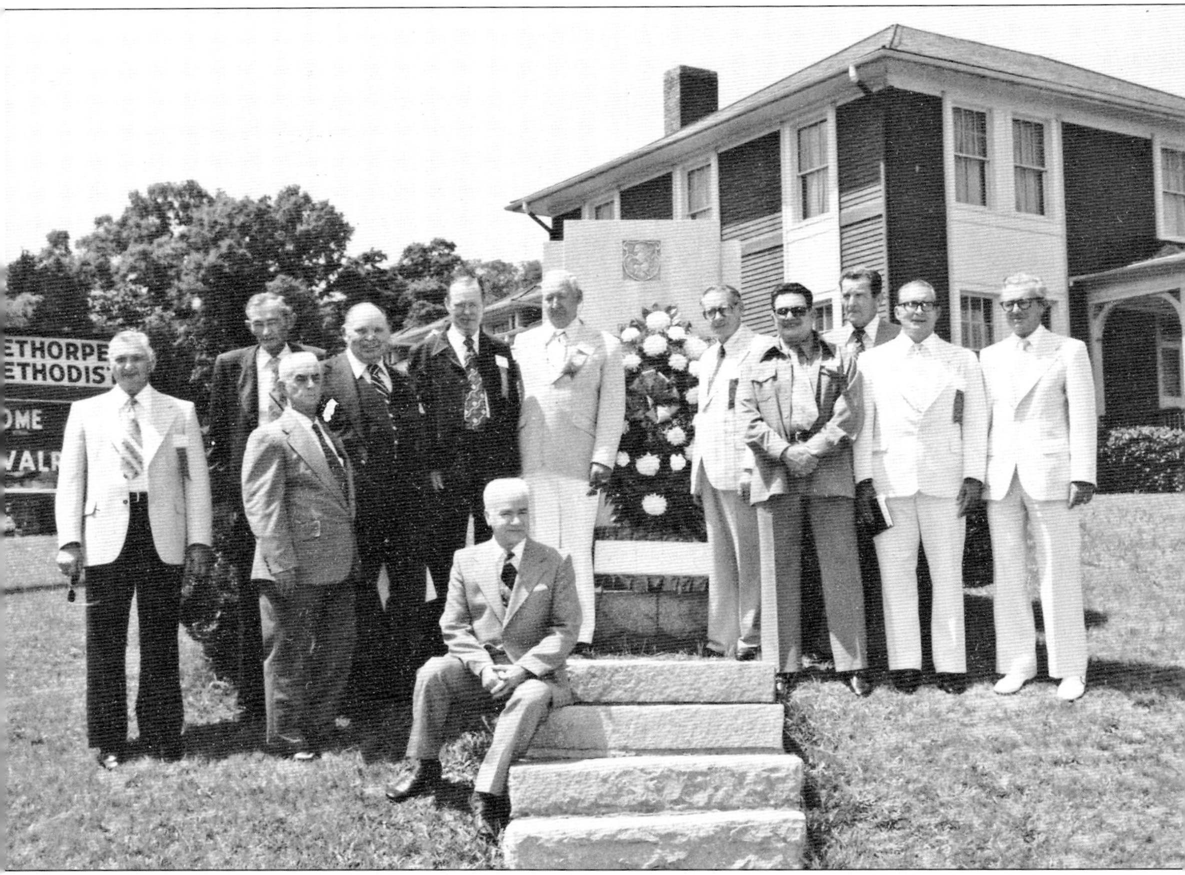

The Sixth U. S. Cavalry Veterans Association held its first reunion in 1900, after the Spanish-American War. After World War II, the association held its annual reunions in Chattanooga and visited the old post in Fort Oglethorpe, which was their unit home for 23 years. In 1950, the veterans dedicated a granite marker to the memory of their fellow cavalrymen: "Dedicated to the Men and Officers of the Sixth U.S. Cavalry Who Have Gone Before to That Unknown Silent Shore." The marker was located on the corner of the post chapel property at the main gate at Harker Road. It was subsequently moved to the base of the post flagpole. Each reunion Sunday, "Taps" is played and the names of those who had died that year are read. (SCM.)

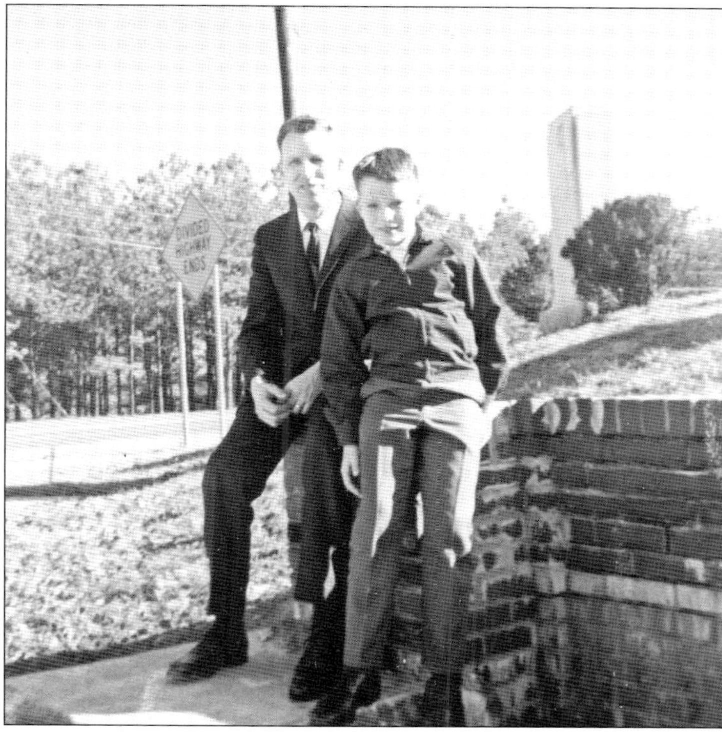

Bobby Brown's dad, Robert Brown Sr., always wanted to visit what he called "10th cousins" in the Chattanooga area. Bobby thinks that his father used the cousins as a reason to visit the post. Once the family neared Chattanooga, his dad would divert them to the parade grounds and he would revisit the buildings and share his memories again. The horse soldiers and the WACs seem drawn back to the old post. (Robert Brown Jr.)

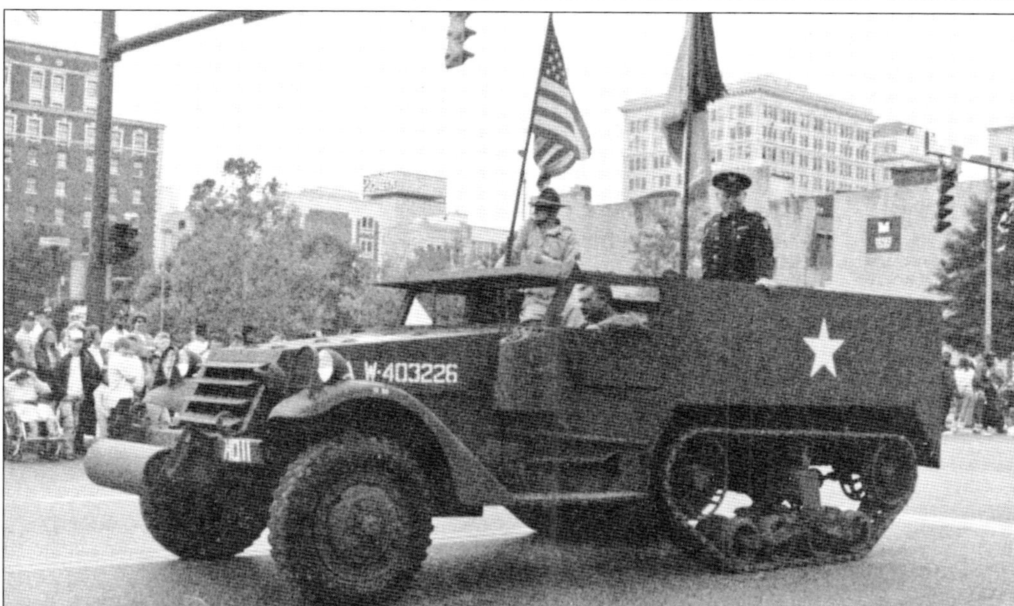

Each spring, ROTC units march, bands play, and military vehicles parade to honor the U.S. Armed Forces. Larry Rose, a Rossville resident and friend of the WAC, drives Joe Hurt, founder of the Sixth Cavalry Museum, and an unidentified veteran. Today the Sixth Cavalry Museum proudly drives a restored World War II jeep, donated by the Veterans Association and restored by Matt Fox. (Larry Rose.)

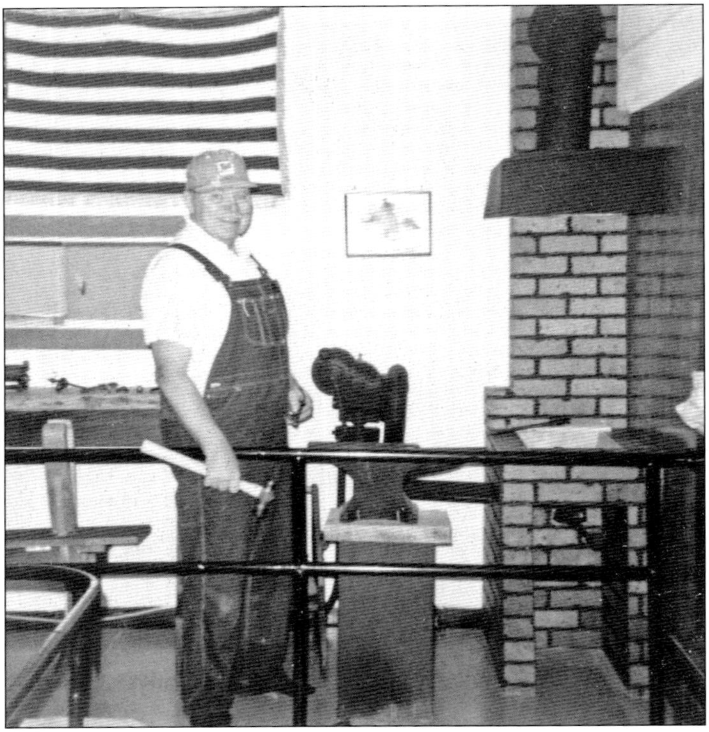

Joe Hurt, prominent in creating the Sixth Cavalry Museum, donned his overalls the day the museum was officially opened in 1981 and posed between the blacksmith display and artifacts. Joe left home in Kansas and, upon joining the 6th, was assigned to the blacksmith shop. His farming background was invaluable for working with the horses. The building, once a county health center, was dedicated to Joe Hurt in 1988. (SCM.)

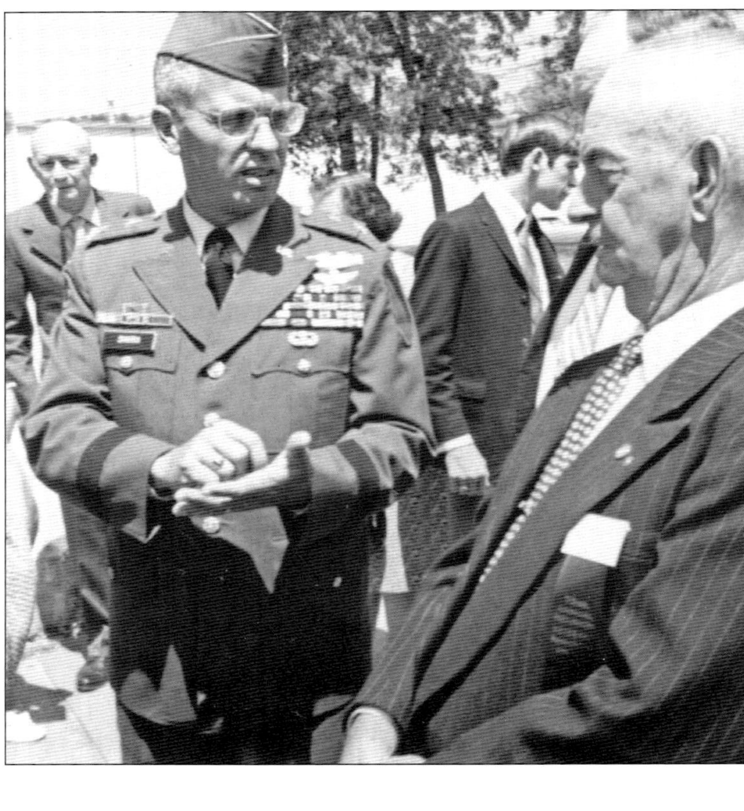

Maj. Gen. James K. Smith (retired) talks with O. C. "Sarge" Churchwell at the 73rd reunion. General Smith was born at the post hospital, son of a sergeant. At a young age, Smith was an accomplished rider. An officer and a gentleman, General Smith appears at the Sunday memorial in his uniform and campaign hat, a silent reminder of the heritage this town shares with these honorable veterans. (SCM.)

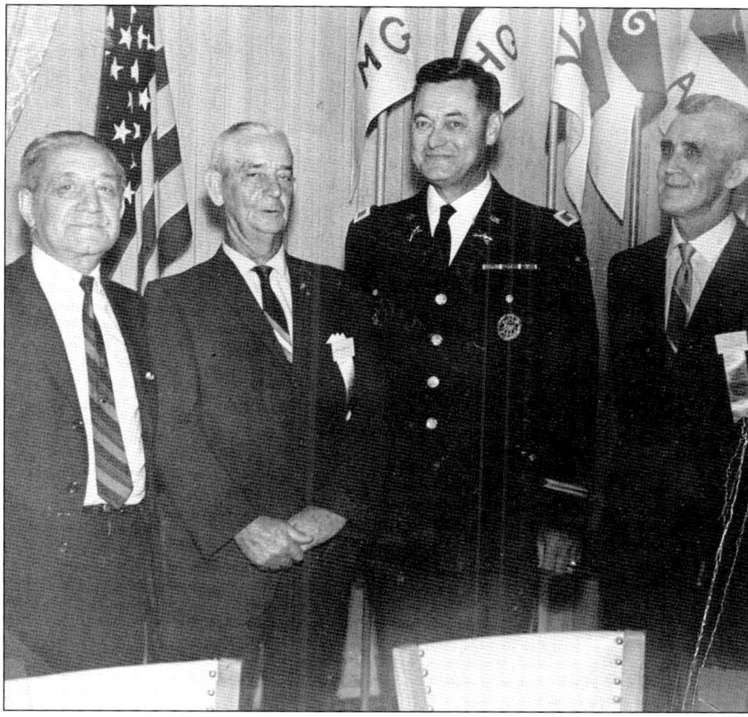

At the 1969 reunion, Colonel Mitchell, Commanding Officer, 6th Cavalry (second from the right), is the guest speaker for the Saturday night dinner. Often the commanding officer would bring a color guard of four men and women who spent much time listening to the stories of the old horse soldiers of the 1930s and 1940s who still attended the reunion. (SCM.)

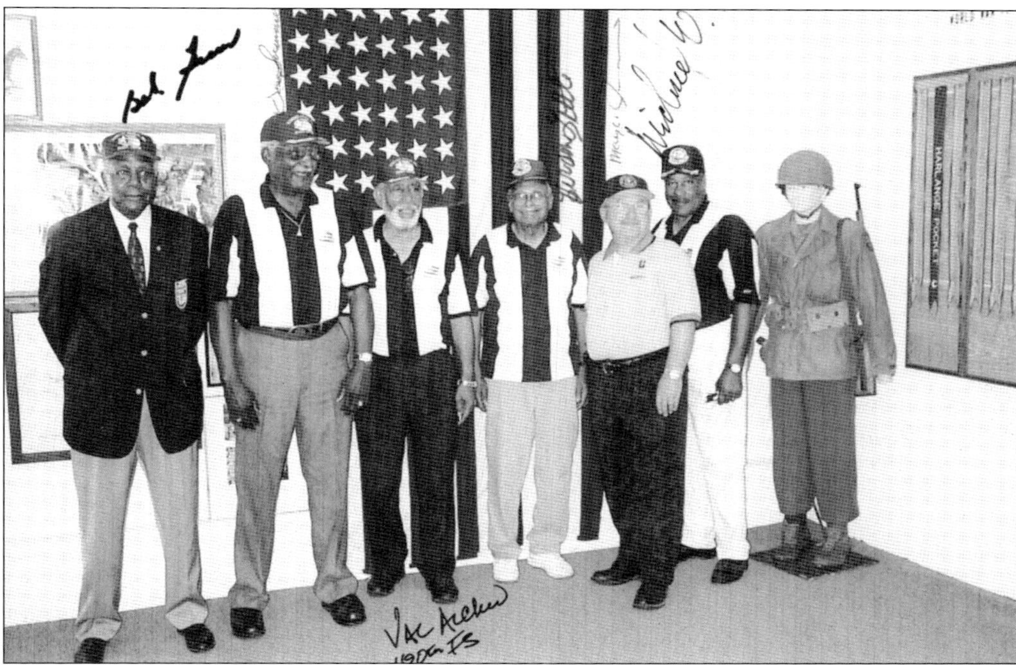

Five members of the Tuskegee Airmen visited the museum during the reunion weekend of 2003. They spoke with the 6th Cavalry veterans, answered questions from visitors, and signed Tuskegee posters. They are pictured here with Mayor Judd Burkart and a World War II GI mannequin in the upstairs exhibit hall. (CFO.)

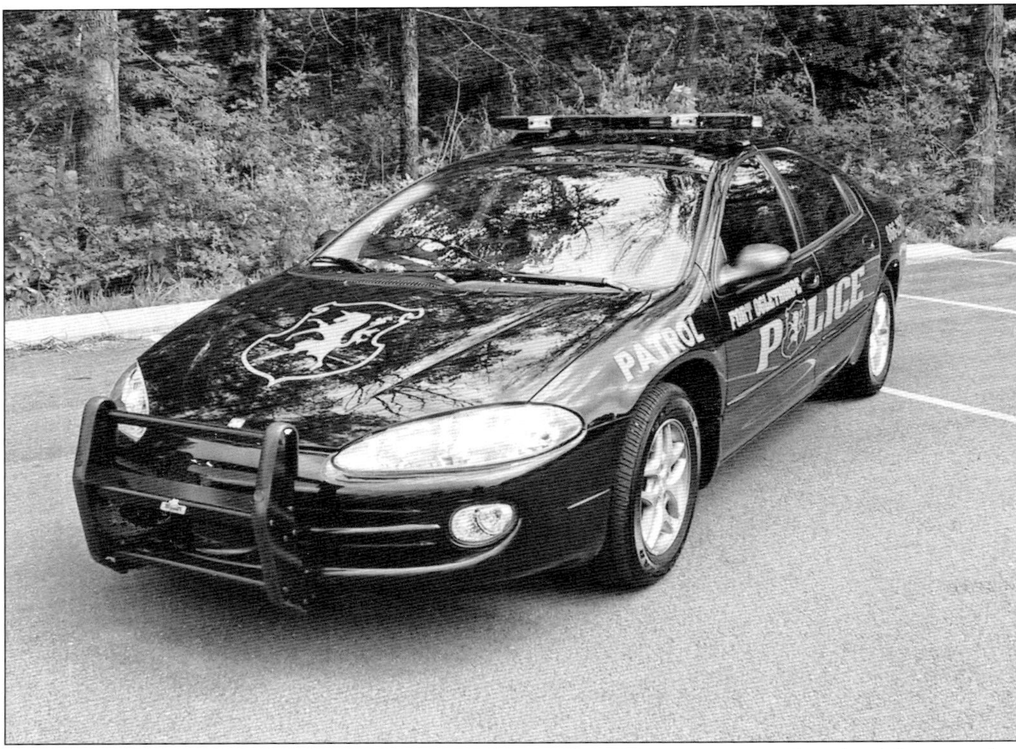

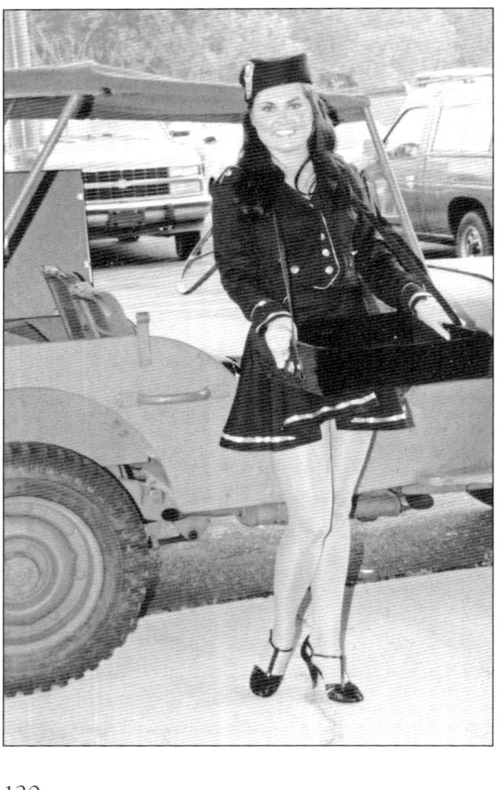

At the 2000 reunion weekend celebrating the 6th Cavalry Association's 100th anniversary, the city and the Sixth Cavalry Museum honored the returning cavalrymen with a parade and a special gift. The city patrol cars, black in color, wore the gold "Fighting 6th Cavalry" shield (modified and adopted as the city emblem) on the engine hoods. It was hard to determine who was more proud—the old cavalrymen or the young policemen. (SCM.)

One of the younger set at a dinner-dance for veterans was Lauren Russell, daughter of Kyle Russell and granddaughter of Roy Russell of the 6th Cavalry. Lauren came as a "cigarette" girl with a saucy hat and a tray of candy. Here she appears in front of the association jeep. (Lauren Russell.)

The loss of the blacksmith shop (below) was no less felt than the loss of this 1930 brick neoclassical house (right). Historic preservationists refer to a "sense of place" to describe the often unconscious feelings people have of a place. Often memories are activated only after that site has been altered to the extreme. Each loss magnifies itself as the memories ripple. A returning WAC mentioned that the battlefield no longer contained any buildings from the WAC South Post. She said, "It was as if we were never there." Thankfully the current fire department understands these feelings. They assure the citizens that they are very gentle with the "ladies" because they understand how important they are to telling the story of the post and the city's heritage. (CFO.)

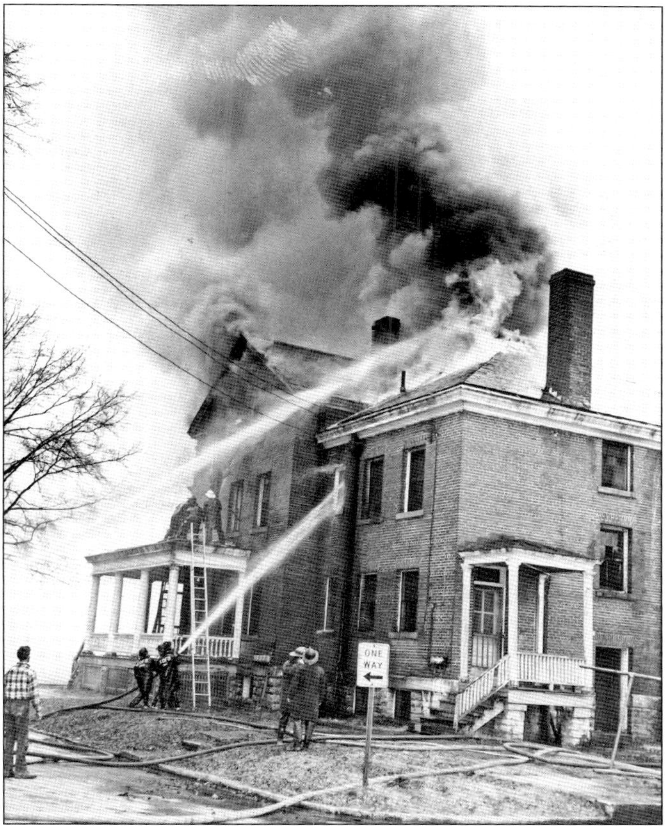

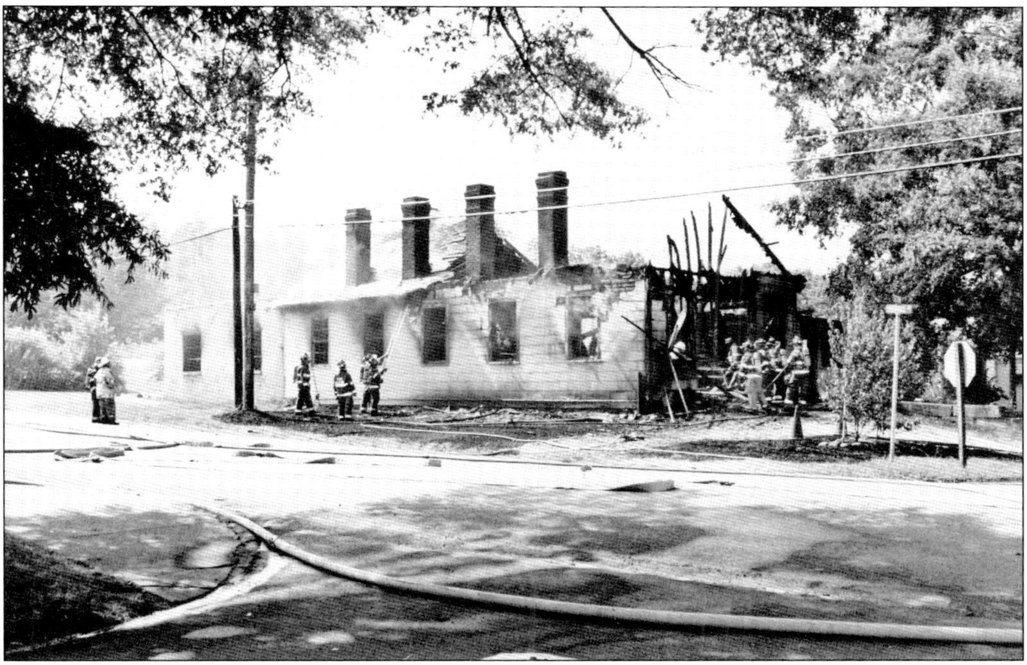

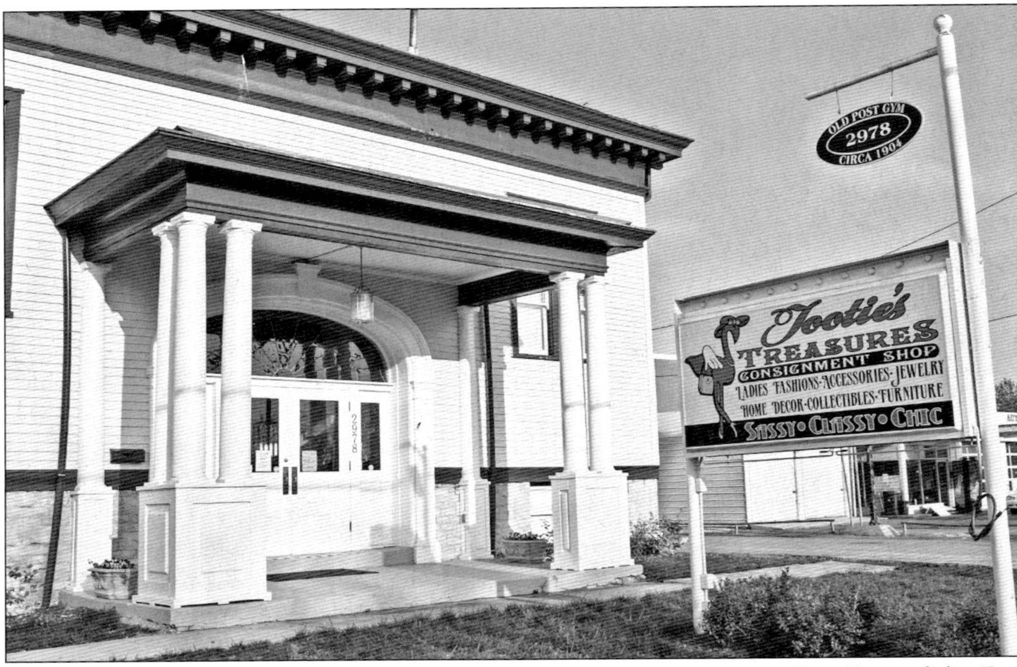

The post gymnasium now contains a consignment shop, but through the efforts of the Fort Oglethorpe Preservation Society, this and many other buildings from the post are now on the National Register of Historic Places and are protected by a local historic preservation ordinance. The exterior beauty speaks to all who drive by. Its previous commercial lives include an antiques and tea shop, a vinyl siding store, and a furniture store. (LP.)

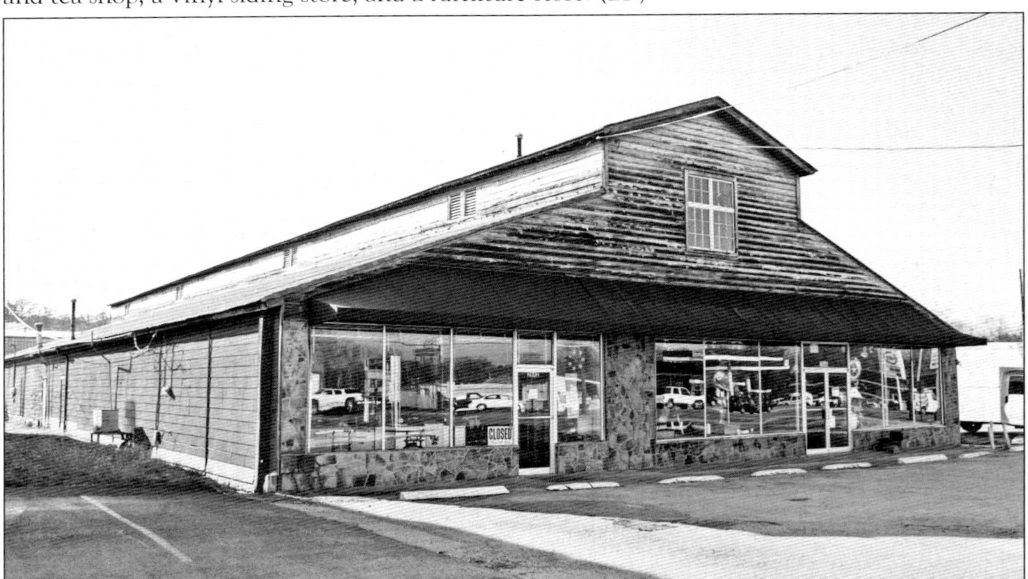

The only stand-alone stable has more windows now but has served a number of commercial businesses, including a fabric store and a gift and gallery shop. Today the occupant sells copies of military pieces and may be well positioned for the 150th anniversary of the Battle of Chickamauga. (LP.)

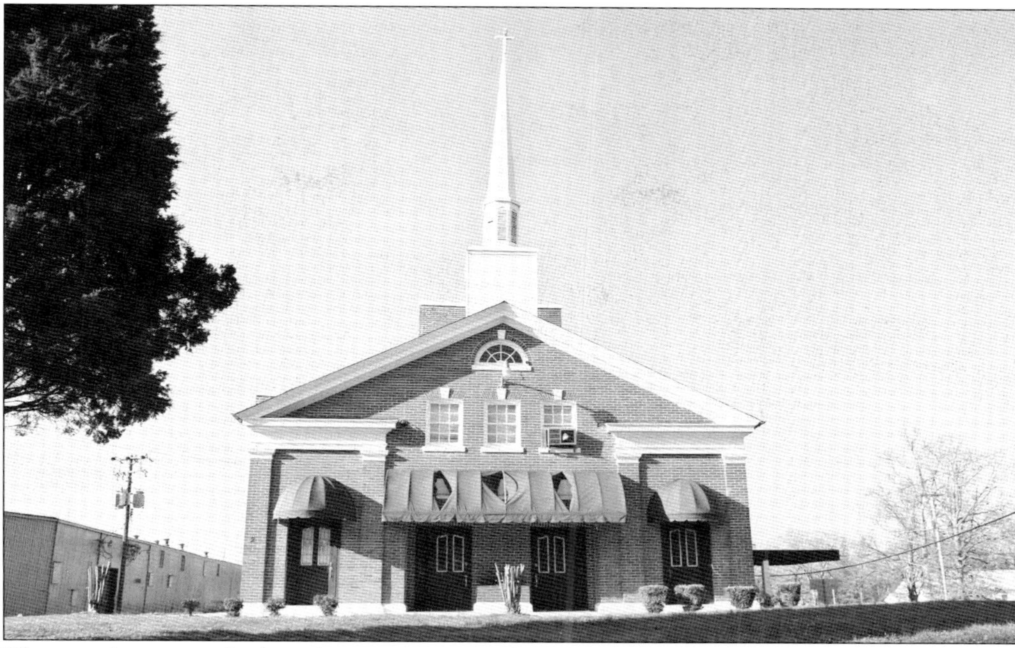

The post theater was built in the 1930s. During the polo seasons, the adults and their guests would go to the Officers Club for tea after the match. The children of these families were gathered together by a sergeant and taken into the movie theater to watch Westerns. Today Calvary Memorial Baptist Church calls the theater home and offers a church service each reunion weekend. (LP.)

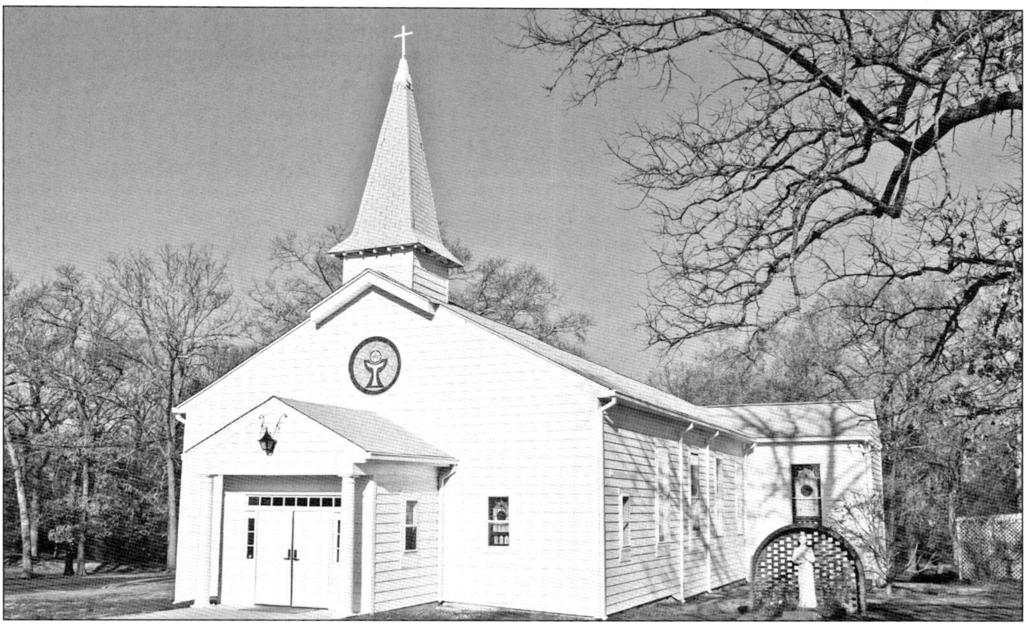

In 1941, St. Gerard's Roman Catholic Church was erected. It seated 500 and would be open and waiting when the men came back from summer maneuvers that year. The church is active but no longer conducts a Catholic school in the town. The large wooded lots to the north of the church reflect the open spaces of the original post site. (LP.)

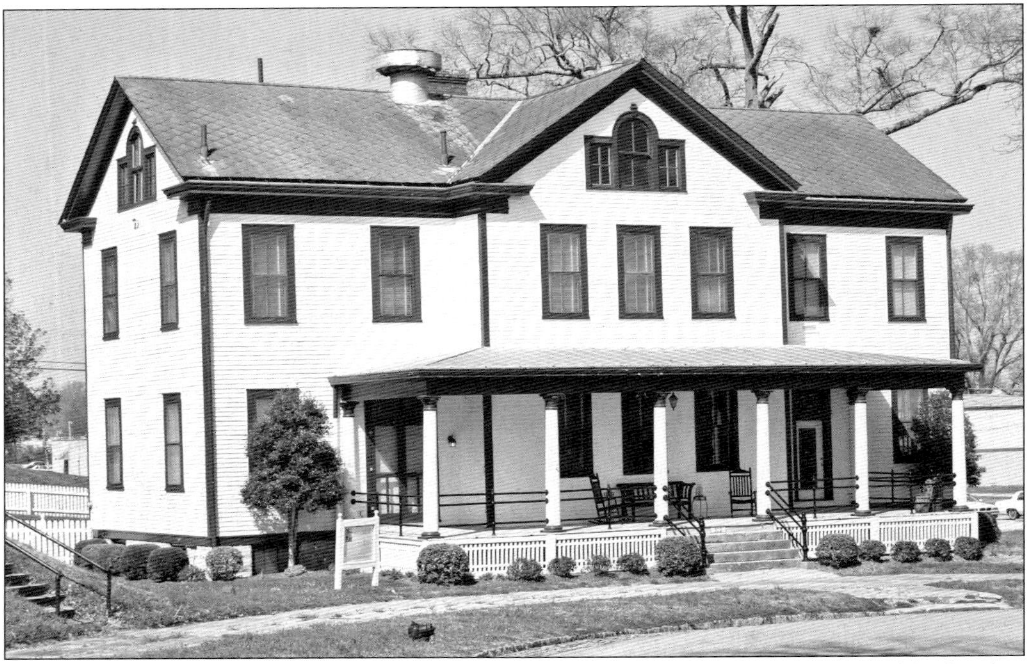

The Band Barracks, above, was restored and today is a vacation rental property used by families for reunions. The Captains' Quarters is a bed-and-breakfast. Both houses are generously opened for the Christmas Tour of Homes. Today the "ladies" around the circle no longer dress in white with green shutters. The colors are more remindful of Easter eggs. There is individualism because these houses are part of a neighborhood and not a caught-in-time concept of life then. (LP.)

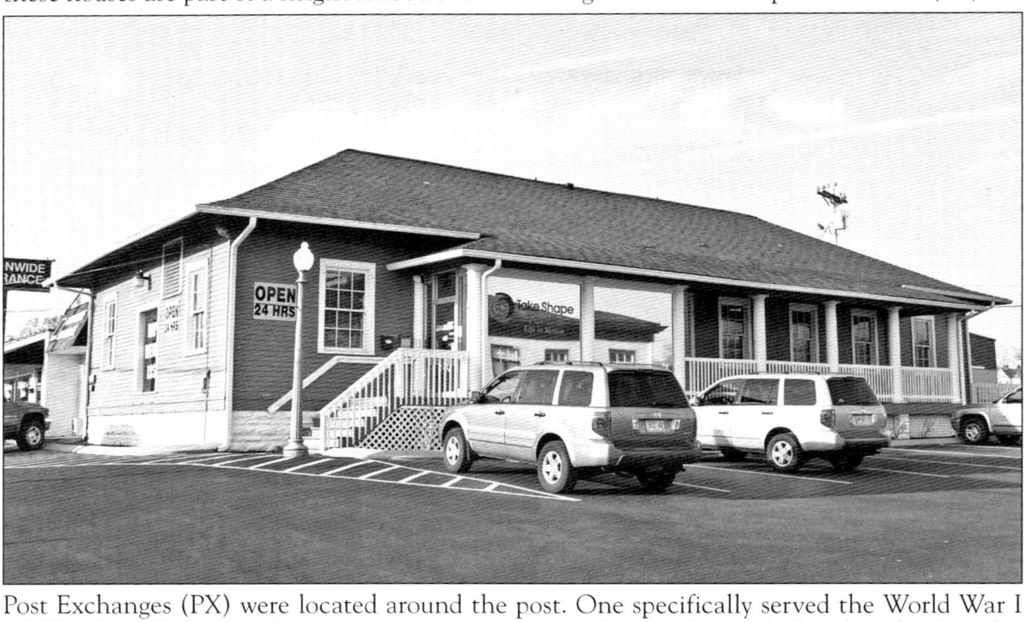

Post Exchanges (PX) were located around the post. One specifically served the World War I POWs. This PX, next to the post gymnasium, was a popular spot during the break at the Saturday night dances for enlisted men and their dates. A cold soda was always available for the thirsty dancers. (LP.)

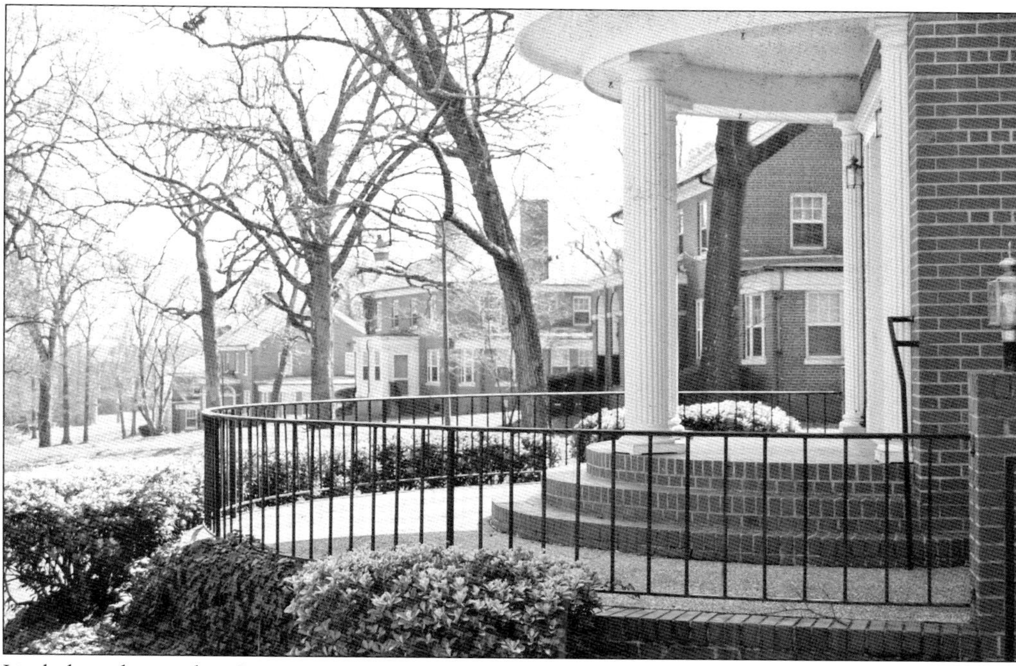

Little has changed at Sergeants Row. Built in the 1930s, the only change has been with this end duplex. The hospital administrator at that time changed the exterior, redesigned the porch, and modified the interior to that of a single-family unit. The hospital administration has maintained the grassy areas around these houses, and the residents and visitors can enjoy the panorama of the dogwoods, hill, and view. (LP.)

Work is slow when a building is being redone. The quartermaster's building is being renovated and window frames will need attention. For most old buildings, often it is more economical to redo the old building than tear it down and rebuild a new structure. Preservation bulletins from the National Park Service can assist a property owner in making good decisions to protect the old structure. (LP.)

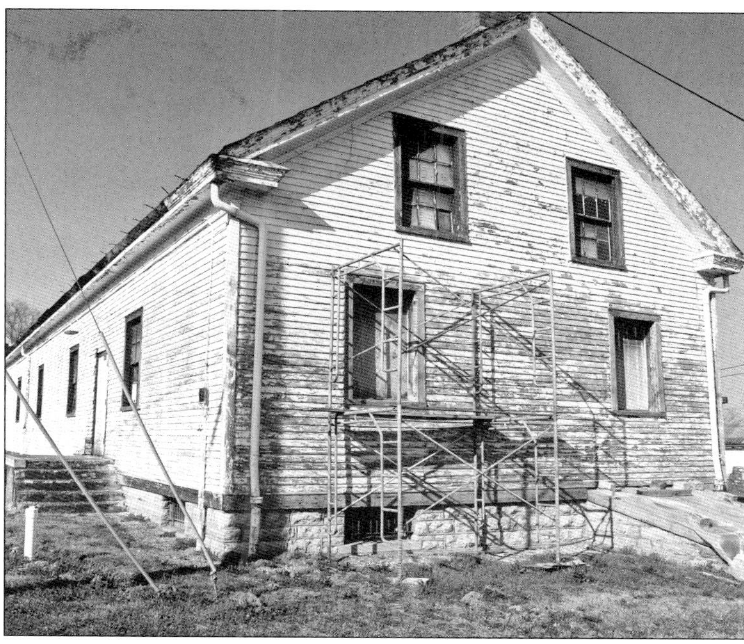

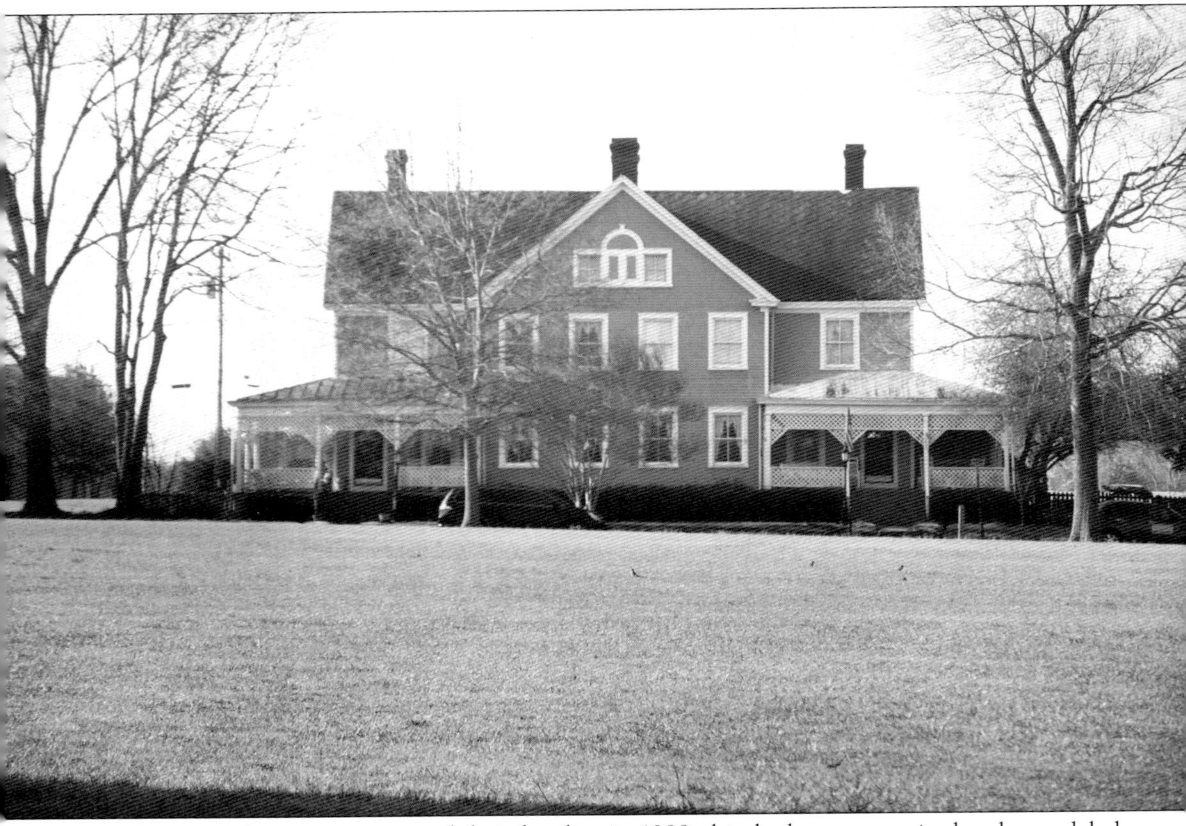

Built in 1902 for two captains and their families, in 1988, this duplex was acquired and remodeled as a bed-and-breakfast. Backing up to the Chickamauga and Chattanooga National Military Park and facing the former parade grounds, the house has welcoming wraparound porches where guests can relax and enjoy the quiet beauty and history of Fort Oglethorpe. (LP.)

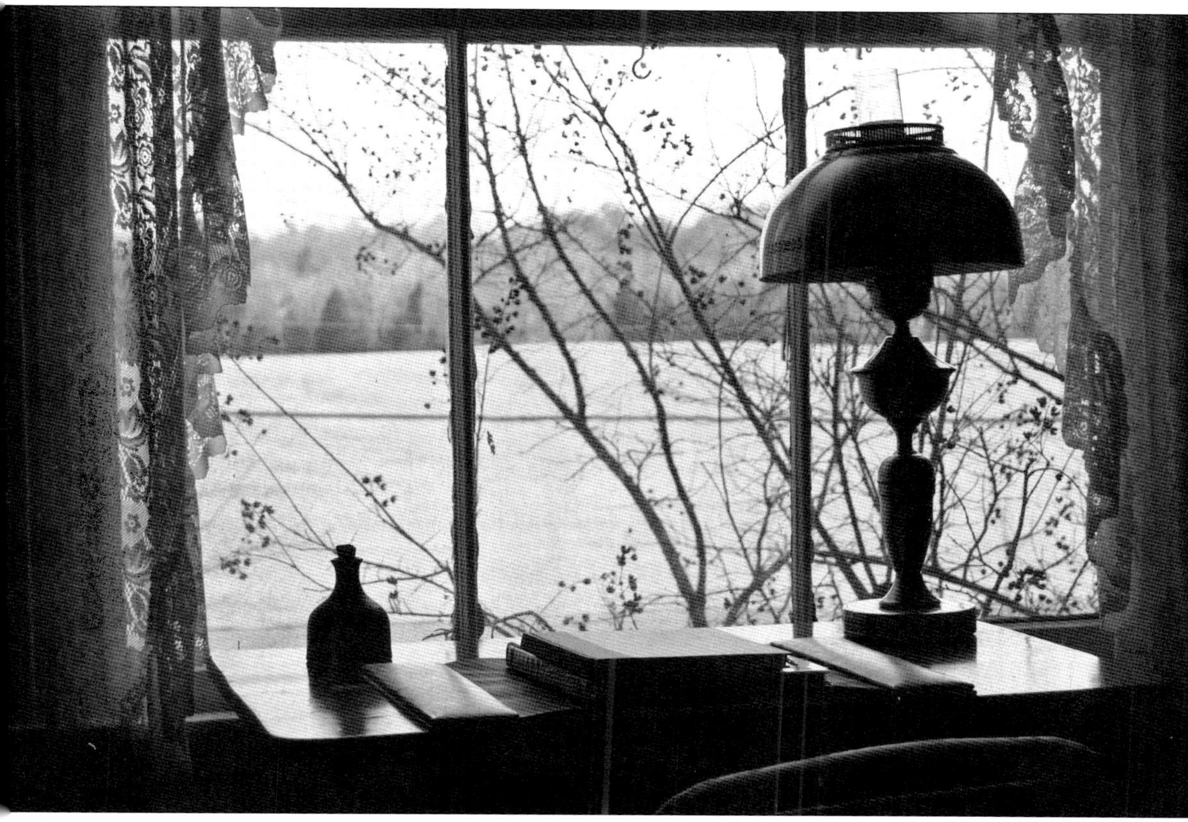

The Civil War reenactor might imagine the Union retreat after Longstreet's breakthrough of the Union lines. A cavalry reenactor might see the 7th Cavalry, its troopers guarding the buildings of the new fort. An engineer might envision how the trenches were dug on the battlefield. A WAC might look for her barracks and her new friends from the Midwest. A historian might imagine all of these times. The authors would prefer that the houseguest simply enjoy the solitude, the view of the woods, and the frequent deer who roam the parklands and take home with himself a "sense of place" called Fort Oglethorpe. (LP.)